Unraveled Mysteries:
The Reality
of
Private Investigation

Unraveled Mysteries: The Reality of Private Investigation
Bruce Nowlin & David Arndt
Copyright © 2024

ISBN: 979-8-218-44801-1

First edition 2024

Printed by Ingram Content Group
Ingram Spark
1 Ingram Blvd
La Vergne, TN 37086
Publisher https://www.ingramspark.com

<u>**Dedication**</u>

This book is for all those who go out into the world day in, day out with the intention and goal in mind and in heart of just doing the right thing and helping someone today.

"No act of kindness, no matter how small, is ever wasted." Aesop

We would like to thank
Family
&
Friends
&
Co-Workers

Index

Preface

Have you ever wondered what it would be like to secretly listen in on your neighbors? To put a GPS tracker on that car in the parking lot? To pick the locks at someone's house? Have you ever dreamt of what it would be like to be involved in a high speed chase? To sneak into an office after hours? This book is designed to help the reader uncover these things and more.

In the world of Private Investigation, there are many theories and even more fables surrounding the work done by those in this unique industry. This book was written with hopes of shedding light on the ever so cloak and dagger field.

According to the Bureau of Labor Statistics (BLS), in 2022 there where only 38,000 Private Investigators in the United States. That's less than one investigator for every 9,000 people in the United States. There are nearly twice as many on-air radio DJ's in the United States than there are Private Investigators. Accordingly, the BLS expects strong growth in the industry. They are forecasting nearly 10% job growth for the Private Investigation industry.

In this book about being a private investigator, we will take a journey back in time to discover the roots of investigation and how the theory and principles have changed through the years. We will delve into the beginning of criminal prosecution and take things all the way up to modern theory. We will look at how psychology, sociology, private investigation and math all work together; from the days of the ancient romans to today.

We will uncover many skills, traits and tools that a private investigator needs. You will learn about using some of the tools an investigator works with on a regular basis and how, as a potential new investigator to the field certain skills and traits are needed to excel in this field of intrigue. We will discuss honing the skills and traits to become a better investigator.

Finally, we will discuss building your network of contacts and narrowing your field of expertise. In the world of private investigation, your network of contacts is vital – the bigger the better. You will learn who you need to add to your list of contacts and why. You will also learn about the number of different fields private investigators work in and why being a solo investigator and not having a specialty is bad business.

Bruce Nowlin

Introduction

When it comes to P.I. work, many people think of a tanned muscular guy with a mustache, driving a red Ferrari 308 GTS across Hawaii or perhaps a gold 1978 Pontiac Firebird around Los Angles working on cold cases or two brothers driving a red and black Dodge Power Wagon around San Diego in search of a missing person. 1980's television crime shows brought to life the idea that being a private investigator can be a somewhat glamorous life and even somewhat enchanting. The reality is, being a private investigator is mystical and challenging, there isn't much glamor and its not very enchanting. It is mystical because according to Webster dictionary the meaning of mystical is leaving one in awe or wonder, something enigmatic. When assigned a new case, immediately the sense of wonder begins and it is up to the investigator to solve the enigma, the puzzle and that my friends is the challenge.

Being a private investigator is all about the chase, figuring it out. As most of us were taught in school when we were children, ask the Who, What, Where, When, Why and How. Who is or was involved, what is or was to be gained, where is it taking place, when did it or will it take place, why did they do it and how did they do it. For each piece of the puzzle, ask the same questions over and over until you absolutely cannot ask them without getting any additional information. For example: a potential client comes to the office wanting an investigator to find out if her husband really is cheating on her. Who is her husband, who does the client think he is cheating on her with, who else may he be fooling around with, who else could he possibly be involved with, is there anyone else that we should consider? What makes these possible people standout? What would they be doing if they were together; not in the sexual nature but would they go bowling, snorkeling, etc. You get the picture. The more information a client can provide you with, the further along you will be in your investigation.

If a potential client cannot provide you with the information you need to work a case properly, it would behove you to not accept the case. The worst case scenario is when a client comes in and wants help but they know nothing. My spouse is fooling around, I don't know with who, I don't know were they are meeting or how. All I know is there is a scent of perfume/cologne on the clothes and its not my spouses normal scent. While you may be able to satisfactorily work a case with only a persons name and address. A photo and vehicle driven would be helpful in closing the case.

While the information provided in this book is thought to be complete, times change, techniques and technology change and laws change. So it is advised to the reader to verify that any tools, gadgets or processes taken from this book for ones own personal use be explored for legality in your own city, county and State before implementation. The author, publisher, manager or any other being and/or entity shall not be held liable for the readers failure to verify legality.

CHAPTER ONE
History of criminology

Crime: *Greek origin Krima* - condemnation

Criminology is the scientific study of crime, criminals, and the criminal justice system, is a multifaceted field that has evolved over the centuries. It encompasses various theories, methodologies, and perspectives aimed at understanding the causes of crime and devising effective strategies for prevention and intervention. This comprehensive exploration of the history of criminology will delve into its origins, key developments, influential thinkers, and contemporary trends.

Ancient Origins and Early Concepts of Crime:

The roots of criminology can be traced back to ancient civilizations where crime and punishment were integral parts of societal norms and governance. In Mesopotamia, Hammurabi's Code (circa 1754 BCE) established one of the earliest known legal systems, prescribing harsh penalties for criminal offenses. Similarly, ancient Egyptian law emphasized retribution and restitution for crimes against individuals and property.

In ancient Greece, philosophers like Plato and Aristotle contemplated the nature of justice and its role in maintaining social order. Plato's "Republic" and Aristotle's "Nicomachean Ethics" laid the groundwork for ethical theories of crime and punishment, emphasizing the importance of virtue, fairness, and the common good.

During the Roman Empire, the concept of law underwent significant development, with the creation of legal codes such as the Twelve Tables and the institution of a complex system of courts and magistrates. Roman law, characterized by its emphasis on legal procedure and precedent, influenced legal systems throughout Europe and beyond.

Medieval and Renaissance Periods:

The Middle Ages witnessed the dominance of religious institutions in matters of law and justice. Canon law, based on the teachings of the Catholic Church, prescribed moral codes and punishments for sinful behavior, often involving penance, excommunication, or public shaming.

Secular authorities, such as feudal lords and monarchs, also wielded power over matters of crime and punishment, often resorting to harsh measures to maintain control and order in their domains. Trial by ordeal, in which the accused underwent a physical test to determine guilt or innocence, was a common practice during this period.

The Renaissance brought about a resurgence of interest in classical thought and philosophy, laying the groundwork for the emergence of modern legal and criminological concepts. Renaissance humanists, such as Niccolò Machiavelli and Francesco Guicciardini, explored themes of power, governance, and justice in their works, contributing to the intellectual ferment of the era.

Enlightenment and the Birth of Modern Criminology:

The Enlightenment of the 17th and 18th centuries marked a pivotal moment in the history of criminology, as scholars began to question traditional notions of crime and punishment and advocate for more rational and humane approaches to justice.

Cesare Beccaria, an Italian philosopher, is often credited as the father of modern criminology for his groundbreaking work "On Crimes and Punishments" (1764). In this influential treatise, Beccaria argued against arbitrary and excessive punishments, advocating instead for proportionality, deterrence, and the reform of criminal laws and institutions.

Jeremy Bentham, another Enlightenment thinker, developed the utilitarian theory of punishment, which posited that the goal of punishment should be to maximize the overall happiness of society by deterring crime and rehabilitating offenders. His concept of the "panopticon," a prison design enabling constant surveillance of inmates, reflected his belief in the efficacy of surveillance and control in preventing crime.

They where most likely opposed to an invention made in 1818 by Sir William Cubitt, an engineer in Britian whom is credited with the invention of a torture device still in use today. The idea behind the device was to make the prisoners work in a manner that would mechanically grind corn or pump water. The device was a hollow cylinder composed of steps built around the cylinder. It is the predecessor to the modern treadmill. The device was used in prisons by having the inmates walk on the treadmill which in turn would generate power to grind grains or pump water.

The Positivist School and the Rise of Scientific Criminology:

The late 19th century saw the emergence of the positivist school of criminology, which sought to apply scientific methods and principles to the study of crime and criminal behavior. Positivist criminologists rejected the classical notion of free will and focused instead on identifying the biological, psychological, and social factors that contribute to criminality.

Cesare Lombroso, an Italian physician and criminologist, is often associated with the positivist school for his pioneering work on the biological roots of crime. In his seminal work "L'Uomo Delinquente" (1876), Lombroso proposed the theory of the "born criminal," suggesting that some individuals were biologically predisposed to criminal behavior due to atavistic traits or physical abnormalities.

Other prominent positivist criminologists, such as Enrico Ferri and Raffaele Garofalo, expanded upon Lombroso's ideas, emphasizing the role of social and environmental factors in shaping criminal behavior. Ferri, in particular, introduced the concept of "social defense" to justify the preventive detention of habitual offenders deemed a threat to society.

The Chicago School and the Study of Urban Crime:

In the early 20th century, the Chicago School of sociology emerged as a leading force in criminological research, focusing on the social and environmental factors that influence crime rates in urban areas. Scholars such as Robert Park, Ernest Burgess, and Clifford Shaw conducted pioneering studies of crime patterns and social disorganization in Chicago neighborhoods.

The Chicago School's ecological approach to crime emphasized the importance of social networks, neighborhood dynamics, and cultural influences in shaping individual behavior. Their research laid the groundwork for theories such as social disorganization theory and differential association theory, which sought to explain how social and environmental factors contribute to the prevalence of crime in certain communities.

Social Disorganization Theory posited that crime rates are highest in neighborhoods characterized by poverty, residential mobility, and social fragmentation, as these conditions undermine the social controls and informal networks that help maintain order and cohesion.

Differential Association Theory, developed by Edwin Sutherland, argued that criminal behavior is learned through interactions with others, particularly in close-knit social groups such as families, peer networks, and subcultures. According to this theory, individuals become delinquent when they are exposed to favorable definitions of crime and deviance and lack adequate socialization into conventional norms and values.

The Emergence of Critical Criminology:

The latter half of the 20th century saw the rise of critical criminology, a theoretical approach that seeks to challenge conventional explanations of crime and justice from a socio-political perspective. Critical criminologists draw on insights from Marxism, feminism, postcolonialism, and other critical theories to analyze the structural inequalities and power dynamics that underlie crime and social control.

Marxist criminologists, inspired by the writings of Karl Marx, view crime as a product of capitalist exploitation and inequality. They argue that laws and law enforcement serve the interests of the ruling class, perpetuating social injustice and reinforcing the status quo.

Feminist criminologists, meanwhile, highlight the gendered nature of crime and justice, emphasizing the need to consider how gender norms, power relations, and patriarchal structures shape individuals' experiences of crime and victimization. They critique male-centric theories of crime for neglecting women's voices and experiences within the criminal justice system.

Postmodern criminologists challenge the validity of grand narratives and universal truths about crime and deviance, arguing instead for a more nuanced and contextual understanding of social phenomena. They emphasize the importance of language, discourse, and representation in shaping perceptions of crime and influencing policy responses.

Contemporary Trends and Future Directions:

In the 21st century, criminology continues to evolve in response to new challenges and developments in society, technology, and globalization. Emerging areas of study include cybercrime, transnational crime, environmental crime, and the intersections of race, ethnicity, and criminal justice.

Advancements in neuroscience, genetics, and psychology have led to a deeper understanding of the biological and psychological factors that contribute to criminal behavior.

Research in behavioral genetics, for example, explores the role of genetic predispositions and gene-environment interactions in shaping antisocial behavior and criminal propensity.

Technological innovations, such as surveillance cameras, DNA analysis, and predictive analytics, have revolutionized law enforcement practices and crime prevention strategies. However, they also raise ethical and privacy concerns regarding the use of surveillance technologies and the potential for biased algorithms to perpetuate social inequalities.

As society grapples with issues such as mass incarceration, police brutality, and systemic injustice, criminologists play a vital role in advocating for reform, promoting social justice, and advancing evidence-based policies. By fostering interdisciplinary collaboration and engaging with diverse perspectives, criminology continues to evolve as a dynamic and relevant field of study.

The history of criminology is a testament to the enduring human quest for understanding and addressing the complex phenomenon of crime. From ancient religious codes to modern scientific inquiry, the study of crime and criminal behavior has undergone profound transformations, reflecting shifts in culture, ideology, and technology.

While criminology has made significant strides in advancing knowledge and informing policy, it remains a dynamic and interdisciplinary field, continuously adapting to new challenges and opportunities. By embracing diverse perspectives, engaging with emerging issues, and promoting social justice, criminologists can contribute to a safer, fairer, and more just society for all.

CHAPTER TWO
Background of P.I.

Investigation: *Latin Origin Investigationem* - Search into

Eugène François Vidocq (1833)

Eugène François Vidocq, a name synonymous with both crime and detection, occupies a unique place in the annals of criminology. Born in 1775 in Arras, France, Vidocq's tumultuous life journey took him from the depths of criminality to the heights of law enforcement innovation, leaving an indelible mark on the history of policing and detective work.

Early Life and Criminal Career:

Vidocq's early years were marked by poverty, adversity, and rebellion against authority. He ran away from home at a young age and soon found himself immersed in the criminal underworld of 18th-century France. His exploits as a thief, forger, and fugitive earned him a notorious reputation and multiple stints in prison.

Despite his criminal activities, Vidocq possessed a keen intellect, charisma, and resourcefulness that set him apart from his peers. During his time behind bars, he honed his skills in deception, disguise, and manipulation, becoming a master of the art of subterfuge.

Transformation and Redemption:

Vidocq's life took a dramatic turn in 1809 when he made a daring escape from prison and decided to turn his back on crime. Determined to redeem himself and prove his worth, he approached the French authorities with an audacious proposal—to use his intimate knowledge of the criminal underworld to assist in the apprehension of fellow offenders.

This proposal caught the attention of Georges Henry, the chief of the Paris police, who saw in Vidocq's offer an opportunity to revolutionize law enforcement tactics and techniques. Henry granted Vidocq a pardon and enlisted him as an informant and undercover agent, marking the beginning of Vidocq's remarkable career as a detective.

The Birth of the Sûreté and Vidocq's Legacy:

In 1811, Vidocq was appointed as the head of the newly established Sûreté, France's first official plainclothes detective force. Under his leadership, the Sûreté pioneered innovative investigative methods, including surveillance, handwriting analysis, and criminal profiling, laying the groundwork for modern detective work.

Vidocq's tenure at the Sûreté was characterized by his unorthodox approach to crime-solving, which often relied on cunning, intuition, and unconventional tactics. He cultivated a network of informants and collaborators from all walks of life, leveraging their knowledge and connections to crack even the most baffling cases.

One of Vidocq's most enduring contributions to criminology was his creation of the first centralized criminal records system, known as the "anthropometric" or "portrait parlé" system. This revolutionary method involved cataloging detailed physical descriptions and distinguishing features of known criminals, enabling law enforcement agencies to identify suspects based on eyewitness accounts and physical evidence.

Vidocq's memoirs, "Memoirs of Vidocq: Master

of Crime," published in 1828, further cemented his reputation as a legendary figure in the world of crime and detection. His colorful anecdotes, daring escapades, and insights into the criminal mind captivated readers and inspired generations of aspiring detectives and writers.

Legacy and Influence:

Vidocq's influence extended far beyond his own lifetime, shaping the development of detective fiction and the popular imagination of the detective as a heroic figure. Authors such as Edgar Allan Poe, Arthur Conan Doyle, and Émile Gaboriau drew inspiration from Vidocq's life and exploits, creating iconic literary detectives such as Sherlock Holmes and Monsieur Lecoq.

Moreover, Vidocq's innovations in forensic science and criminal investigation paved the way for modern law enforcement practices and methodologies. His emphasis on systematic record-keeping, scientific analysis, and collaborative intelligence-gathering laid the foundation for the establishment of professional detective agencies and the standardization of investigative procedures.

Despite his controversial past and occasional brushes with scandal and controversy, Vidocq's legacy endures as a testament to the transformative power of redemption and reinvention. His journey from outlaw to lawman serves as a reminder that even the most unlikely individuals have the capacity for redemption and the potential to leave a lasting impact on the world.

Eugène François Vidocq stands as a towering figure in the history of criminology, his life and career embodying the complex interplay of vice and virtue, crime and justice. Through his ingenuity, perseverance, and relentless pursuit of truth, Vidocq forever changed the landscape of crime-fighting and left an indelible legacy that continues to inspire and captivate to this day.

<u>Allan Pinkerton (1850)</u>
Allan Pinkerton, a name synonymous with detective work and law enforcement, played a pivotal role in shaping the landscape of criminal investigation and security in the United States. Born on August 25, 1819, in Glasgow, Scotland, Pinkerton's life journey took him from humble beginnings to the forefront of the fight against crime and corruption, leaving an enduring legacy as a pioneer of modern private investigation.

Early Life and Career:

Pinkerton's early years were marked by hardship and adversity. Raised in poverty, he received limited formal education and began working at a young age to support his family. Despite these challenges, Pinkerton possessed a natural curiosity and thirst for knowledge that propelled him to seek out new opportunities and experiences.

In 1842, Pinkerton immigrated to the United States, settling in Chicago, Illinois, where he found work as a barrel maker and cooper. His life took a fateful turn when he stumbled upon a group of counterfeiters operating in his neighborhood. Determined to root out this criminal enterprise, Pinkerton embarked on his first foray into detective work, gathering evidence and collaborating with local law enforcement to bring the perpetrators to justice.

The Birth of the Pinkerton Detective Agency:

In 1850, Pinkerton officially launched the Pinkerton National Detective Agency, recognizing the growing demand for private security and investigative services in the rapidly expanding American frontier. Initially operating as a one-man operation, Pinkerton quickly gained a reputation for his skill, resourcefulness, and unwavering commitment to justice.

Under Pinkerton's leadership, the agency expanded rapidly, recruiting a team of skilled operatives and establishing a network of offices across the country. Pinkerton's agents, known as "Pinkerton Men," were renowned for their professionalism, discretion, and effectiveness in solving a wide range of cases, from theft and fraud to espionage and murder.

Pinkerton's approach to detective work was characterized by his innovative use of surveillance, undercover operations, and forensic techniques. He was a firm believer in the power of collaboration and information-sharing, often working closely with law enforcement agencies and government officials to combat crime and maintain public order.

Notable Cases and Contributions:

Throughout his career, Pinkerton and his agency were involved in numerous high-profile cases and investigations that captured the public's imagination and earned him widespread acclaim. One of his most famous cases was the thwarting of an assassination plot against President-elect Abraham Lincoln in 1861.

Pinkerton's agents infiltrated a secret society known as the "Baltimore Plot," uncovering a conspiracy to assassinate Lincoln during his journey to Washington, D.C., for his inauguration. Thanks to Pinkerton's timely intervention and effective intelligence-gathering, the plot was foiled, and Lincoln safely reached the nation's capital.

In addition to his work in crime detection, Pinkerton also made significant contributions to the field of security and risk management. He developed innovative security measures, including the use of alarm systems, safes, and guard patrols, to protect businesses, banks, and railroads from theft and vandalism.

Legacy and Influence:

Allan Pinkerton's legacy as a pioneer of modern private investigation and security continues to reverberate in the field of law enforcement and beyond. His innovative methods and principled approach to detective work laid the groundwork for the professionalization of private investigation and the development of modern policing techniques.

The Pinkerton Detective Agency, which later became known as Pinkerton's National Detective Agency and eventually Pinkerton, Inc., remains one of the oldest and most respected names in the security industry. Over the years, the agency has adapted to changing times and technologies, expanding its services to include corporate risk management, executive protection, and cybersecurity.

Beyond his professional accomplishments, Pinkerton's legacy is also remembered for his commitment to social justice and humanitarian causes. He was an outspoken opponent of slavery and played a key role in the Underground Railroad, assisting fugitive slaves in their quest for freedom and equality.

Allan Pinkerton's life and career stand as a testament to the power of determination, innovation, and integrity in the pursuit of justice. From his humble beginnings as a Scottish immigrant to his rise as a pioneering detective and entrepreneur, Pinkerton's influence on the field of private investigation and security continues to be felt to this day, inspiring generations of law enforcement professionals and private investigators around the world.

<u>Sherlock Holmes (1887)</u>
Sherlock Holmes, the iconic detective created by Sir Arthur Conan Doyle, stands as one of the most recognizable and enduring figures in literature and popular culture. With his razor-sharp intellect, keen powers of observation, and uncanny ability to solve even the most perplexing mysteries, Holmes has captivated readers for generations and left an indelible mark on the genre of detective fiction.

Origins and Evolution:

Sherlock Holmes made his first appearance in Doyle's novel "A Study in Scarlet," published in 1887. Set against the backdrop of Victorian London, the story introduces readers to Holmes, a brilliant but eccentric consulting detective, and his loyal friend and chronicler, Dr. John H. Watson.

Doyle went on to pen three more novels and fifty-six short stories featuring Holmes and Watson, collectively known as the "Canon." These stories, originally serialized in magazines such as The Strand, became immensely popular with readers of all ages, propelling Holmes to literary stardom and establishing him as the archetypal detective.

Holmes's appeal lies not only in his formidable intellect and deductive prowess but also in his complex personality and idiosyncratic habits. He is portrayed as a mercurial and enigmatic figure, prone to bouts of melancholy and boredom interspersed with bursts of frenetic energy and single-minded focus.

Characteristics and Methods:

Holmes is characterized by his keen powers of observation, deductive reasoning, and encyclopedic knowledge of a wide range of subjects, from chemistry and anatomy to literature and philosophy. He approaches each case with a scientific mindset, relying on empirical evidence and logical analysis to unravel the truth behind even the most baffling mysteries.

One of Holmes's most distinctive traits is his remarkable talent for disguise and impersonation. He frequently adopts various personas and alters his appearance to infiltrate criminal circles, gather information, and outwit his adversaries. This chameleon-like ability adds an element of intrigue and theatricality to his investigations, earning him the moniker of the "Master of Disguise."

Holmes's methodical approach to detection is exemplified by his famous maxim, "When you have eliminated the impossible, whatever remains, however improbable, must be the truth." This principle, known as "Holmes's deduction," reflects his reliance on deductive reasoning and logical inference to sift through the evidence and arrive at the correct solution.

Holmes's deductive prowess is complemented by his keen powers of observation, which enable him to glean insights from seemingly mundane details that others overlook. He possesses an extraordinary ability to read people's emotions, habits, and intentions based on their physical appearance, demeanor, and speech—a skill he refers to as "deduction."

Legacy and Influence:

The enduring popularity of Sherlock Holmes can

be attributed to his timeless appeal and universal resonance. Holmes's adventures have been translated into dozens of languages, adapted into countless films, television series, radio dramas, and stage productions, and inspired a vast array of derivative works, pastiches, and parodies.

Holmes's influence extends far beyond the realm of literature and entertainment, shaping the development of forensic science, criminal investigation, and the modern detective profession. His emphasis on empirical evidence, logical reasoning, and systematic inquiry laid the foundation for the scientific approach to crime-solving and the professionalization of law enforcement agencies.

Holmes's legacy can also be seen in the enduring popularity of detective fiction as a genre and the proliferation of fictional detectives inspired by his iconic character. From Agatha Christie's Hercule Poirot to Raymond Chandler's Philip Marlowe, a myriad of sleuths have followed in Holmes's footsteps, each bringing their own unique style and methods to the art of detection.

Moreover, Holmes's influence extends to popular culture, where his image and persona have become iconic symbols of intellect, eccentricity, and adventure. His distinctive deerstalker cap, curved pipe, and magnifying glass have become instantly recognizable symbols of detective work, while his catchphrases and quotes have entered the lexicon of everyday speech.

Sherlock Holmes remains a towering figure in the annals of literature and popular culture, his legacy enduring long after his creator's pen fell silent. With his unparalleled intellect, deductive prowess, and indomitable spirit, Holmes continues to inspire and captivate readers of all ages, inviting them to join him on a journey of mystery, intrigue, and adventure. As long as there are mysteries to solve and puzzles to unravel, the great detective will live on, forever immortalized in the hallowed halls of literary history.

<u>Kate Warne (1856)</u>

In the annals of detective history, few figures stand out as prominently as Kate Warne, the pioneering female detective who broke barriers, shattered stereotypes, and made invaluable contributions to the field of criminal investigation during the 19th century. Despite facing formidable obstacles and entrenched gender biases, Warne's intelligence, resourcefulness, and determination propelled her to prominence and earned her a place of honor in the pantheon of detective legends.

Early Life and Career Beginnings:

Kate Warne was born in 1833 in Erin, New York, into a world where women's roles were largely confined to the domestic sphere. However, Warne possessed an independent spirit and a thirst for adventure that set her apart from her peers. Determined to chart her own course in life, she sought opportunities beyond the traditional confines of womanhood.

In 1856, Warne responded to an advertisement placed by the Pinkerton National Detective Agency, a fledgling detective agency founded by Allan Pinkerton in Chicago. Despite the skepticism and resistance she encountered, Warne's intelligence, poise, and persuasive charm won over Pinkerton, who recognized her potential as a valuable asset to his agency.

Pioneering Role at Pinkerton:

Warne's hiring marked a significant milestone in the history of law enforcement, as she became the first female detective in the United States. Embracing her new role with enthusiasm and dedication, Warne quickly proved her mettle as a skilled investigator and adept undercover operative.

One of Warne's early assignments involved infiltrating a criminal gang suspected of plotting to assassinate Abraham Lincoln, then the president-elect of the United States. Disguised as a Southern belle, Warne gained the trust of the conspirators and successfully foiled the assassination plot, earning the gratitude of Pinkerton and the admiration of her colleagues.

Warne's success in the Lincoln case solidified her reputation as a talented and resourceful detective, paving the way for her involvement in a wide range of high-profile cases. She assumed various aliases and personas to infiltrate criminal organizations, gather intelligence, and gather evidence, often at great personal risk.

Contributions to Detective Work:

Warne's contributions to the field of criminal investigation were manifold and enduring. She pioneered many techniques and methodologies that would later become standard practices in detective work, including surveillance, undercover operations, and the use of disguise and deception.

Warne's skill as an undercover operative was particularly noteworthy, as she possessed a remarkable ability to blend into diverse social circles and gain the confidence of suspects and informants. Her mastery of disguise and her talent for assuming different roles enabled her to extract valuable information and solve complex cases that had baffled her male counterparts.

In addition to her investigative prowess, Warne played a pivotal role in shaping the culture and ethos of the Pinkerton Agency. She advocated for the recruitment and training of female detectives, arguing that women possessed unique abilities and perspectives that could enhance the effectiveness of the agency's operations.

Legacy and Impact:

Despite her groundbreaking achievements, Warne's contributions to detective work were largely overshadowed by the male-dominated narratives of her time. Nevertheless, her legacy endures as a testament to the power of perseverance, ingenuity, and determination in the face of adversity.

Warne's pioneering role as the first female detective paved the way for future generations of women in law enforcement and criminal investigation. Her example inspired countless women to pursue careers in detective work, breaking down barriers and challenging stereotypes in the process.

Warne's story also highlights the importance of diversity and inclusion in the field of criminal justice. Her success as a detective demonstrated that talent and ability are not limited by gender, and that women have a vital role to play in the pursuit of justice and the maintenance of law and order.

In recognition of her trailblazing achievements, Kate Warne was posthumously inducted into the Women in Law Enforcement Hall of Fame in 2017. This honor serves as a fitting tribute to a remarkable woman whose courage, intelligence, and determination helped shape the course of detective history.

Kate Warne's legacy as a pioneering woman of detection remains a source of inspiration and admiration to this day. Her trailblazing achievements, groundbreaking contributions, and unwavering commitment to justice have left an indelible mark on the field of criminal investigation, paving the way for future generations of women in law enforcement.

Warne's story serves as a reminder that courage, resilience, and determination know no bounds, and that barriers can be overcome through perseverance and ingenuity. As we celebrate her achievements and honor her memory, let us also reaffirm our commitment to promoting diversity, equity, and inclusion in the pursuit of justice for all.

Jay J Armes (1958)
In the world of private investigation, Jay J. Armes is a legend. Known for his daring exploits, innovative methods, and larger-than-life persona, Armes has carved out a unique legacy as one of the most celebrated and controversial figures in the field. From rescuing hostages to recovering millions in stolen goods, his career reads like a Hollywood blockbuster, yet every twist and turn is grounded in the gritty reality of crime and justice.

Early Life and Beginnings:

Jay J. Armes was born Julian Armas on August 11, 1932, in Ysleta, Texas, a small community on the outskirts of El Paso. Raised in modest circumstances, he learned the value of hard work and determination from an early age. However, tragedy struck when Armes lost both of his hands in a childhood accident involving a railroad crossing.

Despite this setback, Armes refused to let his disability define him. With unwavering determination and a fierce sense of independence, he adapted to his circumstances and learned to use prosthetic limbs with remarkable dexterity and skill. These prosthetics would later become his trademark, distinguishing him as the "man with the golden arm" in the public imagination.

Armes's entry into the world of private investigation was serendipitous. In the early 1960s, while working as a private security guard, he caught the attention of a local attorney who was impressed by his resourcefulness and tenacity. Recognizing Armes's potential, the attorney offered him a job as an investigator, thus launching his illustrious career in the field.

Rise to Prominence:

Armes quickly made a name for himself as a formidable investigator, employing a combination of street smarts, cunning, and intuition to crack even the most challenging cases. His reputation for getting results attracted a diverse clientele, ranging from high-profile celebrities and wealthy businessmen to ordinary individuals seeking justice.

One of Armes's most famous cases involved the rescue of Marlon Brando's kidnapped son, Christian, in 1972. Brando enlisted Armes's help after receiving ransom demands for his son's safe return. Armes, employing his trademark blend of ingenuity and audacity, orchestrated a daring rescue operation that ultimately led to Christian's safe recovery and the apprehension of the kidnappers.

Another high-profile case that catapulted Armes into the spotlight was his involvement in the Patty Hearst kidnapping saga in 1974. Armes was hired by Hearst's family to assist in the search for the kidnapped heiress, who had been abducted by the radical group known as the Symbionese Liberation Army. While Hearst was eventually apprehended by law enforcement, Armes's efforts played a crucial role in keeping her case in the public eye and providing support to her family during their ordeal.

In addition to his work on high-profile cases, Armes also built a reputation as a pioneering forensic investigator. He was among the first private investigators to employ cutting-edge technology and scientific methods in his work, including DNA analysis, fingerprinting, and ballistics testing. His meticulous attention to detail and relentless pursuit of truth earned him the respect of law enforcement agencies and forensic experts alike.

Controversies and Criticisms:

Despite his many successes, Armes has not been without controversy. His flamboyant style, larger-than-life persona, and penchant for self-promotion have occasionally drawn criticism from some quarters. Critics have accused him of sensationalism and grandstanding, arguing that his public persona sometimes overshadowed the seriousness of the cases he worked on.

Moreover, Armes's unorthodox methods and willingness to push the boundaries of legality have raised eyebrows in the legal and law enforcement communities. His penchant for going undercover and conducting surveillance operations without proper authorization has led to accusations of vigilantism and ethical lapses.

However, supporters of Armes argue that his

methods, while unconventional, are driven by a genuine desire to seek justice for his clients. They point to his long track record of success and the tangible results he has achieved in solving cases that had stymied law enforcement agencies and other private investigators.

Legacy and Influence:

Jay J. Armes's legacy extends far beyond his individual accomplishments as a private investigator. He has inspired countless aspiring detectives and law enforcement professionals with his fearless attitude, resourcefulness, and unwavering commitment to justice.

Moreover, Armes's impact on popular culture cannot be overstated. His larger-than-life persona and daring exploits have been the subject of numerous books, articles, and documentaries, further cementing his status as a true American original.

In conclusion, Jay J. Armes is more than just a private investigator—he is a living legend, a real-life superhero whose exploits have captured the imagination of people around the world. Despite facing seemingly insurmountable odds, he has proven time and again that with determination, ingenuity, and a little bit of luck, anything is possible. As long as there are mysteries to solve and injustices to right, Jay J. Armes will continue to be a beacon of hope and inspiration for generations to come.

Modern Era of Private Investigation

In the vast landscape of contemporary society, private investigation has evolved far beyond trench coats and fedoras. While the image of the solitary detective chasing down leads in dark alleys still persists in popular culture, the reality of modern private investigation is a dynamic blend of traditional sleuthing techniques and cutting-edge technology. In this exploration, we delve into the multifaceted world of private investigation in the digital age, uncovering the diverse roles, tools, and challenges faced by today's investigators.

Private investigation has a long and storied history, dating back to ancient times when individuals were hired to gather information or solve mysteries for wealthy patrons. Over the centuries, the profession has evolved in response to societal changes, technological advancements, and shifting legal landscapes.

In the modern era, private investigators play a crucial role in various sectors, including law enforcement, corporate security, legal defense, and personal matters. While the core principles of investigation remain unchanged—such as gathering evidence, conducting surveillance, and analyzing data —the methods and tools employed have undergone a profound transformation.

Modern private investigators encompass a diverse range of roles and specializations, each tailored to meet the specific needs of clients and industries. Some investigators focus on traditional investigative tasks, such as surveillance, background checks, and witness interviews, while others specialize in niche areas such as digital forensics, cybercrime investigation, or financial fraud detection.

Corporate investigators, for example, are often hired by businesses to uncover internal misconduct, intellectual property theft, or corporate espionage. These investigators may employ a combination of traditional investigative techniques and digital forensics to identify security breaches or unauthorized access to sensitive information.

Legal investigators, on the other hand, work closely with attorneys and law firms to gather evidence, locate witnesses, and conduct thorough research to support legal cases. Their expertise in gathering admissible evidence and navigating complex legal procedures is invaluable in both civil and criminal litigation.

In recent years, the demand for digital investigators has surged as crimes and illicit activities increasingly migrate to the digital realm. These specialists are trained to extract and analyze digital evidence from computers, mobile devices, and online platforms to uncover cybercrimes, data breaches, or online harassment.

The arsenal of tools available to modern private investigators is as diverse as the cases they handle. While some tools remain timeless—such as cameras, binoculars, and voice recorders—others have evolved in tandem with technology.

One of the most indispensable tools for today's investigators is digital forensics software, which allows them to extract, analyze, and interpret data from electronic devices. These tools can uncover deleted files, trace online communications, and reconstruct digital activities, providing invaluable insights into a subject's behavior or intentions.

Surveillance technology has also advanced significantly, with high-definition cameras, GPS tracking devices, and drones enabling investigators to monitor subjects discreetly and gather real-time intelligence. Social media intelligence platforms aggregate publicly available information from social networking sites, enabling investigators to profile individuals, track their online activities, and identify potential leads.

Moreover, data analytics software empowers investigators to sift through vast amounts of data efficiently, identifying patterns, correlations, and anomalies that may not be apparent to the naked eye. By leveraging big data analytics, investigators can uncover hidden connections, track financial transactions, and identify potential risks or threats.

While technology has revolutionized the field of private investigation, it has also introduced new challenges and ethical considerations. The proliferation of surveillance technology and digital tracking tools has raised concerns about privacy rights and civil liberties, prompting lawmakers to enact regulations governing the use of such technology.

Furthermore, the digital landscape is constantly evolving, presenting investigators with the challenge of staying abreast of emerging technologies, cyber threats, and evolving investigative techniques. Continuous training and professional development are essential for investigators to adapt to these changes and maintain their effectiveness in an increasingly complex environment.

Ethical considerations also loom large in the practice of private investigation, particularly when it comes to the collection and use of personal data. Investigators must adhere to strict ethical standards and legal regulations governing data privacy and confidentiality, ensuring that their investigative methods do not infringe upon the rights of individuals or violate applicable laws.

Modern private investigation represents a

synthesis of traditional investigative techniques and cutting-edge technology. From corporate espionage to cybercrime investigation, the role of private investigators has expanded to encompass a wide range of specialties and industries.

As technology continues to evolve and society becomes increasingly interconnected, the demand for skilled investigators adept at navigating the complexities of the digital age will only continue to grow. By embracing innovation, adhering to ethical standards, and continually honing their skills, today's private investigators are poised to unravel the mysteries of the digital age and safeguard the interests of their clients in an ever-changing world.

CHAPTER THREE
Types of P.I. work

Type: Greek *Origin Typos* - To model

Private investigators (PIs) undertake a wide array of tasks and assignments, serving diverse clientele in various industries and sectors. Their work involves gathering information, conducting investigations, and providing insights and evidence to support legal, corporate, and personal matters. In this comprehensive summary, we'll explore the numerous types of work that private investigators can do, examining their roles, responsibilities, and the industries they serve.

Surveillance and Investigations:

Surveillance investigations involve the covert observation and monitoring of individuals, locations, or activities to gather evidence, uncover information, or verify suspicions. These investigations are commonly conducted by private investigators, law enforcement agencies, or corporate security teams.

The primary goal of surveillance investigations is to obtain accurate and reliable evidence that can be used for various purposes, including legal proceedings, criminal investigations, civil litigation, or corporate matters such as employee misconduct or insurance fraud.

Surveillance investigations typically involve the use of specialized equipment such as video cameras, audio recording devices, GPS trackers, and long-range lenses to observe subjects discreetly from a distance. Investigators may also employ various techniques such as stakeouts, undercover operations, and vehicle tracking to gather information while minimizing the risk of detection.

Effective surveillance requires meticulous planning, attention to detail, and adherence to legal and ethical guidelines to ensure that evidence obtained is admissible in court and obtained in a lawful manner.

Mobile Surveillance:

In the realm of private investigation, mobile surveillance stands as a cornerstone technique, allowing investigators to monitor subjects discreetly and gather valuable intelligence while in motion. Whether tracking a suspect in a criminal investigation, conducting corporate espionage surveillance, or gathering evidence for a legal case, mobile surveillance requires a delicate balance of skill, strategy, and technological prowess. In this exploration, we delve into the intricacies of mobile surveillance, from its methodologies to its challenges and ethical considerations.

Mobile surveillance involves the covert observation of individuals or locations while in transit. Unlike static surveillance, which focuses on monitoring a fixed location, mobile surveillance requires investigators to maintain a discreet presence while following a subject who may be moving through various environments.

One of the primary methodologies employed in mobile surveillance is the use of vehicles equipped with specialized surveillance equipment. These surveillance vehicles are outfitted with discreet cameras, GPS tracking devices, and communication systems, enabling investigators to track and observe subjects without attracting undue attention.

Another common technique is foot surveillance, where investigators blend into the surrounding environment and follow subjects on foot. This approach requires a high degree of stealth and situational awareness, as investigators must navigate crowded streets, urban landscapes, and other obstacles while maintaining visual contact with the subject.

In some cases, investigators may utilize a combination of vehicle and foot surveillance to maximize effectiveness and minimize the risk of detection. By alternating between vehicles and pedestrian modes of surveillance, investigators can adapt to changing circumstances and maintain continuous observation of the subject.

Despite its effectiveness, mobile surveillance poses several challenges and considerations for investigators. One of the primary challenges is the need to remain covert and undetected while following a subject in motion. Any suspicion or awareness on the part of the subject could compromise the integrity of the surveillance operation and jeopardize the investigation.

Moreover, mobile surveillance often requires investigators to navigate complex traffic patterns, congested urban areas, and other obstacles while maintaining visual contact with the subject. This requires a combination of skillful driving, strategic planning, and quick thinking to adapt to changing conditions and avoid detection.

Furthermore, mobile surveillance raises ethical considerations regarding privacy rights and the use of surveillance technology. Investigators must adhere to strict ethical standards and legal regulations governing surveillance activities, ensuring that their actions are conducted within the bounds of the law and respect the rights of individuals.

Advancements in technology have transformed the landscape of mobile surveillance, providing investigators with an array of sophisticated tools and equipment to enhance their capabilities. GPS tracking devices enable investigators to monitor the movements of subjects in real-time, providing precise location data and facilitating more effective surveillance operations.

High-definition cameras and wireless video transmission systems allow investigators to capture clear, high-quality footage of subjects while on the move. This footage can be invaluable as evidence in legal proceedings or provide valuable insights into the activities and behavior of the subject.

In addition, mobile surveillance software and applications enable investigators to coordinate surveillance operations, track multiple subjects simultaneously, and analyze data in real-time. These technological advancements streamline the surveillance process, allowing investigators to gather actionable intelligence more efficiently and effectively.

Mobile surveillance represents a critical tool in the arsenal of modern private investigators, enabling them to monitor subjects discreetly and gather valuable intelligence while in motion. By employing a combination of vehicles, foot surveillance, and advanced technology, investigators can adapt to changing circumstances, navigate complex environments, and maintain visual contact with the subject. However, mobile surveillance also poses challenges and ethical considerations that must be carefully navigated to ensure that investigations are conducted with integrity and respect for individual rights.

Background Checks:
Background investigations entail thorough

research into an individual's personal, professional, and criminal history. Conducted by employers, private investigators, or government agencies, these inquiries aim to verify a person's identity, education, employment history, financial records, and criminal record. Background investigations are crucial for pre-employment screening, tenant screening, security clearances, and due diligence in business transactions. They involve accessing public records, conducting interviews, and utilizing databases to gather information, ensuring informed decision-making and risk mitigation. Privacy laws and ethical considerations govern the conduct of background investigations to uphold individual rights and confidentiality.

Missing Persons and Locating Assets:
Missing persons investigations involve efforts to locate individuals who have disappeared under mysterious or unknown circumstances. Conducted by law enforcement agencies, private investigators, or specialized organizations, these investigations utilize various methods such as interviews, forensic analysis, and public appeals to gather information and trace the whereabouts of the missing individual. Asset location investigations, on the other hand, focus on identifying and recovering assets that have been hidden, transferred, or misappropriated. Typically conducted in cases of fraud, divorce, or financial disputes, these inquiries involve examining financial records, conducting surveillance, and tracing the movement of funds or property to uncover hidden assets. Both missing persons and asset location investigations require meticulous research, attention to detail, and collaboration with relevant parties to achieve successful outcomes. They play a crucial role in providing closure to families, solving crimes, and ensuring equitable resolution in legal proceedings.

Infidelity and Domestic Investigations:

Infidelity and domestic investigations involve uncovering evidence of romantic or sexual involvement outside of a committed relationship. Conducted by private investigators or concerned individuals, these inquiries aim to confirm suspicions of cheating, gather evidence for legal proceedings, or facilitate informed decision-making. Infidelity investigations often entail surveillance, background checks, and forensic analysis of communication devices or social media activity to track the actions and interactions of the suspected party. Ethical considerations and privacy laws govern the conduct of these investigations, ensuring that evidence obtained is admissible and obtained in a lawful manner. While emotionally challenging, infidelity investigations can provide closure, facilitate relationship counseling, or inform decisions regarding divorce or separation.

Corporate and Business Investigations:

Corporate and business investigations involve examining internal or external activities within a business to uncover misconduct, fraud, or compliance violations. Conducted by internal audit teams, private investigators, or specialized firms, these inquiries aim to protect the interests and reputation of the company, ensure regulatory compliance, and mitigate financial losses. Corporate investigations may involve forensic accounting, computer forensics, surveillance, and interviews with employees or stakeholders to gather evidence and assess risks. Ethical considerations, confidentiality, and legal requirements guide the conduct of these investigations, which play a vital role in maintaining transparency, accountability, and integrity within organizations.

Insurance and Fraud Investigations:

Insurance and fraud investigations involve the detection, analysis, and prevention of fraudulent activities, such as financial fraud, identity theft, or embezzlement. Conducted by law enforcement agencies, forensic accountants, or private investigators, these inquiries aim to uncover evidence of deceptive practices, identify perpetrators, and recover misappropriated funds or assets. Fraud investigations typically involve reviewing financial records, conducting interviews, and analyzing digital evidence to trace fraudulent transactions or patterns of behavior. Ethical considerations, confidentiality, and legal protocols guide the conduct of these investigations, which play a crucial role in protecting individuals, businesses, and organizations from financial losses and reputational damage. Additionally, fraud investigations contribute to the enforcement of laws and regulations, deterrence of criminal activities, and promotion of transparency and accountability in financial transactions.

Security and Risk Assessment:
        Security and risk assessment investigations involve evaluating potential threats, vulnerabilities, and risks to individuals, organizations, or assets. Conducted by security professionals, risk managers, or specialized firms, these inquiries aim to identify security gaps, implement preventive measures, and mitigate potential hazards.

        Security investigations typically encompass physical security, cybersecurity, personnel security, and operational security. They may involve assessing access controls, conducting vulnerability scans, reviewing security policies and procedures, and analyzing incident reports to identify weaknesses and areas for improvement.

        Risk assessment investigations focus on evaluating the likelihood and impact of various threats and hazards, such as natural disasters, terrorist attacks, or cyber-attacks. They involve conducting risk analyses, scenario planning, and impact assessments to prioritize risks and develop risk mitigation strategies.

Ethical considerations, confidentiality, and legal requirements guide the conduct of security and risk assessment investigations. These investigations play a critical role in safeguarding assets, ensuring business continuity, and protecting individuals and communities from harm. By identifying and addressing potential risks proactively, organizations can enhance their resilience, minimize losses, and maintain a safe and secure environment for stakeholders.

Legal Support and Witness Interviews:
Private investigators assist attorneys and legal firms in preparing for civil and criminal cases. They may conduct witness interviews, gather evidence, serve legal documents, and provide expert testimony in court proceedings. Private investigators play a crucial role in uncovering facts, locating witnesses, and corroborating evidence to support legal arguments and ensure a fair trial.

Computer Forensics and Cyber Investigations:
Cyber and computer forensic investigations involve the collection, analysis, and preservation of digital evidence to uncover cybercrimes, data breaches, or unauthorized activities. Conducted by digital forensic experts, law enforcement agencies, or cybersecurity firms, these inquiries aim to identify perpetrators, gather evidence for legal proceedings, and mitigate security breaches.

Cyber forensic investigations focus on analyzing digital systems, networks, and electronic devices to trace the origin and impact of cyber-attacks, malware infections, or data breaches. They may involve examining network traffic, log files, and system configurations to identify suspicious activities and unauthorized access.

Computer forensic investigations, on the other hand, concentrate on analyzing digital evidence stored on computers, mobile devices, or storage media. Investigators utilize specialized tools and techniques to recover deleted files, examine file metadata, and trace digital footprints to reconstruct events and establish timelines.

Ethical considerations, legal requirements, and chain of custody protocols govern the conduct of cyber and computer forensic investigations. These inquiries play a crucial role in incident response, threat intelligence, and digital risk management, enabling organizations to detect and respond to cyber threats effectively, preserve evidence for legal proceedings, and protect sensitive information from unauthorized access or manipulation.

Undercover Operations and Sting Operations:
Private investigators conduct covert, undercover or sting operations to gather evidence of illegal activities or unethical behavior. This may involve posing as employees, customers, or members of a targeted group to gain access to sensitive information, observe criminal activities, or elicit confessions from suspects. Undercover operations require careful planning, coordination, and adherence to legal and ethical guidelines to ensure the safety of the investigator and the integrity of the investigation.

Covert operations, shrouded in secrecy and intrigue, represent a cornerstone of intelligence gathering, military strategy, and law enforcement tactics. These clandestine operations, carried out with precision and discretion, are designed to achieve strategic objectives, gather critical intelligence, or neutralize threats without alerting adversaries or compromising operational security. In this exploration, we delve into the intricacies of covert operations, from their strategic purpose to their execution and the ethical considerations that accompany them.

At the heart of covert operations lies the strategic imperative to achieve specific objectives while minimizing risk and exposure. These objectives can vary widely depending on the context and the goals of the operation. Covert operations may involve infiltrating enemy organizations, recruiting assets, or intercepting communications to obtain sensitive information, conduct reconnaissance on your subject(s), even gathering of evidence or apprehending suspects.

The execution of covert operations requires meticulous planning, careful coordination, and a high degree of operational security to maintain secrecy and avoid detection. Operational planning begins with intelligence gathering and analysis to identify targets, assess vulnerabilities, and develop strategies for achieving objectives while minimizing risk to personnel and operational integrity.

Once a plan is formulated, operatives are selected, trained, and equipped for the mission ahead. These operatives, often highly trained specialists with expertise in surveillance, reconnaissance, and covert communications, are tasked with executing the mission with precision and discretion.

Operational tactics vary depending on the nature of the mission and the operational environment. Infiltration missions may involve undercover operatives posing as civilians or members of the target organization to gather intelligence or gain access to sensitive locations. Surveillance operations may employ advanced technology, such as drones, satellites, or wiretapping devices, to monitor targets and gather real-time intelligence.

Throughout the execution of the operation, operatives must maintain strict operational security, adhere to protocols for communication and reporting, and adapt to changing circumstances to ensure the success of the mission while minimizing the risk of exposure.

While covert operations serve strategic purposes and may be necessary to achieve certain objectives, they also raise ethical considerations regarding the use of deception, manipulation, and the potential for collateral damage. Covert operations conducted without proper oversight and accountability can lead to abuses of power, violations of human rights, and undermine public trust.

Ethical considerations also arise in the context of target selection, with questions of proportionality, necessity, and the potential for unintended consequences. Covert operations that result in legal challenges can have far-reaching consequences and may ultimately undermine the legitimacy of the operation and the broader strategic objectives it seeks to achieve.

Ultimately, covert operations represent a complex and multifaceted aspect of intelligence gathering and law enforcement tactics. While they play a crucial role in achieving strategic objectives, gathering critical intelligence, they also raise ethical considerations regarding transparency, accountability, and the protection of human rights. By carefully balancing the strategic imperative with ethical considerations and ensuring proper oversight and accountability, covert operations can be conducted effectively and responsibly to achieve desired outcomes while upholding and respecting individual rights.

Personal Protection and Bodyguard Services:
Private investigators provide personal protection and bodyguard services for individuals who require security assistance. Private investigators and bodyguards/personal protection professionals play distinct yet complementary roles in the field of security and investigation. Private investigators specialize in gathering information, conducting surveillance, and uncovering evidence related to legal, corporate, or personal matters. They may be hired to investigate fraud, infidelity, or missing persons cases, among other assignments.

On the other hand, bodyguards and personal protection professionals are tasked with ensuring the safety and security of individuals or groups. They undergo specialized training in threat assessment, defensive tactics, and emergency response to mitigate risks and protect clients from harm. Bodyguards may accompany high-profile individuals, celebrities, or executives, providing close protection and security measures to deter potential threats and ensure their clients' safety in various environments. Both professions require discretion, integrity, and adherence to legal and ethical standards to fulfill their responsibilities effectively.

Process Serving and Legal Support:
Private investigators serve legal documents, such as subpoenas, summonses, and court orders, on behalf of attorneys, legal firms, or individuals involved in legal proceedings. They ensure that legal documents are delivered promptly and accurately to the intended recipients, maintaining proper

documentation and adhering to legal requirements. Process serving may also involve locating individuals who are difficult to find or evasive in order to serve them with legal documents.

Forensic Accounting and Financial Investigations:
Forensic accounting and financial investigations involve the examination, analysis, and interpretation of financial records and transactions to uncover fraud, embezzlement, or financial misconduct. Forensic accountants utilize their expertise in accounting, auditing, and investigative techniques to scrutinize financial data, identify irregularities, and trace the flow of funds. They may conduct interviews, review documentation, and perform forensic analysis of financial statements to gather evidence and reconstruct financial activities. Financial investigations may involve collaboration with law enforcement agencies, regulatory bodies, or legal professionals to support criminal prosecutions, civil litigation, or regulatory enforcement actions. Ethical considerations, confidentiality, and adherence to legal standards guide the conduct of forensic accounting and financial investigations, which play a vital role in detecting financial crimes, recovering assets, and upholding the integrity of financial markets.

Asset Recovery and Debt Collection:
Asset recovery and debt collection involve efforts to reclaim funds or assets owed to individuals, businesses, or organizations. Asset recovery focuses on locating and recovering assets that have been misappropriated, stolen, or hidden. This may involve tracing the movement of funds, conducting forensic accounting, and employing legal measures to recover assets through civil proceedings or restitution orders.

Debt collection, on the other hand, entails pursuing individuals or entities who owe money to creditors. Debt collectors may use various strategies such as negotiation, mediation, or legal action to recover outstanding debts on behalf of their clients. Both asset recovery and debt collection require specialized knowledge of financial laws, negotiation skills, and legal procedures to achieve successful outcomes while adhering to ethical standards and regulatory guidelines.

Executive Due Diligence and Risk Management:
Private investigators provide executive due diligence and risk management services for businesses and organizations. They conduct comprehensive background checks on executives, board members, or key personnel to assess their qualifications, integrity, and potential risks. Private investigators may also evaluate business partners, suppliers, or clients to identify potential threats or vulnerabilities that could impact the organization's operations or reputation.

Child Custody and Family Law Investigations:
Family law and child custody investigations involve conducting inquiries into matters related to divorce, child custody, and family disputes to ensure the well-being and safety of children involved. These investigations are typically conducted by private investigators, social workers, or court-appointed guardians ad litem.

In family law cases, investigations may focus on gathering evidence related to allegations of domestic abuse, neglect, or substance abuse, as well as assessing the fitness of parents or caregivers to provide a stable and nurturing environment for their children. Investigators may conduct interviews with family members, observe interactions between parents and children, and review relevant documentation such as medical records or school reports to gather information.

Child custody investigations, specifically, aim to determine the best interests of the child and make recommendations to the court regarding custody arrangements. Investigators assess factors such as the child's relationship with each parent, living conditions, and parental fitness to provide a safe and supportive environment. These investigations play a crucial role in informing court decisions and ensuring that children's needs and rights are prioritized in family law proceedings. Ethical considerations, confidentiality, and adherence to legal standards are paramount in conducting family law and child custody investigations.

Pre-Employment Screening and Due Diligence:
Private investigators conduct pre-employment screening and due diligence checks for employers seeking to hire new employees or contractors. They verify credentials, employment history, education, and professional qualifications to ensure that candidates meet the requirements for the position. Pre-employment screening may also involve conducting background checks, criminal record searches, and drug testing to assess the suitability and reliability of potential hires.

Intellectual Property and Counterfeit Investigations:
Private investigators specialize in intellectual property and counterfeit investigations, protecting the rights and interests of businesses and individuals. They investigate cases of trademark infringement, copyright violations, product counterfeiting, and unauthorized use of intellectual property. Private investigators may conduct surveillance, gather evidence, and collaborate with private investigation agencies to identify and prosecute perpetrators of

intellectual property crimes.

Workplace Investigations and Employee Misconduct:
Workplace investigations involve examining allegations of misconduct, discrimination, harassment, or other violations of company policies or legal regulations within an organization. Conducted by human resources professionals, legal counsel, or third-party investigators, these inquiries aim to uncover the facts, determine the scope of the issue, and implement appropriate corrective actions.

Workplace investigations may involve interviewing employees, reviewing documentation, and gathering evidence related to the allegations. Investigators must adhere to ethical standards, confidentiality, and legal requirements throughout the process to ensure fairness and objectivity.

The goals of workplace investigations include protecting employee rights, promoting a safe and respectful work environment, and mitigating legal and reputational risks for the organization. Effective communication, transparency, and accountability are essential to maintaining trust and integrity throughout the investigation process. Upon completion, investigators typically provide recommendations for corrective actions, training, or policy revisions to prevent future incidents and foster a culture of compliance and respect within the workplace.

Personal Injury and Accident Investigations:
Personal injury and accident investigations involve examining the circumstances surrounding accidents, injuries, or incidents to determine liability, assess damages, and facilitate legal proceedings or insurance claims. These investigations are typically conducted by private investigators, insurance

adjusters, or legal professionals.

The process of personal injury and accident investigations may include gathering evidence such as witness statements, police reports, photographs, and medical records. Investigators may also conduct site inspections, reconstruct events, and consult with experts in various fields to assess causation and liability.

The goals of personal injury and accident investigations are to establish the facts, determine fault or negligence, and assess the extent of damages suffered by the injured party. This information is crucial for negotiating settlements, pursuing legal action, or resolving insurance claims.

Ethical considerations, adherence to legal standards, and confidentiality are essential in conducting personal injury and accident investigations to ensure fairness and accuracy in the assessment of claims. By uncovering the truth behind accidents and injuries, these investigations play a vital role in ensuring that victims receive appropriate compensation and that responsible parties are held accountable for their actions.

Private investigators perform a wide range of tasks and assignments across various industries and sectors, providing valuable services to their clients. Whether conducting surveillance, gathering evidence, or providing expert testimony, private investigators play a crucial role in uncovering the truth, protecting assets, and ensuring justice in legal, corporate, and personal matters. Their work requires a combination of skills, expertise, and ethical integrity, making them indispensable partners in today's complex and dynamic world.

CHAPTER FOUR
Traits of a P.I.

Trait: Latin *Origin Tractus* - Inherited characteristics

Being a private investigator requires a unique set of character traits, skills, and qualities to succeed in this challenging and demanding profession. Investigative work often involves gathering information, analyzing evidence, and uncovering the truth in a wide range of situations, from criminal cases to corporate investigations to personal matters. In this extensive exploration, we'll delve into the essential character traits required to excel as a private investigator, aside from going hours without a restroom break, we will be examining how the following qualities contribute to success in the field and how they can be cultivated and developed.

Integrity and Ethical Conduct:
Integrity is the cornerstone of being a private investigator. It involves honesty, trustworthiness, and adherence to ethical standards and principles. Investigators must maintain the highest level of integrity in their work, ensuring that they conduct themselves with honesty and transparency at all times. They must adhere to legal and ethical guidelines, respect confidentiality, and avoid conflicts of interest to preserve the integrity of their investigations and uphold the trust of their clients.

Analytical and Critical Thinking:
Analytical and critical thinking skills are essential for investigators to assess situations, evaluate evidence, and draw logical conclusions. Investigators must be able to analyze complex information, identify patterns, and recognize discrepancies or inconsistencies in their investigations. They must approach each case with a skeptical yet open-minded

perspective, carefully weighing evidence and considering alternative explanations to arrive at accurate and objective conclusions.

Attention to Detail:

Attention to detail is a crucial trait for investigators, as even the smallest piece of information or overlooked detail can have significant implications for an investigation. Investigators must be meticulous in their observations, documentation, and analysis of evidence, ensuring that they capture and record every relevant detail accurately. They must pay close attention to nuances, inconsistencies, and discrepancies to uncover hidden clues and solve complex cases.

Perseverance and Determination:

Investigative work can be challenging and time-consuming, often requiring perseverance and determination to overcome obstacles and achieve results. Investigators must possess a strong work ethic and a willingness to persevere through setbacks, delays, and obstacles in their investigations. They must remain focused and tenacious in their pursuit of the truth, never giving up until they have exhausted all avenues and uncovered the answers they seek.

Discretion and Professionalism:

Discretion is essential for investigators to maintain confidentiality, protect sensitive information, and preserve the privacy of individuals involved in their investigations. Investigators must exercise discretion and professionalism in their interactions with clients, witnesses, and subjects, ensuring that they handle sensitive information with care and respect. They must maintain strict confidentiality and avoid disclosing confidential or privileged information to unauthorized parties.

Communication and Interpersonal Skills:
Effective communication and interpersonal skills are essential for investigators to interact with clients, witnesses, private investigation officials, and other stakeholders involved in their investigations. Investigators must be able to communicate clearly and effectively, both orally and in writing, conveying complex information in a concise and understandable manner. They must be skilled at active listening, interviewing, and building rapport to elicit information and gather evidence effectively.

Adaptability and Flexibility:
Investigative work often involves dealing with unpredictable situations, changing circumstances, and evolving challenges. Investigators must be adaptable and flexible, able to adjust their approach, tactics, and strategies to meet the demands of each case. They must be comfortable operating in dynamic and uncertain environments, quickly adapting to new information, changing priorities, and unexpected developments in their investigations.

Creativity and Problem-Solving Skills:
Investigative work often requires creativity and innovative thinking to solve complex problems and overcome obstacles. Investigators must be creative and resourceful in their approach, able to think outside the box and consider alternative solutions to challenges. They must possess strong problem-solving skills, able to analyze situations from multiple perspectives, identify root causes, and develop effective strategies to address them.

Time Management and Organizational Skills:
Time management and organizational skills are essential for investigators to effectively manage their workload, prioritize tasks, and meet deadlines.

Investigators must be able to juggle multiple cases and assignments simultaneously, allocating time and resources efficiently to ensure that each investigation progresses smoothly. They must be highly organized, maintaining detailed records, documentation, and case files to track progress and maintain accountability.

Resilience and Stress Management:
	Investigative work can be emotionally demanding and stressful, requiring investigators to cope with challenging situations, confront difficult truths, and manage their own emotional well-being. Investigators must possess resilience and stress management skills, able to cope with adversity, bounce back from setbacks, and maintain their focus and composure under pressure. They must develop healthy coping mechanisms and self-care strategies to protect their mental and emotional health while navigating the demands of their profession.

Technical Proficiency and Continuous Learning:
	Technical proficiency and a commitment to continuous learning are essential for investigators to stay current with advances in technology, tools, and techniques in their field. Investigators must be proficient in using investigative software, surveillance equipment, forensic tools, and other specialized resources to conduct their work effectively. They must also engage in ongoing training, education, and professional development to expand their skills, stay abreast of industry trends, and enhance their expertise in various areas of investigation.

Leadership and Teamwork:
	Leadership and teamwork skills are important for investigators who work as part of multidisciplinary teams or collaborate with other professionals in their field. Investigators must be able to lead and coordinate investigative teams, delegating tasks, providing

guidance, and fostering collaboration to achieve common goals. They must also be effective team players, able to work collaboratively with others, share information, and contribute their expertise to collective efforts.

Legal Knowledge and Understanding:
A solid understanding of the legal system, procedures, and regulations is essential for investigators to conduct their work effectively within the bounds of the law. Investigators must possess a working knowledge of relevant laws, regulations, and legal principles governing investigative practices, evidence collection, and privacy rights. They must also adhere to ethical guidelines and professional standards to ensure that their investigations are conducted lawfully and ethically.

Physical Fitness and Well-being:
Physical fitness and well-being are important for investigators who may be required to work in physically demanding or hazardous environments. Investigators must maintain good physical health and stamina to perform tasks such as surveillance, fieldwork, or evidence collection effectively. They must also prioritize their well-being, practicing self-care, managing stress, and maintaining a healthy work-life balance to sustain their energy and focus over the course of their careers.

Cultural Sensitivity and Diversity Awareness:
Cultural sensitivity and diversity awareness are essential for investigators who work with individuals from diverse backgrounds, cultures, and communities. Investigators must demonstrate respect, tolerance, and sensitivity to cultural differences, avoiding stereotypes, biases, or discriminatory attitudes in their interactions with others. They must strive to foster an inclusive and supportive environment that values diversity and

promotes understanding and collaboration among all stakeholders involved in their investigations.
Financial Responsibility and Accountability:
Financial responsibility and accountability are important for investigators who manage budgets, expenses, and resources for their investigations. Investigators must exercise prudent financial management, allocating funds and resources efficiently to maximize the impact and effectiveness of their work. They must maintain accurate records, documentation, and accountability for expenses, ensuring transparency and compliance with financial regulations and ethical standards.

Confidence and Professionalism:
Confidence and professionalism are essential for investigators to instill trust and credibility in their work and interactions with clients, witnesses, and stakeholders. Investigators must project confidence and competence in their abilities, demonstrating professionalism, authority, and expertise in their field. They must maintain a professional demeanor, appearance, and communication style, projecting credibility and trustworthiness to inspire confidence and respect in others.

Compassion and Empathy:
Compassion and empathy are essential qualities for investigators to understand the perspectives, emotions, and experiences of the individuals involved in their investigations. Investigators must demonstrate empathy and compassion when interacting with clients, witnesses, and victims, acknowledging their feelings, concerns, and needs with sensitivity and understanding. They must be able to provide support, reassurance, and assistance to those affected by the circumstances of their investigations, showing kindness and empathy in their interactions.

Being a private investigator requires a diverse range of character traits, skills, and qualities to excel in this challenging and dynamic profession. From integrity and analytical thinking to empathy and adaptability, investigators must possess a unique blend of attributes to navigate complex situations, solve challenging problems, and achieve successful outcomes in their investigations. By cultivating and developing these essential qualities, investigators can uphold the highest standards of professionalism, integrity, and ethical conduct, making a positive impact in their field and serving the needs of their clients and communities.

To touch on a subject from the beginning of this book being a private investigator is not exactly what is seen on the silver screen. Television has long been enamored with the archetype of the private investigator, portraying these characters as charismatic, resourceful, and always one step ahead of the game. From the iconic trench-coat-clad detectives of film noir to the tech-savvy sleuths of contemporary crime dramas, television has created a rich tapestry of fictional private investigators that captivate audiences worldwide. However, the depiction of private investigation on television often diverges significantly from the reality of the profession. In this comparison, we unravel the truth behind the fiction, exploring the similarities and differences between television private investigators and their real-life counterparts.

Television private investigators are often portrayed as larger-than-life characters, endowed with a combination of wit, charm, and cunning that enables them to solve the most perplexing of cases. Whether it's Sherlock Holmes deducing clues with uncanny precision or Veronica Mars outsmarting adversaries with her quick wit and resourcefulness, television PIs are typically depicted as master detectives capable of unraveling even the most intricate mysteries.

These fictional portrayals often emphasize the glamorous aspects of the profession, showcasing sleek offices, high-tech surveillance equipment, and daring undercover missions. Television PIs are frequently depicted as lone wolves, operating outside the confines of law enforcement and answering only to their own moral code.

In reality, private investigation is a far cry from its glamorous portrayal on television. While some elements of the fictional depiction may ring true—such as the need for keen observation skills, attention to detail, and perseverance—the day-to-day work of real-life private investigators is often less dramatic and more methodical.

Unlike their television counterparts, real-life private investigators must adhere to strict ethical guidelines and legal regulations governing their profession. They often work closely with law enforcement agencies, legal teams, and corporate clients to gather evidence, conduct background checks, and provide investigative support for a wide range of cases.

The reality of private investigation is also far less glamorous than its television portrayal. Instead of high-speed car chases and dramatic confrontations, much of the work involves conducting surveillance, analyzing data, and compiling reports. It can be tedious and time-consuming, requiring patience, attention to detail, and a willingness to sift through mountains of information to uncover the truth.

One area where television and reality converge is in the use of technology and tools. While television PIs may have access to futuristic gadgets and cutting-edge surveillance equipment, real-life investigators also leverage technology to enhance their capabilities.

Modern private investigators use a variety of tools and techniques to gather evidence, including surveillance cameras, GPS tracking devices, and computer forensics software. They may also employ social media monitoring, database searches, and open-source intelligence gathering to gather information and track down leads.

However, while technology can be a valuable asset in the investigative process, it is not a substitute for good old-fashioned detective work. Real-life private investigators must still rely on their instincts, experience, and interpersonal skills to navigate complex cases and uncover the truth. Despite all these differences, both fictional and real-life private investigators share a common goal: to uncover the truth and bring closure to their clients' cases, albeit through different means and methods.

CHAPTER FIVE
Education/Skills needed

Education: Old Norse *Origin Knowledge* - aptitude

Becoming a private investigator is a career path that requires a combination of education, training, and specific skills to excel in the role. private investigators play a crucial role in a highly regulated field, investigating crimes, gathering evidence, and solving cases. In this comprehensive guide, we'll explore the education and skills needed to become a private investigator, examining the academic requirements, specialized training, and essential qualities that contribute to success in this challenging and rewarding profession.

Education Requirements:

High School Diploma or Equivalent:
The journey to becoming a private investigator often begins with obtaining a high school diploma or equivalent qualification. While there are no specific educational prerequisites for entering private investigation, a solid foundation in subjects such as English, mathematics, social studies, and science can be beneficial for aspiring private investigators.

Bachelor's Degree:
Many private investigation agencies require candidates to have a bachelor's degree from an accredited college or university. While the specific field of study may vary, common areas of study for aspiring private investigators include criminal justice, criminology, psychology, sociology, or forensic science. A bachelor's degree provides a comprehensive understanding of the criminal justice system, investigative techniques, and relevant legal principles.

Advanced Degrees:
	While not always required, obtaining an advanced degree, such as a master's or doctoral degree, can enhance a private investigator's qualifications and career prospects. Advanced degrees in fields such as criminal justice administration, forensic psychology, or private investigation leadership can provide specialized knowledge and skills that are valuable for leadership positions within private investigation agencies.

Specialized Training:

Police Academy:
	Upon completing their education, aspiring private investigators typically undergo training at a police academy to gain the necessary skills and knowledge for a career in private investigation. Police academy training covers a wide range of topics, including criminal law, investigative techniques, firearms training, defensive tactics, and emergency response procedures. Graduates of the police academy are equipped with the foundational skills and training needed to begin their careers as private investigators.

Field Training:
	After completing schooling, new investigator's typically undergo field training under the supervision of experienced investigators. Field training provides hands-on experience in real-world private investigation situations, allowing recruits to apply their knowledge and skills in practical settings. Field training programs vary in duration but typically last several weeks, during which recruits work alongside seasoned agents to learn the ropes of work, crime scene investigation, and surveillance.

Specialized Investigative Training:

Aspiring private investigators often undergo specialized training in investigative techniques, evidence collection, and case management to prepare for their roles as independent investigators. This training may be provided by private investigation agencies, specialized training academies, or professional organizations. Topics covered in specialized investigative training may include interview and interrogation techniques, crime scene processing, forensic analysis, surveillance methods, and legal procedures related to investigations.

Being that private investigation is a multifaceted field requiring a diverse skill set and specialized knowledge. A strong foundation in investigation techniques is essential, staying competitive in the industry often demands continuous learning and development. Specialized training courses play a crucial role in honing the expertise of private investigators, enabling them to tackle complex cases and excel in their profession.

Here we will explore various specialized training courses available to private investigators. From digital forensics to undercover operations, each course equips professionals with specific skills tailored to different investigative needs. By delving into these courses, aspiring and seasoned private investigators alike can identify opportunities for growth and advancement in their careers.

1. Digital Forensics

In today's digital age, the importance of digital forensics in investigations cannot be overstated. Private investigators often encounter cases involving cybercrimes, data breaches, or digital evidence. Specialized training in digital forensics equips professionals with the knowledge and tools necessary to collect, analyze, and preserve digital evidence effectively.

Courses in digital forensics cover a range of topics, including:

- Understanding file systems and data storage mechanisms
- Techniques for data acquisition and preservation
- Forensic analysis of computers, mobile devices, and network traffic
- Legal considerations and chain of custody protocols
- Recovery of deleted or encrypted data
- Cybersecurity best practices

Certifications such as Certified Digital Forensics Examiner (CDFE) or Certified Computer Forensics Examiner (CCFE) validate proficiency in this specialized area and enhance credibility in the field of private investigation.

2. Surveillance Techniques

Surveillance is a fundamental aspect of private investigation, often employed to gather evidence, monitor subjects, or conduct reconnaissance. Specialized training in surveillance techniques provides investigators with the skills to conduct covert observations discreetly and effectively.

Courses in surveillance techniques cover:

- Principles of surveillance and counter-surveillance
- Covert photography and videography
- Vehicle and foot surveillance tactics
- Use of surveillance equipment such as GPS trackers and hidden cameras
- Legal and ethical considerations in surveillance

operations
- Report writing and evidence documentation

Advanced surveillance courses may also include specialized training in mobile surveillance, rural surveillance, or surveillance in high-risk environments.

3. Forensic Accounting

Financial investigations are common in both corporate and private sectors, often involving fraud, embezzlement, or asset tracing. Forensic accounting courses provide private investigators with the expertise to analyze financial records, identify discrepancies, and uncover illicit activities.

Key topics covered in forensic accounting courses include:

- Principles of financial investigation and auditing
- Analysis of financial statements and transaction records
- Tracing assets and identifying hidden or offshore accounts
- Investigating money laundering schemes
- Expert testimony and litigation support

Certifications such as Certified Fraud Examiner (CFE) or Certified Forensic Accountant (Cr.FA) validate proficiency in forensic accounting and enhance credibility in investigative matters involving financial fraud.

4. Interview and Interrogation Techniques

Effective interviewing and interrogation skills are essential for extracting information, eliciting confessions, and building rapport with witnesses and suspects. Specialized training in interview and interrogation techniques equips private investigators with the communication skills and psychological insights necessary to conduct successful interviews.

Courses in interview and interrogation techniques cover:

- Psychological principles of communication and persuasion
- Establishing rapport and gaining cooperation
- Questioning strategies and active listening techniques
- Detecting deception and evaluating verbal and nonverbal cues
- Ethical considerations and legal safeguards

Advanced courses may focus on specialized interviewing techniques for specific populations, such as juveniles, victims of trauma, or individuals with mental health issues.

5. Undercover Operations

Undercover operations play a vital role in gathering intelligence, infiltrating criminal organizations, and uncovering illicit activities. Specialized training in undercover operations prepares private investigators for the challenges and risks associated with assuming covert identities.

Courses in undercover operations cover:

- Fundamentals of undercover work and covert communication
- Techniques for building and maintaining cover identities
- Risk assessment and safety protocols
- Surveillance and counter-surveillance tactics
- Psychological aspects of undercover operations

- Legal considerations and ethical dilemmas

Simulation exercises and real-world scenarios may be incorporated into training programs to provide practical experience in undercover operations.

Specialized training courses offer private investigators the opportunity to expand their skill set, enhance their expertise, and stay abreast of emerging trends and technologies in the field. Whether it's digital forensics, surveillance techniques, forensic accounting, interview and interrogation skills, or undercover operations, each course provides valuable knowledge and practical tools for conducting thorough and effective investigations.

By investing in continuous learning and professional development, private investigators can distinguish themselves in a competitive industry, deliver exceptional results for their clients, and contribute to the pursuit of justice and truth. As industries evolve, technologies advance, and societal needs change, the acquisition of new knowledge and skills becomes essential for personal growth, career advancement, and societal progress.

In many professions, staying stagnant is not an option. Continued education enables individuals to stay relevant and competitive in their fields by acquiring new skills, certifications, or qualifications. Whether it's mastering emerging technologies, keeping up with industry best practices, or gaining expertise in specialized areas, ongoing learning enhances one's professional profile and opens doors to new opportunities for career advancement.

The pace of change in today's world is rapid, and industries are constantly evolving. Continued education fosters adaptability by equipping individuals with the flexibility and resilience needed to navigate shifting landscapes. By embracing new ideas, methodologies, and technologies, lifelong learners remain agile and better prepared to tackle challenges and seize opportunities in a rapidly changing environment.

Education is not solely about professional advancement; it also contributes significantly to personal growth and fulfillment. Lifelong learning expands individuals' horizons, stimulates intellectual curiosity, and fosters a deeper understanding of the world around them. Whether pursuing a new hobby, exploring a different field of study, or engaging in self-improvement activities, continued education enriches lives and enhances overall well-being.

Continued education hones critical thinking, analytical, and problem-solving skills, which are valuable across all aspects of life. By exposing individuals to diverse perspectives, challenging them to think creatively, and encouraging them to question assumptions, ongoing learning enables more effective problem-solving and decision-making in both professional and personal contexts.

From a societal perspective, continued education contributes to economic growth and prosperity. A well-educated workforce drives innovation, productivity, and competitiveness, ultimately leading to higher standards of living and greater social mobility. Moreover, individuals with higher levels of education tend to earn higher incomes and enjoy better job security, thereby contributing to overall economic stability and prosperity.

Lifelong learning fosters a culture of curiosity, collaboration, and continuous improvement within communities. By participating in educational programs, workshops, or community initiatives, individuals not only enhance their own knowledge and skills but also contribute to the collective learning and development of society. This shared pursuit of knowledge strengthens social bonds, fosters empathy and understanding, and promotes positive societal change.

CHAPTER SIX
Similar Jobs that Help in the P.I. Field

Similar: Greek *Origin homalos* - Equal like

Police Officers / Military Police

Private investigators and policemen (including military police) share several similarities despite their different roles and contexts within law enforcement. Both professions are dedicated to upholding the law, ensuring public safety, and seeking justice, albeit through distinct avenues.

First, both private investigators and policemen possess investigative skills essential for gathering evidence and solving cases. They are adept at conducting interviews, analyzing data, and employing surveillance techniques to uncover information crucial to their investigations. Whether pursuing leads on a missing person or probing a criminal activity, both professionals rely on their keen observational abilities and analytical minds to piece together complex puzzles.

Second, a commitment to ethics and integrity underpins the work of both private investigators and policemen. While private investigators often operate within the constraints of legal boundaries specific to their jurisdiction, they adhere to codes of conduct that prioritize honesty, confidentiality, and respect for individuals' rights. Similarly, policemen are bound by the law and sworn to uphold justice impartially, demonstrating integrity in their interactions with the public and handling of evidence.

Furthermore, teamwork and collaboration are integral to the success of investigations in both domains. Private investigators may work independently or as part of a team within their agency, pooling resources and expertise to tackle challenging cases effectively. Likewise, policemen operate within hierarchical structures within law enforcement agencies, coordinating efforts with colleagues, forensic experts, and other agencies to solve crimes and maintain public order.

Additionally, both professions require a commitment to ongoing training and professional development. Private investigators may undergo specialized training in areas such as surveillance techniques, digital forensics, or undercover operations to enhance their investigative skills. Similarly, policemen receive continuous training in areas such as firearms proficiency, crisis intervention, and legal updates to stay abreast of evolving law enforcement practices and technologies.

While private investigators and policemen operate in different spheres of law enforcement, they share fundamental similarities in their dedication to justice, investigative prowess, ethical conduct, teamwork, and professional development. These commonalities underscore the essential role both professions play in safeguarding communities and upholding the rule of law.

Health Safety & Environment
Private investigators and safety management professionals may seem to operate in disparate realms, but a closer look reveals striking similarities in their approach, skill sets, and objectives, particularly concerning risk mitigation and protection of assets.

Firstly, both professions require a keen eye for detail and analytical thinking. Private investigators meticulously analyze evidence, scrutinize behavior patterns, and follow leads to uncover the truth behind various situations, whether it's a case of fraud, theft, or infidelity. Similarly, safety management professionals employ systematic risk assessments, hazard analyses, and incident investigations to identify potential threats to workplace safety and develop effective mitigation strategies.

Secondly, effective communication is paramount for both private investigators and safety management professionals. Private investigators must adeptly interview witnesses, gather statements, and convey findings to clients or legal authorities clearly and concisely. Likewise, safety management professionals must communicate safety protocols, policies, and procedures to employees at all levels of an organization, fostering a culture of safety and ensuring compliance with regulatory standards.

Furthermore, both professions require a comprehensive understanding of applicable laws, regulations, and industry standards. Private investigators must navigate complex legal frameworks governing surveillance, privacy rights, and evidence collection to ensure their actions remain within legal boundaries. Similarly, safety management professionals must stay abreast of occupational health and safety regulations, building codes, and industry-specific guidelines to implement effective safety measures and prevent workplace incidents.

Moreover, both private investigators and safety management professionals emphasize proactive measures to mitigate risks and prevent incidents before they occur. Private investigators may conduct background checks, security assessments, or vulnerability analyses to identify potential threats and vulnerabilities. Similarly, safety management professionals implement safety training programs, conduct safety audits, and develop emergency response plans to minimize workplace hazards and ensure swift and effective responses to emergencies.

While private investigators and safety management professionals operate in distinct contexts, they share fundamental similarities in their approach to risk management, attention to detail, communication skills, legal knowledge, and emphasis on proactive measures to safeguard individuals, assets, and organizations from harm. These commonalities underscore the vital role both professions play in promoting safety, security, and peace of mind in various settings.

Insurance

Private investigators and insurance agents may seem like they operate in entirely different realms, but upon closer examination, it becomes evident that they share significant similarities in their roles, responsibilities, and objectives, particularly in the realm of risk assessment and mitigation.

Firstly, both professions involve a thorough investigation process. Private investigators meticulously gather evidence, conduct interviews, and analyze information to uncover the truth behind various situations, whether it involves fraud, theft, or other criminal activities. Similarly, insurance agents assess risks by evaluating factors such as the applicant's health, lifestyle, and driving record, aiming to determine the likelihood of future insurance claims accurately.

Secondly, effective communication skills are essential for both private investigators and insurance agents. Private investigators must adeptly communicate their findings to clients or legal authorities, often translating complex information into understandable reports. Similarly, insurance agents need to explain policy terms, coverage options, and claim processes clearly and accurately to clients, ensuring they make informed decisions about their insurance needs.

Furthermore, both professions require a keen understanding of legal and ethical considerations. Private investigators must navigate laws and regulations governing surveillance, privacy rights, and evidence collection to ensure their actions remain within legal boundaries. Similarly, insurance agents must adhere to regulatory standards and industry best practices, ensuring compliance with insurance laws and ethical guidelines while serving the best interests of their clients.

Moreover, both private investigators and insurance agents play proactive roles in risk management. Private investigators may conduct background checks, security assessments, or fraud investigations to identify potential risks and vulnerabilities for their clients. Similarly, insurance agents help clients mitigate risks by recommending appropriate insurance coverage tailored to their individual needs and circumstances, aiming to protect them financially from unforeseen events.

In conclusion, while private investigators and insurance agents operate in different spheres, they share fundamental similarities in their investigative processes, communication skills, legal knowledge, and proactive approach to risk management. These commonalities highlight the crucial roles both professions play in uncovering truths, assessing risks, and protecting the interests of their clients in various contexts.

Bail Enforcement
Bail enforcement agents, commonly known as bounty hunters, and private investigators may seem to operate in distinct realms within the field of law enforcement, but they share several fundamental

similarities in their roles, methods, and objectives.

First, both professions involve conducting thorough investigations to locate individuals. Bail enforcement agents track down fugitives who have skipped bail, using various investigative techniques such as surveillance, background checks, and interviews with acquaintances to locate their targets. Similarly, private investigators are often tasked with finding missing persons, whether for legal, personal, or professional reasons, employing similar investigative methods to gather information and locate individuals.

Second, both bail enforcement agents and private investigators must possess strong observational skills and attention to detail. They meticulously analyze evidence, observe behavioral patterns, and follow leads to piece together the puzzle of a case. Whether searching for a fugitive or gathering evidence for a legal case, both professions require keen observation and the ability to uncover crucial details that others may overlook.

In addition, effective communication is essential for both bail enforcement agents and private investigators. They often need to interact with a diverse range of individuals, including witnesses, informants, and law enforcement officials, to gather information and collaborate on cases. Clear and concise communication is crucial in conveying findings, coordinating efforts with relevant parties, and ensuring successful outcomes.

Finally, both professions require a solid understanding of legal regulations and procedures. Bail enforcement agents must navigate the legal framework surrounding bail bonds, fugitive recovery, and apprehension procedures to ensure their actions remain within legal boundaries. Similarly, private investigators must adhere to laws and regulations governing surveillance, privacy rights, and evidence collection to conduct their investigations ethically and lawfully.

In conclusion, while bail enforcement agents and private investigators may have distinct objectives and operate in different contexts within law enforcement, they share fundamental similarities in their investigative techniques, observational skills, communication abilities, and legal knowledge. These commonalities underscore the essential roles both professions play in locating individuals, gathering evidence, and upholding the principles of justice and public safety.

Debt Collections
Debt collectors and private investigators, although operating in different realms, share several fundamental similarities in their approach, methods, and objectives, particularly concerning information gathering and locating individuals.

Firstly, both professions require adeptness in locating individuals. Debt collectors often track down debtors who have defaulted on their payments, utilizing various investigative techniques such as skip tracing, database searches, and contacting acquaintances or references to locate their targets. Similarly, private investigators may be tasked with finding individuals for various reasons, including legal proceedings, asset recovery, or locating witnesses, employing similar investigative methods to gather information and locate individuals.

Secondly, effective communication skills are crucial for both debt collectors and private investigators. They must interact with a diverse range of individuals, including debtors, witnesses, family members, and employers, to gather information and pursue leads. Clear and persuasive communication is essential in negotiating payment arrangements, eliciting cooperation from sources, and obtaining crucial information to further their objectives.

Likewise, both professions require a thorough understanding of legal regulations and ethical guidelines. Debt collectors must adhere to strict regulations such as the Fair Debt Collection Practices Act (FDCPA) to ensure fair and lawful debt collection practices, avoiding harassment or deceptive tactics. Similarly, private investigators must operate within legal boundaries, respecting privacy rights, and adhering to laws governing surveillance, evidence collection, and information disclosure.

What's more, both debt collectors and private investigators rely on investigative techniques to gather information and assess situations effectively. They analyze financial records, conduct background checks, and employ surveillance methods to uncover relevant details and verify the accuracy of information provided. Whether assessing a debtor's financial situation or investigating an individual's background, both professions rely on thorough research and analysis to achieve their objectives.

While debt collectors and private investigators may have distinct objectives and operate within different contexts, they share fundamental similarities in their investigative techniques, communication skills, legal knowledge, and ethical considerations. These commonalities underscore the essential roles both professions play in locating individuals, gathering information, and achieving their respective objectives within the realm of financial transactions and legal proceedings.

Positive traits, when taken to extremes or applied in inappropriate contexts, can often transmute into negative attributes. Consider empathy, a quintessential quality that fosters understanding and compassion. Yet, when excessively indulged, it can lead to emotional exhaustion and burnout.

Take the case of an empathetic individual working in a caregiving profession. Initially, their empathy drives them to provide unparalleled support and comfort to those in need. However, without proper boundaries, they might absorb the emotional burdens of their patients to the extent that it compromises their own well-being. Continuously internalizing others' pain can lead to compassion fatigue, rendering them less effective in their role and jeopardizing their mental health.

Similarly, ambition, typically lauded as a trait that propels individuals toward success, can spiral into obsession and ruthlessness. A person driven by ambition may prioritize their goals above all else, including ethical considerations and personal relationships. They may resort to unethical means to achieve their ends, disregarding the consequences on others. Their relentless pursuit of success can lead to alienation from loved ones, burn bridges in their professional sphere, and even result in a hollow victory devoid of fulfillment.

Even humility, revered for its ability to foster modesty and cooperation, can backfire when excessively practiced. While acknowledging one's limitations is commendable, an overly humble individual may undermine their own abilities and downplay their accomplishments. This could impede their career progression and limit their potential for growth, as they shy away from opportunities that require self-assertion and confidence.

In essence, the boundary between a positive trait and a negative attribute is often blurred, contingent upon the context and degree of expression. It underscores the importance of balance and self-awareness in harnessing these traits constructively. Awareness of when these traits veer into detrimental territory is key to mitigating their adverse effects and fostering personal and professional development.

While any of the above mentioned career fields can help a person excel in the private investigation industry, experience in any of the same career fields could also create problems for a potential private investigator. A person with a police or military background may find it difficult to separate private investigation with law enforcement investigation. Someone with Health, Safety & Environment experience may rely too much on standard workplace investigation skills and overlook critical clues; same goes for someone that has worked in insurance. As with everything, there is a fine line between being passion and obsession. Find that fine line for yourself in the field of private investigation and walk that line all the way to a lasting successful career.

Transitioning between legal, law enforcement, or private investigation careers can present unique challenges and conflicts as individuals navigate the intricacies of different roles, responsibilities, and professional cultures. These transitions require careful consideration of the skills, knowledge, and ethical considerations inherent in each field, as well as the potential conflicts that may arise during the transition process.

One significant area of conflict when transitioning between legal, law enforcement, and private investigation careers is the divergence in professional norms, practices, and priorities. For example, attorneys are bound by strict ethical guidelines and legal regulations governing client confidentiality, conflict of interest, and attorney-client privilege. Transitioning from a legal career to a law enforcement or private investigation role may require individuals to adapt to different standards of evidence, investigative techniques, and ethical considerations.

Conversely, individuals transitioning from law enforcement or private investigation careers to legal roles may encounter conflicts related to their previous experiences, biases, or perspectives. While their investigative skills and knowledge of criminal justice processes may be valuable assets in a legal career, individuals may need to reconcile any conflicts between their roles as objective legal advocates and their previous roles as investigators or law enforcement officers.

Also, transitioning between legal, law enforcement, and private investigation careers can raise conflicts related to professional identity and career trajectory. Individuals may struggle to reconcile their previous roles and experiences with their new career paths, leading to feelings of uncertainty, identity crisis, or imposter syndrome. Additionally, transitioning between these fields may entail changes in job responsibilities, work environments, and professional networks, further complicating the transition process.

Another area of conflict when transitioning between legal, law enforcement, and private investigation careers is the potential for conflicts of interest or ethical dilemmas. Individuals may encounter situations where their loyalties or obligations to former clients, colleagues, or employers conflict with their current roles and responsibilities. Negotiating these conflicts requires individuals to uphold the highest standards of integrity, transparency, and professionalism, while ensuring compliance with legal and ethical obligations.

It goes without saying that transitioning between legal, law enforcement, and private investigation careers may entail practical challenges such as acquiring new skills, certifications, or licenses, or adapting to different organizational cultures and hierarchies. Individuals may need to invest time and resources in professional development, networking, or education to successfully transition between these fields and mitigate potential conflicts.

In closing, transitioning between legal, law enforcement, and private investigation careers can present unique challenges and conflicts related to professional norms, identity, ethics, and practical considerations. By acknowledging these conflicts and proactively addressing them through thoughtful planning, reflection, and adaptation, individuals can navigate the transition process with integrity, resilience, and a commitment to upholding the highest standards of professionalism and ethical conduct.

CHAPTER SEVEN
Center of Influence

Investigation: Medieval Latin *Origin Influentia* - Flow into

Attorney's

Lawyers; especially divorce, accident and criminal defense attorneys are vital contacts. They, and private investigators often collaborate closely to gather evidence, build cases, and achieve successful outcomes for their clients. Their collaboration is particularly vital in legal matters where thorough investigation is essential to uncovering facts, verifying claims, and strengthening arguments.

Lawyers may engage private investigators to gather information and evidence relevant to their cases. Private investigators have specialized skills in conducting research, surveillance, and interviews, which can provide lawyers with crucial insights and evidence to support their legal strategies. Whether it's locating witnesses, uncovering financial records, or conducting background checks, private investigators can offer valuable assistance in gathering information that may be challenging for lawyers to obtain on their own.

Private investigators often work under the direction of lawyers to ensure that their investigations adhere to legal and ethical standards. Lawyers provide guidance on the specific information or evidence needed to support their legal arguments, ensuring that private investigators conduct their inquiries within the bounds of the law and respect individuals' rights to privacy.

Lawyers rely on private investigators to provide expert testimony or assist with witness preparation in legal proceedings. Private investigators may offer their insights into the credibility of witnesses, help attorneys craft effective lines of questioning, and provide support during cross-examination to strengthen their cases in court.

Private investigators may also assist lawyers in identifying potential issues or weaknesses in their cases early on, allowing them to adjust their legal strategies accordingly. By conducting thorough investigations and uncovering pertinent information, private investigators help lawyers anticipate challenges, assess risks, and develop effective solutions to achieve favorable outcomes for their clients.

The collaboration between lawyers and private investigators is a symbiotic relationship built on trust, expertise, and mutual respect. Together, they form a formidable team dedicated to uncovering the truth, advocating for their clients' interests, and achieving justice within the legal system. By leveraging their complementary skills and resources, lawyers and private investigators play vital roles in ensuring fair and effective legal representation for individuals and organizations alike.

Businesses / Corporations
Businesses often rely on private investigators for a variety of reasons, ranging from mitigating risks to uncovering crucial information that can protect their interests, assets, and reputation. Private investigators provide specialized skills and expertise that businesses can leverage to address a wide range of challenges and achieve their objectives effectively.

One primary way businesses utilize private investigators is for conducting background checks on potential employees, partners, or clients. By verifying individuals' credentials, employment history, criminal records, and financial backgrounds, private investigators help businesses make informed decisions about hiring, partnerships, or financial transactions. These background checks can mitigate the risk of fraud, theft, or other liabilities that could harm the company's reputation or financial well-being.

Businesses often engage private investigators to conduct due diligence investigations before entering into new partnerships, mergers, or acquisitions. Private investigators can uncover hidden risks, liabilities, or discrepancies that may not be apparent through conventional means, enabling businesses to assess potential risks and negotiate terms with full transparency and confidence.

Private investigators also play a crucial role in corporate security and risk management. Businesses may hire private investigators to assess vulnerabilities in their physical security systems, conduct surveillance to identify potential threats or security breaches, or investigate instances of employee misconduct or corporate espionage. By identifying and addressing security threats proactively, businesses can safeguard their employees, assets, and confidential information from harm.

In addition to security and due diligence, businesses often rely on private investigators for litigation support and asset recovery. Private investigators can gather evidence, locate witnesses, and conduct surveillance to support legal proceedings, whether it's in civil litigation, intellectual property disputes, or insurance claims. Furthermore, private investigators can assist businesses in locating and recovering assets in cases of fraud, embezzlement, or other financial crimes, helping to minimize losses and preserve the company's financial integrity.

Businesses may engage private investigators to investigate instances of corporate fraud, theft, or misconduct within the organization. Private investigators can conduct undercover operations, forensic accounting, and digital forensics to uncover evidence of fraud, employee theft, or other unethical behavior. By identifying and addressing internal issues promptly, businesses can protect their reputation, maintain trust with stakeholders, and ensure compliance with legal and regulatory standards.

Businesses rely on private investigators for a wide range of services, including background checks, due diligence, corporate security, litigation support, and asset recovery. Private investigators provide valuable expertise and resources that enable businesses to mitigate risks, protect their interests, and maintain integrity in an increasingly complex and competitive business environment. By leveraging the specialized skills of private investigators, businesses can make informed decisions, address challenges effectively, and achieve their objectives with confidence.

Law Enforcement

Private investigators often cultivate professional relationships and networks with law enforcement agencies to enhance their investigative capabilities, access resources, and collaborate on cases. While private investigators and law enforcement officers have distinct roles and jurisdictions, their collaboration can be mutually beneficial in solving crimes, gathering evidence, and upholding the principles of justice.

One primary benefit of networking with law enforcement for private investigators is access to information and resources. Law enforcement agencies possess databases, records, and investigative tools that may not be available to private investigators. By establishing relationships with law enforcement officers, private investigators can gain access to valuable resources such as criminal records, police reports, surveillance footage, and forensic analysis, which can significantly enhance their investigative efforts and provide crucial insights into cases.

Furthermore, private investigators often collaborate with law enforcement to exchange information and intelligence on criminal activities, suspects, or ongoing investigations. By sharing information and coordinating efforts, private investigators and law enforcement officers can leverage their respective expertise and resources to solve crimes more efficiently and effectively. This collaboration can lead to successful outcomes in cases involving complex criminal activities, organized crime, or cross-jurisdictional investigations.

Private investigators may assist law enforcement agencies with their investigations as consultants or subcontractors. Private investigators often possess specialized skills, such as surveillance, undercover operations, or digital forensics, that can complement law enforcement's investigative efforts. By collaborating with private investigators, law enforcement agencies can tap into additional expertise and resources to gather evidence, track down suspects, and build stronger cases.

Private investigators also play a crucial role in providing support to law enforcement in cases where their involvement may be limited due to resource constraints or jurisdictional issues. Private investigators can conduct parallel investigations, gather additional evidence, or provide surveillance support to supplement law enforcement's efforts. This collaboration allows law enforcement agencies to focus their resources on high-priority cases while private investigators handle ancillary tasks or provide specialized assistance as needed.

In addition to case-specific collaboration, private investigators and law enforcement officers often participate in professional associations, conferences, and training programs where they can network, share best practices, and build relationships. These professional networks provide opportunities for private investigators and law enforcement officers to exchange ideas, discuss emerging trends, and collaborate on mutual interests, fostering a culture of cooperation and collaboration within the investigative community.

However, it's essential to recognize the limitations and ethical considerations associated with private investigators networking with law enforcement. Private investigators must adhere to legal and ethical guidelines governing their profession, including respecting individuals' rights to privacy and due process. While collaboration with law enforcement can be beneficial, private investigators must maintain independence, objectivity, and impartiality in their investigations to uphold the integrity of their work and the legal system.

Lastly, networking with law enforcement can provide numerous benefits for private investigators, including access to information, resources, and opportunities for collaboration. By cultivating professional relationships with law enforcement agencies, private investigators can enhance their investigative capabilities, support law enforcement efforts, and contribute to the pursuit of justice in their communities. Collaboration between private investigators and law enforcement fosters a culture of cooperation, mutual respect, and shared responsibility for public safety and the rule of law.

Bail Bond Agents

Private investigators often establish professional relationships with bail bond agents to collaborate on cases involving bail enforcement, fugitive recovery, and locating individuals who have skipped bail. These partnerships can be mutually beneficial, leveraging the expertise and resources of both parties to achieve successful outcomes in apprehending fugitives and ensuring the integrity of the bail bond system.

One primary benefit of networking with bail bond agents for private investigators is access to information and leads on fugitive cases. Bail bond agents often work closely with defendants and their families, providing bail bonds and monitoring compliance with court appearances. When defendants fail to appear in court, bail bond agents become responsible for locating and apprehending them to avoid financial losses. Private investigators can leverage their investigative skills and resources to assist bail bond agents in locating fugitives, gathering intelligence, and tracking their movements, significantly enhancing the chances of successful apprehension.

Likewise, private investigators and bail bond agents often collaborate on cases involving skip tracing, where individuals have absconded to evade legal obligations or authorities. Private investigators possess specialized skills in conducting surveillance, background checks, and database searches to locate individuals, complementing the efforts of bail bond agents in tracking down fugitives. By combining their expertise and resources, private investigators and bail bond agents can pursue leads, follow up on tips, and deploy effective strategies to locate and apprehend fugitives efficiently.

Alas, private investigators can provide valuable support to bail bond agents in preparing for apprehensions and ensuring their safety during enforcement operations. Private investigators can conduct risk assessments, gather intelligence on potential threats or hazards, and provide surveillance support to assist bail bond agents in executing apprehensions safely and effectively. By collaborating with private investigators, bail bond agents can mitigate risks, maximize operational efficiency, and achieve successful outcomes in apprehending fugitives.

In addition to case-specific collaboration, private investigators and bail bond agents often participate in professional associations, conferences, and training programs where they can network, share best practices, and build relationships. These professional networks provide opportunities for private investigators and bail bond agents to exchange ideas, discuss emerging trends, and collaborate on mutual interests, fostering a culture of cooperation and collaboration within the bail enforcement community.

However, it's essential to recognize the limitations and ethical considerations associated with private investigators networking with bail bond agents. Private investigators must adhere to legal and ethical guidelines governing their profession, including respecting individuals' rights to privacy and due process. While collaboration with bail bond agents can be beneficial, private investigators must maintain independence, objectivity, and impartiality in their investigations to uphold the integrity of their work and the legal system.

Networking with bail bond agents can provide numerous benefits for private investigators, including access to information, resources, and opportunities for collaboration in cases involving bail enforcement and fugitive recovery. By cultivating professional relationships with bail bond agents, private investigators can enhance their investigative capabilities, support bail bond agents' efforts, and contribute to ensuring the integrity of the bail bond system. Collaboration between private investigators and bail bond agents fosters a culture of cooperation, mutual respect, and shared responsibility for upholding the rule of law and ensuring public safety.

News Reporters
Networking with news reporters can be a strategic move for private investigators, offering opportunities for collaboration, information exchange, and mutual benefit. While maintaining ethical boundaries and respecting privacy rights, private investigators can leverage their investigative expertise to assist reporters in uncovering stories, verifying information, and providing valuable insights, while also gaining access to potential leads, sources, and exposure for their own investigations.

One primary benefit of networking with news reporters for private investigators is access to information and leads on news stories and events. Reporters often cover a wide range of topics, including crime, corruption, corporate scandals, and human interest stories, which may overlap with the investigative interests of private investigators. By establishing relationships with reporters, private investigators can gain insights into breaking news stories, receive tips on potential leads or sources, and access information that may not be publicly available, providing valuable opportunities to advance their investigations.

Private investigators can offer valuable assistance to news reporters in verifying information, conducting background checks, and providing expert analysis on investigative matters. Private investigators possess specialized skills in conducting research, surveillance, and interviews, which can complement the work of reporters in gathering evidence and uncovering the truth behind complex stories. By collaborating with private investigators, reporters can enhance the credibility and accuracy of their reporting, ensuring that their stories are thoroughly researched and fact-checked before publication.

To boot, private investigators can provide reporters with access to sources, witnesses, and experts who may be reluctant to speak to the media directly. Private investigators often cultivate relationships with a wide range of individuals, including law enforcement officers, industry insiders, and whistleblowers, who may possess valuable information or insights relevant to news stories. By connecting reporters with these sources, private investigators can facilitate access to exclusive information, interviews, and perspectives that can enrich news reporting and contribute to the public's understanding of important issues.

In addition to assisting with news reporting, private investigators can also benefit from networking with reporters by gaining exposure for their own investigations and expertise. Reporters may be interested in covering stories related to the work of private investigators, such as high-profile cases, groundbreaking discoveries, or investigative techniques. By establishing relationships with reporters, private investigators can pitch story ideas, offer insights into newsworthy topics, and provide expert commentary on investigative matters, raising awareness of their work and enhancing their professional reputation within the media industry.

Private investigators can leverage their relationships with reporters to generate publicity and media coverage for their investigations. By sharing updates, milestones, and breakthroughs in their cases with reporters, private investigators can attract attention to their work, attract potential clients, and generate interest in their services. Additionally, media coverage can help private investigators build credibility, establish trust with clients, and differentiate themselves from competitors in a crowded marketplace.

It's essential for private investigators to approach networking with reporters ethically and responsibly, respecting the principles of journalistic integrity, privacy rights, and confidentiality. Private investigators must ensure that they do not compromise the integrity of their investigations or disclose sensitive information that could harm their clients or jeopardize ongoing cases. By maintaining professional boundaries and adhering to ethical guidelines, private investigators can build productive relationships with reporters based on trust, respect, and mutual benefit.

Networking with news reporters can provide numerous benefits for private investigators, including access to information, collaboration opportunities, and exposure for their investigations and expertise. By establishing relationships with reporters, private investigators can gain access to valuable leads, sources, and insights, enhance the credibility and accuracy of news reporting, and generate publicity for their own investigations. Collaboration between private investigators and reporters fosters a culture of transparency, accountability, and truth-seeking, contributing to the public's understanding of important issues and ensuring that investigative efforts are conducted with integrity and professionalism.

Coroners Office

Private investigators often network with coroners to gather valuable information, insights, and expertise relevant to their investigations. Coroner offices play a vital role in determining the cause and manner of death in cases involving suspicious or unexplained circumstances. By collaborating with coroners, private investigators can access forensic expertise, autopsy reports, and other resources that can shed light on the circumstances surrounding deaths and assist in their investigations.

One primary benefit of networking with coroners for private investigators is access to forensic expertise and resources. Coroners and forensic pathologists possess specialized knowledge and training in analyzing evidence, conducting autopsies, and determining the cause and manner of death. By establishing relationships with coroners, private investigators can gain access to valuable insights into forensic science, forensic pathology, and the interpretation of autopsy findings, which can provide crucial evidence and support their investigative efforts.

Private investigators can collaborate with coroners to gather information and evidence relevant to their cases. Coroners conduct thorough investigations into deaths, examining medical records, conducting autopsies, and interviewing witnesses to determine the circumstances surrounding a death. By working closely with coroners, private investigators can access autopsy reports, toxicology results, and other forensic evidence that can provide valuable leads and insights into the circumstances surrounding deaths and assist in their investigations.

Moreover, private investigators may engage coroners as expert witnesses in legal proceedings or investigations involving suspicious deaths. Coroners can provide expert testimony on forensic matters, autopsy findings, and the cause and manner of death, offering valuable insights and expertise that can strengthen the case and support the investigator's findings. By collaborating with coroners as expert witnesses, private investigators can enhance the credibility and persuasiveness of their investigations and provide compelling evidence to support their conclusions.

In addition to accessing forensic expertise, private investigators can also benefit from networking with coroners by gaining access to contacts and resources within the coroner's office. Coroner offices often maintain databases, records, and other resources that can be valuable sources of information for private investigators. By establishing relationships with coroners and their staff, private investigators can gain access to valuable contacts, resources, and information that can assist in their investigations and help them achieve successful outcomes.

Finally, networking with coroners can provide numerous benefits for private investigators, including access to forensic expertise, autopsy reports, and other resources relevant to their investigations. By collaborating with coroners, private investigators can gain valuable insights into the circumstances surrounding deaths, access crucial evidence, and strengthen their investigative efforts. Collaboration between private investigators and coroners fosters a culture of cooperation, transparency, and expertise-sharing, contributing to the pursuit of justice and the resolution of cases involving suspicious or unexplained deaths.

Skip Tracers
Private investigators often network with skip tracers to collaborate on cases involving locating

individuals who have absconded, skipped bail, or evaded legal obligations. Skip tracing is a specialized field within investigation that involves tracing the whereabouts of individuals who are difficult to find. By collaborating with skip tracers, private investigators can access specialized skills, databases, and resources that can enhance their efforts in locating fugitives and individuals of interest.

One primary benefit of networking with skip tracers for private investigators is access to specialized skills and techniques for locating individuals. Skip tracers possess expertise in conducting comprehensive searches, analyzing data, and following leads to track down individuals who have disappeared or gone into hiding. By collaborating with skip tracers, private investigators can leverage their specialized skills and techniques to uncover valuable information, verify leads, and locate individuals more efficiently and effectively.

On top of that, skip tracers often have access to databases, records, and other resources that can be valuable sources of information for private investigators. Skip tracers utilize a wide range of tools and resources, including public records, social media, databases, and proprietary software, to gather information and track down individuals. By networking with skip tracers, private investigators can gain access to these resources and leverage them to enhance their own investigative efforts in locating individuals and gathering intelligence.

Plus, skip tracers and private investigators often collaborate on cases involving skip tracing, sharing information, leads, and insights to maximize the chances of success. Skip tracers may provide private investigators with leads or information on individuals of interest, while private investigators may assist skip tracers in conducting surveillance, verifying information, or gathering additional evidence to support their efforts. By collaborating on cases, skip tracers and private investigators can combine their expertise and resources to achieve successful outcomes in locating individuals and resolving cases.

In addition to collaborating on specific cases, skip tracers and private investigators may also participate in professional associations, forums, and online communities where they can network, share best practices, and exchange information. These professional networks provide opportunities for skip tracers and private investigators to build relationships, learn from each other's experiences, and stay updated on the latest developments and trends in skip tracing and investigation.

However, it's essential for private investigators to approach networking with skip tracers ethically and responsibly, respecting privacy rights and legal boundaries. Private investigators must ensure that they comply with applicable laws and regulations governing skip tracing and investigation, including obtaining consent when conducting searches or accessing personal information. By maintaining professional integrity and ethical standards, private investigators can build productive relationships with skip tracers based on trust, respect, and mutual benefit.

Networking with skip tracers can provide numerous benefits for private investigators, including access to specialized skills, databases, and resources for locating individuals. By collaborating with skip tracers, private investigators can enhance their efforts in skip tracing, gather valuable information, and achieve successful outcomes in locating fugitives and individuals of interest. Collaboration between skip tracers and private investigators fosters a culture of cooperation, expertise-sharing, and mutual support, contributing to the effectiveness and professionalism of the investigation industry.

Car Dealerships
Networking with car dealerships can be advantageous for private investigators, offering access to valuable information, resources, and potential leads relevant to their investigations. While maintaining ethical boundaries and respecting privacy rights, private investigators can leverage their relationships with car dealerships to gather information on vehicle sales, ownership, and history, which can be crucial in cases involving fraud, theft, or other criminal activities.

One primary benefit of networking with car dealerships for private investigators is access to information on vehicle sales and ownership. Car dealerships maintain records of vehicle sales, including information on buyers, sellers, and vehicle registration. By establishing relationships with car dealerships, private investigators can gain access to these records and obtain valuable information on vehicle transactions, ownership history, and potential leads related to their investigations.

More than that, private investigators can collaborate with car dealerships to gather information on specific vehicles of interest. Car dealerships often have access to databases and resources that can provide insights into vehicle history, including previous owners, maintenance records, and accident reports. By networking with car dealerships, private investigators can leverage these resources to gather crucial information on vehicles involved in their investigations, such as stolen cars, fraudulent sales, or vehicles used in criminal activities.

Also, private investigators can assist car

dealerships in identifying and preventing fraudulent activities, such as identity theft, odometer fraud, or title washing. Private investigators possess specialized skills in conducting research, surveillance, and background checks, which can be valuable in detecting and investigating fraudulent transactions. By collaborating with private investigators, car dealerships can enhance their fraud prevention efforts, protect their customers, and safeguard their reputation in the industry.

In addition to assisting with fraud prevention, private investigators can also support car dealerships in recovering stolen vehicles or resolving disputes related to vehicle sales. Private investigators can conduct investigations, gather evidence, and work with law enforcement to track down stolen vehicles, identify suspects, and recover stolen property. By networking with private investigators, car dealerships can access additional expertise and resources to address security concerns, protect their assets, and ensure the integrity of their business operations.

Furthermore, private investigators can provide car dealerships with insights and intelligence on emerging trends, threats, and risks in the automotive industry. Private investigators often stay updated on developments in the field of investigation, including new techniques, technologies, and best practices for fraud prevention and risk management. By networking with private investigators, car dealerships can gain access to this valuable information and leverage it to enhance their security measures, improve customer service, and stay ahead of potential threats and challenges in the industry.

However, it's essential for private investigators to approach networking with car dealerships ethically and responsibly, respecting confidentiality and privacy rights. Private investigators must ensure that they comply with applicable laws and regulations governing the use of vehicle information and customer data, including obtaining consent when conducting investigations or accessing personal information. By maintaining professional integrity and ethical standards, private investigators can build productive relationships with car dealerships based on trust, respect, and mutual benefit.

By networking with car dealerships they can provide numerous benefits for private investigators, including access to information, resources, and potential leads relevant to their investigations. By collaborating with car dealerships, private investigators can gather valuable information on vehicle sales, ownership, and history, assist in fraud prevention and resolution, and provide insights and intelligence on emerging trends and risks in the automotive industry. Collaboration between private investigators and car dealerships fosters a culture of cooperation, expertise-sharing, and mutual support, contributing to the effectiveness and professionalism of the investigation industry.

Insurance Agents
Networking with insurance agents can be highly beneficial for private investigators, as it provides access to valuable information, resources, and potential leads relevant to their investigations. By collaborating with insurance agents, private investigators can leverage their expertise and connections within the insurance industry to gather intelligence, verify claims, and uncover fraudulent activities.

One primary benefit of networking with insurance agents for private investigators is access to information on insurance claims and policyholders. Insurance agents have access to databases and records containing information on policyholders, insurance claims, and coverage details. By establishing relationships with insurance agents, private investigators can gain access to these records and obtain valuable information on individuals involved in their investigations, such as claimants, witnesses, or suspects.

Equally, private investigators can assist insurance agents in investigating suspicious or fraudulent insurance claims. Private investigators possess specialized skills in conducting research, surveillance, and interviews, which can be valuable in uncovering evidence of insurance fraud, exaggeration, or misrepresentation. By collaborating with private investigators, insurance agents can enhance their fraud detection efforts, reduce losses, and protect the integrity of their insurance business.

Nevertheless, private investigators can provide insurance agents with insights and intelligence on emerging trends, risks, and threats in the insurance industry. Private investigators often stay updated on developments in the field of investigation, including new techniques, technologies, and best practices for fraud prevention and risk management. By networking with private investigators, insurance agents can gain access to this valuable information and leverage it to enhance their fraud detection capabilities, improve customer service, and stay ahead of potential threats and challenges in the industry.

In addition to assisting with fraud detection, private investigators can also support insurance agents in investigating claims involving complex or high-value losses. Private investigators can conduct thorough investigations, gather evidence, and provide expert analysis to help insurance agents determine the validity of claims and assess the extent of damages. By collaborating with private investigators, insurance agents can streamline the claims process, expedite claim resolution, and ensure fair and accurate outcomes for policyholders.

However, it's essential for private investigators to approach networking with insurance agents ethically and responsibly, respecting confidentiality and privacy rights. Private investigators must ensure that they comply with applicable laws and regulations governing the use of insurance information and customer data, including obtaining consent when conducting investigations or accessing personal information. By maintaining professional integrity and ethical standards, private investigators can build productive relationships with insurance agents based on trust, respect, and mutual benefit.

In summary, networking with insurance agents can provide numerous benefits for private investigators, including access to information, resources, and potential leads relevant to their investigations. By collaborating with insurance agents, private investigators can gather valuable intelligence, assist in fraud detection and claim resolution, and provide insights and expertise to help insurance agents protect their business and serve their customers effectively. Collaboration between private investigators and insurance agents fosters a culture of cooperation, expertise-sharing, and mutual support, contributing to the effectiveness and professionalism of both industries.

Other Private Investigator's
Networking among private investigators is not just a professional courtesy; it's a vital strategy for success in the field. Collaboration and cooperation among private investigators can yield numerous

benefits, including access to specialized expertise, sharing of resources, and opportunities for professional development and growth.

One of the primary advantages of networking with other private investigators is the opportunity to access specialized expertise and knowledge. Private investigators often specialize in specific areas such as surveillance, digital forensics, background checks, or corporate investigations. By networking with other private investigators, individuals can tap into a wealth of expertise and insights that may not be available within their own practice. For example, a private investigator specializing in digital forensics may collaborate with a colleague who specializes in surveillance to gather evidence for a complex case, leveraging each other's skills and expertise to achieve successful outcomes.

Even more, networking with other private investigators provides opportunities for sharing resources and pooling resources for collaborative efforts. Private investigators often require access to specialized tools, databases, and resources to conduct their investigations effectively. By building relationships with other investigators, individuals can access shared resources, such as research databases, surveillance equipment, or forensic software, reducing costs and improving efficiency in their investigations.

In the same way, networking with other private investigators can lead to referrals and new business opportunities. Private investigators often receive inquiries or cases that fall outside their area of expertise or geographical coverage. By building a network of trusted colleagues, individuals can refer clients to other investigators who are better suited to handle their specific needs, enhancing client satisfaction and building goodwill within the industry.

Additionally, networking can lead to collaborative opportunities where private investigators team up to pursue larger or more complex cases, expanding their capabilities and enhancing their reputation in the field.

Networking among private investigators also provides opportunities for professional development and growth. Private investigators often face unique challenges and obstacles in their work, ranging from legal and ethical issues to technological advancements and changes in industry standards. By networking with other investigators, individuals can learn from each other's experiences, share best practices, and stay updated on the latest developments and trends in the field. Networking events, conferences, and online forums provide opportunities for private investigators to connect with colleagues, participate in training sessions, and exchange ideas, fostering a culture of continuous learning and improvement within the industry.

Moreover, networking among private investigators promotes collaboration and cooperation in addressing common challenges and advocating for the interests of the profession. Private investigators face various challenges, including legislative changes, regulatory requirements, and public perception issues. By networking with other investigators, individuals can work together to address these challenges, share resources, and advocate for policies and practices that benefit the profession as a whole. Collaborative efforts, such as joining professional associations, participating in industry forums, or organizing advocacy campaigns, can amplify the voices of private investigators and strengthen their collective impact on the industry.

Albeit, effective networking among private investigators requires a commitment to professionalism, integrity, and ethical conduct. Private investigators must respect confidentiality, privacy rights, and legal boundaries when sharing information or collaborating on cases. Additionally, individuals should approach networking with an open mind, willingness to learn, and willingness to contribute to the success of others in the profession. By building trust, fostering mutual respect, and upholding the highest standards of professionalism, private investigators can create a vibrant and supportive network that benefits individuals, clients, and the profession as a whole.

Finally, networking among private investigators is essential for success in the field, providing opportunities for access to specialized expertise, sharing of resources, and collaboration on cases. By building relationships with other investigators, individuals can expand their capabilities, enhance their reputation, and grow their businesses. Moreover, networking promotes professional development, fosters cooperation, and strengthens the collective impact of private investigators on the industry. By embracing networking as a strategic tool for success, private investigators can thrive in a dynamic and competitive profession while upholding the highest standards of professionalism and integrity.

CHAPTER EIGHT
<u>Needed to Get Started</u>

Start: German *Origin Starzen* - Move swiftly

When starting out and working under another P.I. it's not imperative for you to do immediately but at some point you will want to setup a P.O. Box and register your vehicle to that P.O. Box. The last thing you want is to be working a case and have someone run your license plates and show up at your personal residence.

If you are in the State of Texas and intend on operating your own P.I. agency you must be 18 years of age or older and possess three consecutive years of investigation experience OR a possess a bachelors degree in criminal justice and have six months consecutive investigation experience OR an possess an associate degree in criminal justice and have twelve months of investigation experience. Additionally, you must meet all requirements pertaining to criminal records. You must pass the State's exam and show the required proof of insurance and obtain a State Sales Tax permit.

If you do not meet the above requirements you need to locate a licensed P.I. agency that is hiring and willing to train you.

Liability Insurance

Business liability insurance is crucial for protecting companies from financial ruin in the face of lawsuits. It shields against claims of bodily injury, property damage, or negligence arising from business operations. Without it, legal fees and settlements can devastate finances, jeopardizing the continuity of operations. Liability coverage provides peace of mind, ensuring businesses can focus on growth without the

constant threat of litigation-induced bankruptcy.
Errors & Omissions Insurance
	Errors and omissions (E&O) insurance is vital for professionals providing services or advice. It safeguards against claims of negligence, mistakes, or failure to perform. In today's litigious society, even minor errors can lead to costly lawsuits. E&O coverage provides financial protection, covering legal expenses and settlements, preserving the reputation and financial stability of businesses and professionals, fostering trust and confidence among clients.

Firearms Liability Insurance
	Private investigator firearms liability insurance is paramount for professionals who may need to carry firearms during their investigations. This specialized coverage protects against legal liabilities arising from the use of firearms, including injuries, property damage, or wrongful death claims. Without it, investigators face substantial financial risks, including legal fees, settlements, and damage to their reputation. Firearms liability insurance provides peace of mind, allowing investigators to focus on their work without the constant fear of litigation-induced financial ruin. Moreover, it demonstrates a commitment to safety and responsibility, enhancing the professionalism and credibility of private investigators. In today's litigious environment, this insurance is not just beneficial but essential for safeguarding both the investigator and their clients' interests.

Work Vehicle
	Vehicle selection is a critical aspect of private investigation work, directly impacting the efficiency, safety, and success of operations. Choosing the right vehicle tailored to the specific needs of the investigation is paramount. For surveillance, inconspicuous models with tinted windows and ample space for equipment are preferable, enabling

investigators to blend into their surroundings while maintaining a clear view of their subjects. In contrast, for rural or off-road investigations, vehicles with robust off-road capabilities may be necessary to navigate challenging terrain effectively.

Secondly, the vehicle's reliability and performance are crucial. Investigators often need to travel long distances or navigate challenging terrain, so a dependable vehicle minimizes the risk of breakdowns or delays that could compromise an investigation.

At that, the vehicle's size and features should align with the specific needs of the investigation. For example, smaller vehicles may be more suitable for urban surveillance, while larger ones offer greater comfort and equipment storage for stakeouts or transporting surveillance gear.

It goes without saying, fuel efficiency is a practical consideration, as it reduces operational costs and minimizes the need for frequent refueling, which could disrupt surveillance efforts. Safety is another vital consideration. Vehicles with advanced safety features can protect investigators during stakeouts or pursuits, minimizing the risk of accidents or injuries.

Ultimately, the right vehicle enhances the effectiveness and professionalism of private investigation services. It enables investigators to execute their tasks with precision, discretion, and safety, ultimately leading to more successful outcomes for their clients.

Finally, a few items recommended to outfit your vehicle with include a power inverter capable of powering and charging multiple devices at once. Preferably an inverted of at least 400 watts. Also, a high power air supply for tire inflation that connects to the battery rather than a 12 volt low power plug. Plus a battery jump box for instances of unexpected dead batteries. Lastly, storage boxes for equipment required for work.

Still Camera

A mirrorless camera represents a revolution in digital photography, offering photographers a compact, lightweight, and versatile alternative to traditional DSLR cameras. Unlike DSLRs, which use a complex system of mirrors to reflect light into an optical viewfinder, mirrorless cameras employ an electronic viewfinder or a rear LCD screen to preview images in real-time. This innovative design eliminates the need for a bulky mirror mechanism, allowing mirrorless cameras to achieve a more compact and lightweight form factor without compromising image quality or performance.

One of the key advantages of mirrorless cameras is their portability and ease of use, making them ideal for photographers who value mobility and flexibility. With their smaller size and weight, mirrorless cameras are well-suited for travel photography, street photography, and other situations where portability is paramount. Additionally, their silent shooting mode and inconspicuous design make them well-suited for discreet or candid photography, allowing photographers to capture authentic moments without drawing attention to themselves.

Likewise, mirrorless cameras offer a range of advanced features and capabilities that rival those of traditional DSLRs. Many mirrorless cameras boast high-resolution sensors, fast autofocus systems, and advanced image processing algorithms, allowing photographers to capture stunning images with exceptional clarity, detail, and dynamic range.

Additionally, mirrorless cameras often incorporate innovative technologies such as in-body image stabilization, 4K video recording, and customizable shooting modes, empowering photographers to unleash their creativity and push the boundaries of their craft.

Another advantage of mirrorless cameras is their compatibility with a wide range of interchangeable lenses, giving photographers the flexibility to adapt to different shooting conditions and creative preferences. Whether shooting landscapes with a wide-angle lens, portraits with a prime lens, or wildlife with a telephoto lens, photographers can easily swap lenses to achieve their desired results without being encumbered by heavy gear.

Despite all of the positives a mirrorless camera offers, for those, like a private investigator the cost of a mirrorless camera can be prohibitive compared to the cost of a DSLR camera. A basic mirrorless camera costs 2 to 3 times that of a basic DSLR camera.

A DSLR camera is a vital tool for private investigators, offering versatility, image quality, and discreetness crucial for surveillance, evidence gathering, and documentation. Unlike standard point-and-shoot cameras or smartphone cameras, DSLRs provide superior image quality, enabling investigators to capture clear, high-resolution photos and videos even in challenging lighting conditions.

One of the most significant advantages of DSLR cameras is their interchangeable lens system, allowing investigators to adapt to various surveillance scenarios. Telephoto lenses enable long-range photography, ideal for discreetly capturing subjects from a distance during surveillance operations. Wide-angle lenses, on the other hand, are useful for documenting scenes or conducting covert investigations in confined spaces.

DSLR lenses filters serve various purposes in photography. UV filters protect the lens from scratches and dust while reducing haze and UV light. Neutral density (ND) filters control exposure by reducing the amount of light entering the lens, allowing for longer exposures in bright conditions. Polarizing filters reduce glare and reflections, enhancing color saturation and contrast, ideal for landscape photography. Graduated ND filters balance exposure between the sky and foreground in landscapes. Close-up filters enable macro photography by decreasing the minimum focusing distance. Each filter offers unique benefits, enhancing creativity and achieving desired photographic results.

Moreover, DSLRs offer advanced manual settings and controls, empowering investigators to adjust exposure, aperture, and shutter speed for optimal results in different environments. This level of control is invaluable for capturing crucial details or evidence while maintaining discretion.

Another critical aspect of DSLR cameras is their low-light performance. Many investigations occur in low-light conditions or at night, requiring cameras capable of capturing clear images without compromising quality. DSLRs equipped with large image sensors and high ISO capabilities excel in such situations, ensuring that investigators can gather evidence effectively regardless of the lighting conditions.

Additionally, DSLR cameras provide a level of professionalism and credibility essential for private investigators. When presenting evidence in court or to clients, high-quality images captured with DSLRs carry more weight and legitimacy, enhancing the credibility of the investigation findings.

Also, DSLR cameras offer the advantage of discretion. Unlike bulky or conspicuous surveillance equipment, DSLRs are relatively compact and can be easily concealed, allowing investigators to operate covertly without drawing unnecessary attention.

In the end, a DSLR camera is an indispensable tool for private investigators, offering superior image quality, versatility, and discretion crucial for surveillance, evidence gathering, and documentation. Investing in a high-quality DSLR enables investigators to conduct their work more effectively, enhance the credibility of their findings, and ultimately achieve better outcomes for their clients.

Video Camera
The adoption of 4K video cameras by private investigators represents a significant advancement in surveillance and evidence gathering capabilities. These cameras offer several advantages that make them invaluable tools for investigative work.

First and foremost, the higher resolution of 4K video provides superior image quality compared to traditional surveillance cameras. This means that investigators can capture more details, such as facial features, license plate numbers, or other critical evidence, even when recording from a distance or in challenging lighting conditions.

The increased resolution of 4K video allows for enhanced digital zoom capabilities without sacrificing image clarity. This is particularly beneficial during post-processing and analysis, as investigators can zoom in on specific areas of interest without compromising the integrity of the footage.

Additionally, 4K video cameras often feature advanced image stabilization technology, which helps minimize camera shake and ensure smooth, steady footage. This is essential for surveillance operations, where maintaining a clear view of the subject is paramount, especially when recording from a moving vehicle or in crowded environments.

Another advantage of 4K video cameras is their ability to capture a wider dynamic range, resulting in more detailed and lifelike images. This is particularly useful in situations where there are significant contrasts in lighting, such as outdoor surveillance during the day or night.

What's more, 4K video cameras typically offer improved low-light performance, allowing investigators to capture clear footage even in dimly lit environments. This is crucial for conducting covert surveillance operations during nighttime or in poorly lit areas.

Plus, the use of 4K video cameras enhances the credibility of the evidence collected by private investigators. High-resolution footage is more compelling and persuasive when presented in court or to clients, increasing the likelihood of achieving favorable outcomes.

When said and done, the importance of 4K video cameras for private investigators cannot be overstated. These advanced tools provide superior image quality, enhanced zoom capabilities, improved image stabilization, and better low-light performance, ultimately enabling investigators to gather more compelling evidence and achieve better results for their clients.

Spare Batteries
It is paramount that private investigators carry

spare batteries for all of their electronic equipment, as well as tripods and monopods for all camera's. Even better get a universal adapter so that you can use the same tri-pod and monopod for both devices. If you are new to SLR camera's and you need to learn how to use a manual focus camera to take professional style photographs I highly recommend taking photography classes. At the time of this writing Stack Skills master class offers a quality program for a reasonable price.

Covert Eyeglasses
	Video camera eyeglasses offer private investigators a discreet and hands-free method for capturing audio and video during covert operations. These inconspicuous devices allow investigators to record interactions with subjects without drawing attention, enhancing the authenticity of evidence. With built-in storage and battery, they offer extended recording capabilities, crucial for lengthy surveillance sessions. The covert nature of video camera eyeglasses enables investigators to gather valuable intelligence while remaining inconspicuous, facilitating smoother investigations and reducing the risk of detection. This innovative tool empowers private investigators to conduct surveillance operations with increased efficiency, flexibility, and discretion.

Covert Wrist Watch
	Video camera watches are invaluable tools for private investigators conducting covert operations. These discreet devices allow investigators to capture audio and video evidence without raising suspicion. With a camera seamlessly integrated into the watch face, they offer a covert method of recording interactions with subjects or documenting surveillance activities. The inconspicuous nature of video camera watches enables investigators to gather crucial evidence discreetly, enhancing the success and credibility of their investigations. Additionally, these

watches often feature built-in storage and long battery life, ensuring extended recording capabilities essential for surveillance operations. The hands-free design of video camera watches allows investigators to focus on their tasks without the need for additional equipment, maximizing efficiency and minimizing the risk of detection. Overall, video camera watches provide private investigators with a powerful tool for gathering covert evidence, enhancing the professionalism and effectiveness of their work.

Covert Body Camera

Body cameras have become integral tools for both law enforcement officers and private investigators, revolutionizing evidence gathering, accountability, and transparency in their respective fields.

For law enforcement, body cameras provide an unbiased record of interactions between officers and the public, offering valuable evidence in investigations and legal proceedings. These cameras promote accountability and professionalism among officers, encouraging adherence to protocols and best practices. Additionally, body camera footage enhances transparency, fostering trust and legitimacy within communities.

Similarly, private investigators benefit from the use of body cameras during surveillance operations and fieldwork. These devices offer a discreet and hands-free method of capturing audio and video evidence, providing invaluable documentation for investigative purposes. Body cameras enable investigators to maintain a clear and accurate record of their activities, enhancing the credibility and effectiveness of their work.

Body cameras serve as a deterrent to

misconduct or inappropriate behavior, whether in law enforcement or private investigation settings. Knowing that their actions are being recorded encourages officers and investigators to adhere to ethical standards and follow proper procedures.

The use of body cameras also facilitates the review and analysis of incidents, aiding in the resolution of disputes and the identification of areas for improvement. By capturing real-time footage of events as they unfold, body cameras provide a comprehensive perspective that can help inform decision-making and enhance situational awareness.

Overall, the adoption of body cameras by law enforcement and private investigators represents a significant step forward in promoting accountability, transparency, and professionalism in both fields. These devices serve as valuable tools for evidence gathering, documentation, and dispute resolution, ultimately contributing to safer, more effective, and more trustworthy practices.

Drones

Drones have revolutionized surveillance operations, offering unprecedented capabilities in gathering intelligence, monitoring activities, and enhancing situational awareness. These unmanned aerial vehicles (UAVs) provide a versatile and cost-effective solution for a wide range of surveillance tasks, both in law enforcement and private investigation settings.

One of the primary advantages of drones in surveillance operations is their ability to access remote or hard-to-reach areas with ease. Equipped with advanced navigation systems and high-resolution cameras, drones can capture detailed imagery and video footage from vantage points that would be otherwise inaccessible or impractical for human surveillance teams.

In law enforcement, drones play a crucial role in enhancing public safety and security. They can be deployed to monitor large crowds during public events, assess emergency situations in real-time, and conduct aerial reconnaissance in high-risk environments such as disaster zones or crime scenes. Drones provide law enforcement agencies with valuable situational awareness, enabling faster response times and more informed decision-making.

Similarly, private investigators leverage drones to gather intelligence and conduct surveillance operations with greater efficiency and discretion. Whether tracking a subject's movements, documenting activities at a remote location, or conducting aerial surveys for investigative purposes, drones offer a versatile and non-intrusive method of gathering valuable evidence.

More than that, drones equipped with advanced sensors, such as thermal imaging cameras or night vision capabilities, can provide enhanced surveillance capabilities in low-light conditions or adverse weather environments. This allows for round-the-clock surveillance operations, maximizing the effectiveness of investigative efforts.

The use of drones in surveillance operations also enhances safety for both law enforcement officers and private investigators. By reducing the need for ground-based surveillance teams to enter potentially hazardous or hostile environments, drones minimize the risk of injury or exposure to dangerous situations.

However, the use of drones in surveillance operations also raises privacy and ethical concerns.

The ability of drones to capture high-resolution imagery and video footage from aerial perspectives raises questions about the potential invasion of privacy and the appropriate use of surveillance technology. It is essential for law enforcement agencies and private investigators to adhere to strict guidelines and regulations governing the use of drones to ensure compliance with legal and ethical standards.

Drones have become invaluable tools in surveillance operations, offering enhanced capabilities in gathering intelligence, monitoring activities, and improving situational awareness. Whether in law enforcement or private investigation settings, drones provide a versatile, cost-effective, and non-intrusive solution for conducting surveillance operations safely and effectively. However, it is essential for users to address privacy and ethical considerations and adhere to regulatory requirements to ensure responsible and lawful use of drone technology in surveillance activities.

Night Vision

Night vision technology has transformed surveillance operations, enabling law enforcement agencies and private investigators to conduct covert surveillance and gather critical intelligence during low-light conditions. By amplifying ambient light or detecting infrared radiation, night vision devices provide enhanced visibility in darkness, allowing surveillance teams to monitor activities, track subjects, and gather evidence with increased effectiveness and precision.

One of the primary advantages of night vision in surveillance operations is its ability to extend the operational capabilities of surveillance teams beyond daylight hours. Whether conducting stakeouts, monitoring suspicious activities, or patrolling high-risk areas, night vision technology enables surveillance teams to maintain constant vigilance and respond swiftly to emerging threats or incidents.

In law enforcement, night vision is particularly valuable for conducting covert operations, apprehending suspects, and ensuring officer safety during nighttime patrols. By providing law enforcement officers with enhanced situational awareness and visibility in darkness, night vision technology enhances their ability to detect and deter criminal activity, ultimately contributing to public safety and security.

Similarly, private investigators utilize night vision technology to gather intelligence, conduct surveillance operations, and document activities during nighttime hours. Whether monitoring a subject's movements, observing clandestine meetings, or documenting suspicious behavior, night vision devices offer private investigators a discreet and effective means of gathering valuable evidence while minimizing the risk of detection.

Night vision technology is invaluable for surveillance operations in rural or remote areas where artificial lighting is limited or nonexistent. By enabling surveillance teams to operate covertly in natural darkness, night vision devices provide a tactical advantage in monitoring remote locations, tracking wildlife, or conducting border surveillance.

The use of night vision technology in surveillance operations also enhances safety for both law enforcement officers and private investigators. By improving visibility and situational awareness in low-light environments, night vision devices help mitigate the risks associated with nighttime operations, such as accidents, injuries, or hostile encounters.

However, it is essential to recognize the limitations and challenges associated with night vision technology, including reduced visibility in adverse weather conditions, potential glare from artificial light sources, and the risk of detection by individuals equipped with counter-surveillance measures.

At last, night vision technology has become an indispensable tool in surveillance operations, providing law enforcement agencies and private investigators with enhanced visibility and situational awareness during low-light conditions. Whether conducting covert operations, monitoring remote areas, or gathering evidence at night, night vision devices offer a versatile and effective solution for enhancing the effectiveness and safety of surveillance activities. However, it is essential for users to consider the limitations and ethical implications of night vision technology and to employ it responsibly and lawfully in accordance with applicable regulations and guidelines.

Binoculars
Binoculars are indispensable tools for private investigators, offering enhanced observation capabilities crucial for gathering intelligence, conducting surveillance, and documenting activities discreetly and effectively. These optical instruments provide magnified views of distant subjects, enabling investigators to maintain a safe distance while monitoring targets with precision and clarity.

One of the primary advantages of binoculars in private investigation is their versatility and portability. Compact and lightweight models can be easily carried and deployed in various surveillance scenarios, whether observing subjects from a vehicle, monitoring activities in public spaces, or conducting covert operations in urban or rural environments.

Binoculars also offer a wide range of magnification options, allowing investigators to adapt to different surveillance situations and environments. High-powered binoculars provide long-range capabilities, enabling investigators to observe subjects from a distance without compromising image clarity or detail. On the other hand, wide-angle binoculars offer a broader field of view, making them ideal for scanning large areas or monitoring multiple subjects simultaneously.

Moreover, binoculars equipped with advanced features such as image stabilization, low-light performance, and waterproofing enhance their effectiveness and reliability in various surveillance conditions. Image stabilization technology minimizes hand tremors and vibrations, ensuring steady and clear views even in challenging environments or when observing moving targets. Enhanced low-light performance enables investigators to conduct surveillance during dusk, dawn, or nighttime hours, expanding the operational capabilities of surveillance teams.

Furthermore, binoculars play a crucial role in maintaining discretion and minimizing the risk of detection during surveillance operations. Unlike other surveillance equipment such as cameras or drones, binoculars do not emit any visible or audible signals, allowing investigators to observe subjects discreetly from a safe distance without drawing attention.

Additionally, binoculars offer a non-intrusive method of gathering intelligence and documenting activities without the need for direct interaction with subjects. By providing investigators with a magnified view of distant subjects, binoculars enable them to observe behaviors, interactions, and movements discreetly, facilitating the collection of valuable evidence for investigative purposes.

Binoculars are essential tools for private investigators, offering enhanced observation capabilities crucial for gathering intelligence, conducting surveillance, and documenting activities discreetly and effectively. Whether observing subjects from a distance, scanning large areas, or monitoring activities in low-light conditions, binoculars provide investigators with a versatile and reliable solution for enhancing the effectiveness and efficiency of surveillance operations.

Audio Recorders
High-resolution audio recorders are indispensable tools for private investigators, offering enhanced capabilities in gathering evidence, conducting interviews, and documenting conversations crucial for investigative purposes. These advanced recording devices provide clear and accurate audio recordings with superior fidelity, enabling investigators to capture and preserve critical information with precision and clarity.

One of the primary advantages of high-resolution audio recorders is their ability to capture detailed and nuanced soundscapes, allowing investigators to distinguish between voices, background noises, and other audio elements with greater accuracy. Unlike standard audio recording devices, which may produce recordings with limited frequency response and dynamic range, high-resolution recorders offer superior audio quality, capturing subtle nuances and nuances that may be missed by lower-quality equipment.

Anyway, high-resolution audio recorders are equipped with advanced features such as noise reduction, microphone sensitivity adjustments, and audio compression algorithms, further enhancing their effectiveness and reliability in various surveillance and investigative scenarios. Noise reduction technology helps minimize background noise and interference, ensuring clear and intelligible recordings even in noisy environments or adverse conditions. Adjustable microphone sensitivity allows investigators to optimize recording settings based on the distance to the sound source, ensuring optimal signal-to-noise ratio and audio clarity. Additionally, audio compression algorithms help reduce file sizes without compromising audio quality, facilitating efficient storage, and sharing of recordings.

Equally, high-resolution audio recorders offer extended recording capabilities, allowing investigators to capture lengthy conversations, stakeouts, or surveillance operations without interruption. With ample storage capacity and long battery life, these devices enable investigators to document activities and gather evidence over extended periods, ensuring that no crucial information is missed or lost due to recording limitations.

In addition to their surveillance and investigative applications, high-resolution audio recorders are invaluable tools for conducting interviews, gathering witness statements, and documenting testimonies in legal proceedings. By providing clear and accurate recordings of interviews and conversations, these devices offer a reliable record of events, ensuring the accuracy and integrity of witness testimony and facilitating the resolution of disputes or legal proceedings.

High-resolution audio recorders play a crucial role in maintaining the confidentiality and privacy of sensitive information obtained during investigations. Unlike video recording devices, which may raise privacy concerns or legal issues, audio recorders offer a non-intrusive method of gathering evidence without the need for visual surveillance or direct interaction with subjects. By capturing audio recordings discreetly and unobtrusively, these devices help protect the privacy rights of individuals while enabling investigators to gather valuable evidence for investigative purposes.

High-resolution audio recorders are essential tools for private investigators, offering enhanced capabilities in gathering evidence, conducting interviews, and documenting conversations crucial for investigative purposes. With their superior audio quality, advanced features, and extended recording capabilities, these devices provide investigators with a versatile and reliable solution for capturing and preserving critical information with precision and clarity. Whether conducting surveillance operations, gathering witness statements, or documenting testimonies in legal proceedings, high-resolution audio recorders play a crucial role in enhancing the effectiveness and efficiency of investigative efforts.

Telephones
Private investigators often rely on burner phones and business phone lines as essential tools for conducting their work discreetly, efficiently, and legally. These communication resources serve various purposes, from maintaining anonymity and confidentiality to managing client interactions and coordinating surveillance operations. Understanding the distinct advantages and considerations associated with burner phones and business phone lines is crucial for private investigators to navigate their professional responsibilities effectively.

Burner phones, also known as disposable or prepaid phones, are temporary mobile devices purchased without a long-term contract. They offer several benefits for private investigators, particularly in situations where anonymity and discretion are paramount. By using burner phones, investigators can conduct communications related to sensitive investigations without revealing their personal or primary contact information. This helps protect their identity and maintain confidentiality, reducing the risk of compromising ongoing operations or attracting unwanted attention.

In the same way, burner phones enable investigators to establish separate lines of communication for specific tasks or clients, facilitating organization and compartmentalization of their professional activities. This segmentation helps prevent cross-contamination of information and ensures that sensitive data remains isolated and secure. Additionally, burner phones can be easily disposed of or deactivated once their utility is no longer needed, minimizing the risk of exposure or surveillance by adversaries.

Not only is it essential for private investigators to use burner phones responsibly and ethically, in compliance with applicable laws and regulations governing telecommunications and privacy. While burner phones offer a degree of anonymity, they are not immune to legal scrutiny, and their misuse can have serious legal and ethical consequences. Investigators must exercise caution when using burner phones to avoid engaging in unlawful activities or violating the privacy rights of individuals.

In contrast, business phone lines are permanent or semi-permanent telecommunications resources established for professional use. Private investigators often maintain dedicated business phone lines to manage client communications, coordinate team activities, and conduct administrative tasks related to their investigative practice. Business phone lines offer several advantages over burner phones, including greater reliability, consistency, and legitimacy.

With a dedicated business phone line, investigators can establish a professional presence and brand identity, enhancing their credibility and trustworthiness among clients and colleagues. A business phone line also provides a centralized point of contact for clients to reach investigators, streamlining communication and facilitating client management and engagement.

Moreover, business phone lines offer enhanced features and capabilities compared to burner phones, such as call forwarding, voicemail, and caller ID customization. These features help improve efficiency and responsiveness in managing incoming calls and messages, ensuring that important communications are promptly addressed and prioritized.

Additionally, business phone lines can be integrated with other communication tools and technologies used by private investigators, such as email, text messaging, and voice-over-internet-protocol (VoIP) services. This integration enables investigators to leverage multiple channels of communication to reach clients and collaborators efficiently, regardless of their preferred method of contact.

However, maintaining a business phone line requires ongoing investment and management, including subscription fees, maintenance costs, and compliance with regulatory requirements. Private investigators must ensure that their business phone lines are operated in accordance with applicable laws and industry standards, including those related to telecommunications, privacy, and data protection.

In summation, burner phones and business phone lines are essential communication resources for private investigators, offering distinct advantages and considerations in managing their professional communications. While burner phones provide anonymity and discretion for sensitive investigations, business phone lines offer reliability and legitimacy for client management and administrative tasks. By understanding the roles and responsibilities associated with each type of phone line, private investigators can effectively navigate the complexities of their profession and uphold ethical and legal standards in their communication practices.

Word Processors

Word processors are indispensable tools for private investigators, facilitating efficient documentation, report writing, and case management. With features like spell check, formatting options, and document templates, word processors streamline the creation of detailed investigation reports, witness statements, and case summaries. Additionally, they enable investigators to organize and store information securely, ensuring easy access and retrieval of critical documents when needed. Word processors enhance productivity and professionalism, enabling investigators to communicate findings effectively to clients, legal teams, and law enforcement agencies. Overall, word processors play a vital role in supporting the investigative process and maintaining accurate and thorough documentation.

Photo / Video Editing

Photo and video editing software are indispensable tools for private investigators, offering advanced capabilities for enhancing, analyzing, and presenting visual evidence. These software tools enable investigators to manipulate images and videos, clarify details, and highlight relevant information crucial for investigative purposes.

One primary use of photo and video editing software is to enhance image quality and clarity. Investigators can adjust brightness, contrast, and color balance to improve visibility and reveal hidden details in surveillance footage or photographs. Additionally, they can crop, zoom, and enhance specific areas of interest to focus on key elements of the evidence.

Photo and video editing software enable investigators to annotate images and videos, adding text, arrows, or other markers to highlight important details or provide context. This helps clarify complex scenes, document findings, and present evidence effectively to clients, legal teams, or law enforcement agencies.

These software tools offer advanced analysis features, such as facial recognition, object tracking, and metadata extraction, enabling investigators to identify subjects, track movements, and extract valuable information from digital evidence.

Overall, photo and video editing software play a crucial role in the investigative process, enabling private investigators to enhance, analyze, and present visual evidence with precision and clarity. By leveraging these advanced tools, investigators can strengthen their cases, uncover critical insights, and achieve successful outcomes for their clients.

Time/Date Stamp
Time and date stamps on photo and video images are crucial for establishing the authenticity and chronology of evidence presented in court. They provide irrefutable proof of when the images were captured, ensuring accuracy and credibility. Time-stamped evidence helps establish timelines,

corroborate witness testimonies, and refute false alibis. In legal proceedings, accurate timestamps strengthen the reliability of evidence, enhancing its admissibility and persuasiveness. Judges and juries rely on this metadata to make informed decisions, ensuring justice is served fairly and accurately. Time and date stamps thus serve as essential markers of truth and accountability in the courtroom.

Databases

Access to public records databases is a cornerstone of private investigation work, providing invaluable resources for gathering information, conducting background checks, and uncovering critical details relevant to a wide range of cases. These databases contain a wealth of information collected and maintained by various government agencies at the local, state, and federal levels, offering private investigators access to a vast repository of public records, including court documents, property records, criminal histories, business registrations, and more.

One of the primary benefits of public records database access for private investigators is the ability to conduct comprehensive background checks on individuals, businesses, or properties involved in investigations. By searching through public records, investigators can uncover important details such as criminal records, civil litigation history, financial assets, liens, and judgments, providing valuable insights into a subject's background, character, and potential risks.

Public records databases enable private investigators to locate and verify key information, such as addresses, phone numbers, and social media profiles, facilitating the process of locating and contacting witnesses, parties involved in legal proceedings, or individuals of interest to the investigation.

Additionally, public records database access allows private investigators to gather evidence and documentation to support their findings and conclusions. Whether compiling evidence for legal proceedings, due diligence investigations, or insurance claims, access to public records enables investigators to obtain official documents, court filings, and other records necessary to build a strong case and substantiate their findings.

Public records database access enhances the efficiency and effectiveness of private investigation work by providing a centralized platform for accessing a wide range of information quickly and conveniently. Instead of having to visit multiple government offices or agencies to obtain records manually, investigators can access many types of public records online or through specialized databases, saving time and resources.

In addition to traditional public records databases maintained by government agencies, private investigators also leverage specialized investigative databases and proprietary tools designed specifically for their profession. These databases often contain curated collections of public records and proprietary data sources, offering additional insights and capabilities tailored to the unique needs of private investigators.

However, it is essential for private investigators to use public records databases responsibly and ethically, adhering to legal and regulatory requirements governing the access and use of public information. While public records are generally accessible to the public, there are restrictions and limitations on the use of certain types of information, such as sensitive personal data protected by privacy laws or classified government records.

Moreover, private investigators must exercise caution when interpreting and presenting information obtained from public records databases, ensuring accuracy, relevance, and context. Misuse or misrepresentation of public records could have serious legal and ethical consequences, undermining the credibility of the investigation and potentially exposing investigators to liability.

Lastly, access to public records databases is essential for private investigators, providing valuable resources for gathering information, conducting background checks, and uncovering critical details relevant to a wide range of cases. By leveraging public records, investigators can conduct comprehensive background checks, locate and verify key information, gather evidence, and enhance the efficiency and effectiveness of their investigation work. However, it is crucial for investigators to use public records responsibly and ethically, adhering to legal and regulatory requirements and exercising caution in interpreting and presenting information obtained from public records databases.

Computers

Private investigators rely heavily on computers for personal, business, and open-source intelligence (OSINT) research. These devices serve as powerful tools for gathering information, conducting analysis, managing cases, and communicating with clients and collaborators. Understanding the distinct roles and requirements of personal, business, and OSINT research computers is essential for private investigators to effectively navigate their professional responsibilities and achieve successful outcomes in their investigations.

Personal Computers:

Personal computers are the backbone of a

private investigator's digital toolkit, serving as the primary platform for conducting research, organizing case files, and managing administrative tasks. These devices are typically equipped with powerful hardware and software capabilities tailored to the specific needs of investigators.

Personal computers enable investigators to access a wide range of online resources, databases, and research tools essential for gathering information and conducting analysis. From public records databases and social media platforms to specialized investigative software and research databases, personal computers provide investigators with the tools they need to uncover critical details and insights relevant to their cases.

Personal computers serve as centralized hubs for organizing case files, managing evidence, and tracking investigative progress. With specialized case management software, investigators can create digital case files, document findings, and collaborate with team members seamlessly. These tools help streamline workflow, enhance productivity, and ensure that critical information is organized and accessible when needed.

Personal computers facilitate communication with clients, colleagues, and collaborators through email, messaging platforms, and video conferencing tools. These devices enable investigators to maintain regular contact with clients, provide updates on case progress, and coordinate activities with team members effectively. Additionally, personal computers serve as platforms for drafting reports, preparing presentations, and delivering findings to clients in a professional and timely manner.

Business computers are dedicated devices used

exclusively for professional purposes within a private investigator's practice. These devices are equipped with specialized software, security features, and communication tools tailored to the specific needs of investigative work.

Business computers are equipped with robust security features and encryption tools to protect sensitive information and ensure client confidentiality. These devices are often configured with firewalls, antivirus software, and encryption protocols to safeguard against cyber threats and unauthorized access.

Business computers are configured to comply with legal and regulatory requirements governing the handling and storage of sensitive information. Private investigators must adhere to strict guidelines and regulations governing data privacy, confidentiality, and security, particularly when handling sensitive personal data and confidential information related to their cases.

Business computers facilitate collaboration and teamwork among investigative teams, enabling seamless communication, file sharing, and project management. With collaborative software tools and cloud-based platforms, investigators can work together effectively, share information securely, and coordinate activities across multiple locations.

OSINT research computers are specialized devices used exclusively for conducting open-source intelligence (OSINT) research and gathering information from online sources. These devices are equipped with specialized software, tools, and resources tailored to the unique requirements of OSINT research.

OSINT research computers enable investigators

to collect, analyze, and organize vast amounts of information from online sources, including websites, social media platforms, forums, and public records databases. These devices are equipped with specialized software tools and web scraping utilities designed to automate data collection and streamline analysis.

OSINT research computers are configured to prioritize anonymity and security, protecting investigators' identities and ensuring the confidentiality of their research activities. These devices are often equipped with virtual private network (VPN) software, anonymizing tools, and secure browsing protocols to conceal investigators' IP addresses and encrypt data transmissions.

OSINT research computers are optimized for performance and resource efficiency, enabling investigators to conduct research tasks quickly and efficiently. These devices are equipped with high-speed internet connections, powerful processors, and ample storage capacity to handle large volumes of data and conduct complex analysis tasks.

In summary, personal, business, and OSINT research computers play distinct yet complementary roles in the work of private investigators. Personal computers serve as versatile platforms for conducting research, managing cases, and communicating with clients and collaborators. Business computers provide dedicated resources for professional use, ensuring compliance with legal and regulatory requirements, and facilitating collaboration and teamwork among investigative teams. OSINT research computers are specialized devices optimized for conducting open-source intelligence research, gathering information from online sources, and ensuring anonymity and security. By leveraging these distinct computing resources effectively, private investigators can enhance their capabilities, streamline workflow, and achieve successful outcomes in their investigations.

Virtual Private Network (VPN)

Using a Virtual Private Network (VPN) is crucial for private investigators to safeguard their online activities, protect sensitive information, and maintain anonymity while conducting investigations. VPNs offer several benefits that are essential for ensuring privacy, security, and confidentiality in the digital realm.

One of the primary advantages of using a VPN is the protection of sensitive data and communications from prying eyes. By encrypting internet traffic and routing it through secure servers, VPNs prevent third parties, such as hackers, government agencies, or internet service providers, from intercepting or monitoring online activities. This ensures that sensitive information, such as case files, client communications, and investigative findings, remains confidential and secure from unauthorized access or surveillance.

At that, VPNs help maintain anonymity and conceal the true identity and location of users when accessing the internet. By masking IP addresses and routing connections through remote servers located in different geographic regions, VPNs enable investigators to browse the web anonymously, preventing websites, advertisers, or malicious actors from tracking their online activities or identifying their physical location. This is particularly important for private investigators who may need to conduct research or gather information discreetly without revealing their identity or intentions.

Additionally, VPNs provide access to restricted or geo-blocked content by circumventing censorship and bypassing geographic restrictions. This allows investigators to access online resources, databases, and websites that may be blocked or inaccessible from their location, facilitating research, data collection, and information gathering for investigative purposes.

VPNs enhance security and protect against cyber threats such as malware, phishing attacks, and data breaches. By encrypting internet traffic and providing secure connections, VPNs minimize the risk of unauthorized access to sensitive information and mitigate the impact of cyber attacks on investigative operations.

Overall, using a VPN is essential for private investigators to safeguard their online activities, protect sensitive information, and maintain anonymity while conducting investigations. VPNs offer privacy, security, and confidentiality in the digital realm, ensuring that investigators can conduct research, gather information, and communicate with clients and collaborators safely and securely. By leveraging the benefits of VPN technology, private investigators can enhance their capabilities, protect their interests, and achieve successful outcomes in their investigations. There are hundreds of types of VPN's to pick from, the big three are Nord, Express and Proton.

Scanners
The use of police, fire, and EMS scanners by private investigators is a common practice that serves various purposes in investigative work. These scanners allow investigators to monitor public safety communications, such as police dispatches, emergency response activities, and firefighter communications, in real-time. By staying informed about incidents, emergencies, and law enforcement activities as they unfold, private investigators can gather valuable intelligence, coordinate surveillance operations, and respond effectively to evolving

situations. However, the use of scanners in private investigation raises ethical, legal, and practical considerations that investigators must navigate responsibly to ensure compliance with regulations and ethical standards while maximizing the benefits of this technology.

Police, fire, and EMS scanners are radio receivers capable of tuning into frequencies used by public safety agencies to communicate with their personnel in the field. These scanners are equipped with antennas and receivers that pick up radio signals transmitted by police, fire, and EMS dispatch centers, enabling users to listen to live broadcasts of emergency calls, incident reports, and operational communications.

Benefits of Using Scanners in Private Investigation:

1. **Real-time Intelligence Gathering**: Scanners provide private investigators with access to real-time information about incidents, emergencies, and law enforcement activities as they unfold. By monitoring police, fire, and EMS communications, investigators can gather valuable intelligence about ongoing operations, crime trends, and public safety concerns in specific areas.

2. **Coordination of Surveillance Operations**: Scanners enable investigators to coordinate surveillance operations and respond effectively to developments in the field. By staying informed about law enforcement activities and emergency response efforts, investigators can adjust their surveillance strategies, avoid detection, and gather evidence discreetly.

3. **Enhanced Situational Awareness**: Scanners help private investigators maintain situational awareness

and anticipate potential risks or challenges in their investigative work. By monitoring public safety communications, investigators can identify emerging threats, assess the severity of incidents, and take proactive measures to ensure their safety and the success of their operations.

4. **Access to Critical Information**: Scanners provide private investigators with access to critical information, such as suspect descriptions, vehicle descriptions, and incident locations, that can aid in their investigations. By listening to dispatches and officer communications, investigators can gather details about suspects, victims, and witnesses involved in criminal activities or emergencies.

5. **Professional Development**: Using scanners can contribute to the professional development of private investigators by enhancing their understanding of law enforcement procedures, protocols, and terminology. By listening to police, fire, and EMS communications, investigators can gain insights into the inner workings of public safety agencies and improve their knowledge of investigative techniques and strategies.

While the use of scanners can provide private investigators with valuable insights and advantages in their work, it also raises ethical, legal, and practical considerations that must be addressed responsibly.

1. **Privacy Concerns**: Private investigators must respect the privacy rights of individuals and avoid intercepting or monitoring communications that are intended to be private or confidential. While public safety communications are generally considered to be in the public domain, investigators should exercise caution to avoid intruding on the privacy of individuals involved in emergencies or law enforcement activities.

2. **Regulatory Compliance**: Private investigators must comply with laws and regulations governing the use of scanners and radio equipment in their jurisdiction. In some areas, the use of scanners may be subject to restrictions or licensing requirements imposed by local authorities or regulatory agencies. Investigators should familiarize themselves with applicable laws and obtain any necessary permits or licenses before using scanners in their work.

3. **Avoiding Interference**: Private investigators should use scanners responsibly and avoid interfering with public safety communications or emergency response efforts. Investigators should refrain from transmitting or rebroadcasting radio signals picked up by scanners, as this can disrupt communications and interfere with law enforcement operations.

4. **Respect for Law Enforcement**: Private investigators should maintain professional and ethical conduct when using scanners to monitor police, fire, and EMS communications. Investigators should refrain from interfering with law enforcement activities, obstructing emergency responders, or attempting to impede the performance of their duties.

In addition to ethical and legal considerations, private investigators should also address practical considerations when using scanners in their work:

1. **Equipment Selection**: Private investigators should choose scanners that are capable of tuning into the frequencies used by public safety agencies in their area. Investigators should consider factors such as frequency coverage, channel capacity, and audio quality when selecting scanners for their investigative work.

2. **Antenna Placement**: Proper antenna placement

is essential for maximizing the range and effectiveness of scanners. Private investigators should position antennas in locations with clear line-of-sight to transmission towers and away from sources of interference, such as electronic devices and metal objects.

3. **Operational Security**: Private investigators should exercise operational security when using scanners to monitor public safety communications. Investigators should avoid discussing sensitive information or revealing operational details over unsecured channels that may be intercepted or monitored by adversaries.

4. **Continued Monitoring**: Private investigators should make a habit of regularly monitoring police, fire, and EMS communications to stay informed about developments in their area of operation. By maintaining continuous surveillance of public safety channels, investigators can remain alert to emerging threats, incidents, or opportunities for investigative action.

Lastly, the use of police, fire, and EMS scanners by private investigators can provide valuable insights, intelligence, and advantages in their investigative work. By monitoring public safety communications in real-time, investigators can gather critical information, coordinate surveillance operations, and maintain situational awareness while navigating ethical, legal, and practical considerations. By addressing these considerations responsibly and leveraging scanners effectively, private investigators can enhance their capabilities, improve their investigative outcomes, and contribute to the success of their clients' cases.

Firearms
        Using primary and backup firearms is a critical

aspect of the operational toolkit for both law enforcement officers and private investigators. These weapons serve as essential tools for self-defense, maintaining public safety, and carrying out lawful duties in potentially dangerous situations. Understanding the roles, responsibilities, and considerations associated with primary and backup firearms is crucial for ensuring the safety and effectiveness of both law enforcement and private investigation personnel.

Law enforcement officers and some private investigators are authorized to carry primary firearms as part of their official duties. These firearms are typically standard-issue weapons selected by the agency or organization and are carried openly or concealed, depending on jurisdictional regulations and operational requirements.

The primary role of firearms is to respond to emergencies where the use of lethal force may be necessary to neutralize a threat or apprehend a suspect. Training to use firearms judiciously, following strict protocols and legal guidelines governing the use of force and deadly force is imperative.

Anyone carrying firearms should undergo extensive training and certification in firearms proficiency, marksmanship, and tactical shooting techniques. This training should includ classroom instruction, range practice, and scenario-based simulations to prepare the person for real-world encounters and ensure they can use their firearms safely and effectively under stress.

Any person that carries firearm(s) regularly should take responsibility for maintaining their firearms to ensure they are in proper working condition, conduct regular inspections, daily cleaning, and maintenance to ensure reliability and performance.

Backup firearms, also known as secondary or concealed carry weapons, are carried by both law enforcement officers and some private investigators as a supplemental means of self-defense and protection. These weapons serve as a contingency option in case the primary firearm is inaccessible, malfunctioning, or out of ammunition.

The primary role of backup firearms is to provide officers and investigators with a reliable means of self-defense and protection in situations where their primary weapon may be unavailable or impractical to deploy. Backup firearms are typically carried concealed on the officer's person or in a discreet holster, allowing for quick and discreet access when needed.

Carrying and using firearms can have a significant psychological and emotional impact on law enforcement officers and private investigators. Officers and investigators are trained to manage stress, anxiety, and adrenaline responses in high-pressure situations, using techniques such as mindfulness, deep breathing, and mental rehearsal to stay focused and composed under duress.

Law enforcement agencies and private investigation firms have systems in place to ensure accountability and oversight in the use of firearms by their personnel. This includes internal review processes, external oversight mechanisms, and transparent reporting of incidents involving the use of force to ensure accountability and maintain public trust.

Finally, the use of primary and backup firearms is an essential aspect of the operational toolkit for both law enforcement officers and private investigators.

These weapons serve as critical tools for self-defense, protection, and maintaining public safety in potentially dangerous situations. Understanding the roles, responsibilities, and considerations associated with primary and backup firearms is crucial for ensuring the safety, effectiveness, and accountability of personnel who carry and use firearms in the line of duty.

Firearms Holster

Choosing the proper firearms holster is a critical decision for private investigators, as it directly impacts their safety, accessibility, and effectiveness in carrying and deploying their firearms. With a wide range of holster options available, selecting the right one requires careful consideration of factors such as comfort, retention, accessibility, concealment, and compatibility with the firearm and attire.

First and foremost, comfort is paramount when choosing a firearms holster. Investigators may be required to wear their holsters for extended periods during surveillance operations or fieldwork, so selecting a holster that is ergonomically designed and comfortable to wear is essential. Holsters with padded linings, breathable materials, and adjustable straps or belt loops can help minimize discomfort and prevent chafing or irritation during prolonged use.

Retention is another crucial factor to consider when choosing a firearms holster. The holster must securely hold the firearm in place, preventing it from falling out or being easily accessed by unauthorized individuals. Holsters with adjustable retention mechanisms, such as thumb breaks, retention screws, or retention straps, allow investigators to customize the level of retention to their preference while ensuring that the firearm remains securely in place until needed.

Accessibility is also a key consideration when

selecting a firearms holster. Investigators need to be able to access their firearms quickly and efficiently in emergency situations, so choosing a holster that allows for smooth and intuitive draws is essential. Holsters with adjustable cant angles, quick-release mechanisms, and index finger releases facilitate fast and reliable access to the firearm, enabling investigators to respond swiftly to threats or emergencies.

Concealment is particularly important for private investigators who may need to carry firearms discreetly in various environments. Choosing a holster that offers effective concealment while still providing accessibility and retention is crucial for maintaining a low profile and avoiding detection. Holsters with low-profile designs, adjustable ride heights, and customizable cant angles help minimize printing and ensure that the firearm remains hidden from view, whether worn inside the waistband (IWB), outside the waistband (OWB), or in an ankle or shoulder holster.

Compatibility with the firearm and attire is another essential factor to consider when choosing a firearms holster. The holster must be specifically designed to fit the make and model of the investigator's firearm, ensuring a secure and snug fit without unnecessary movement or rattling. Additionally, the holster should be compatible with the investigator's attire and preferred carry position, whether wearing casual or professional clothing, allowing for comfortable and discreet carry without compromising accessibility or retention.

So remember, choosing the proper firearms holster is a critical decision for private investigators, as it directly impacts their safety, accessibility, and effectiveness in carrying and deploying their firearms. By considering factors such as comfort, retention, accessibility, concealment, and compatibility with the firearm and attire, investigators can select a holster that meets their specific needs and preferences, enhancing their ability to carry and deploy their firearms safely and effectively in the field.

Firearms Magazines
Having spare firearms magazines is crucial for private investigators, ensuring they can effectively and safely carry out their duties. These additional magazines serve as backups in case of malfunctions, extended engagements, or emergencies, providing a reliable source of ammunition when needed most.

Firstly, spare magazines offer redundancy and reliability in critical situations. Malfunctions or failures can occur unexpectedly, and having spare magazines readily available allows investigators to quickly address these issues without interruption to their operations. In high-stress situations, such as confrontations or engagements, the ability to swiftly reload can make a significant difference in ensuring personal safety and achieving successful outcomes.

Moreover, spare magazines provide increased ammunition capacity, enhancing the investigator's ability to sustain fire and respond to threats effectively. In dynamic and unpredictable environments, having extra rounds readily available can provide a tactical advantage and increase the investigator's confidence in their ability to handle potential threats or engage multiple targets.

Additionally, spare magazines facilitate efficient training and practice sessions. By having multiple magazines on hand, investigators can engage in realistic and immersive training scenarios, practicing reload drills, malfunction clearances, and tactical maneuvers. This hands-on training helps maintain proficiency and readiness, ensuring investigators are prepared to handle real-world situations effectively.

Spare magazines offer versatility and adaptability in various operational settings. Whether conducting surveillance operations, providing security details, or responding to emergencies, having spare magazines allows investigators to tailor their loadout to meet the specific requirements of each mission or assignment. This flexibility enables investigators to optimize their equipment for maximum effectiveness and readiness.

To close, having spare firearms magazines is essential for private investigators to ensure readiness, reliability, and effectiveness in carrying out their duties. These additional magazines provide redundancy, increased ammunition capacity, and versatility in various operational settings, enhancing the investigator's ability to respond to threats, address malfunctions, and sustain fire effectively. By prioritizing the availability of spare magazines and integrating them into their equipment setup, private investigators can enhance their preparedness, confidence, and safety in the field.

Self-defense Ammunition
Choosing the proper self-defense ammunition is a critical decision for anyone concerned with personal safety, including private investigators. The right choice of ammunition can mean the difference between life and death in a self-defense situation. There are various factors to consider when selecting self-defense ammunition, including caliber, bullet type, weight, velocity, and terminal performance. Understanding the essence of each of these factors is crucial for making an informed decision that maximizes effectiveness and minimizes risks.

One of the first considerations when choosing self-defense ammunition is caliber. Caliber refers to the diameter of the bullet, and different calibers offer varying levels of stopping power, recoil, and capacity. Common handgun calibers for self-defense include 9mm, .40 S&W, and .45 ACP, each with its own advantages and drawbacks. While larger calibers may offer more stopping power, they also tend to have heavier recoil and lower magazine capacity. Conversely, smaller calibers like 9mm offer manageable recoil and higher capacity but may sacrifice some stopping power.

Bullet type is another crucial consideration in self-defense ammunition selection. The two primary types of bullets are full metal jacket (FMJ) and hollow point (HP). FMJ bullets are typically used for target shooting and practice, while HP bullets are designed for self-defense purposes. Hollow point bullets are engineered to expand upon impact, creating a larger wound cavity and transferring more energy to the target. This expansion increases stopping power and reduces the risk of overpenetration, making HP bullets the preferred choice for self-defense scenarios.

Weight and velocity are also important factors to consider when selecting self-defense ammunition. Heavier bullets tend to penetrate deeper but may sacrifice some velocity and expansion. Conversely, lighter bullets may offer higher velocity and expansion but may not penetrate as deeply. Balancing weight and velocity is crucial for achieving optimal terminal performance and stopping power.

Terminal performance refers to how the bullet behaves upon impact with the target. The ideal self-defense ammunition should deliver consistent and reliable terminal performance, ensuring effective incapacitation of the threat. Factors such as expansion, penetration, and energy transfer all contribute to terminal performance. Hollow point bullets are designed to expand upon impact, creating a larger wound channel and maximizing tissue damage. This expansion increases the likelihood of incapacitating the threat quickly and efficiently.

Reliability and consistency are also essential considerations when choosing self-defense ammunition. The selected ammunition should function reliably in the chosen firearm and deliver consistent performance across various conditions. Reliability is crucial for ensuring that the ammunition feeds, fires, and ejects properly, especially in high-stress situations where failure is not an option.

incidentally, legal considerations may influence the choice of self-defense ammunition. Some jurisdictions have restrictions on the type of ammunition that civilians can possess or use for self-defense purposes. It is essential to familiarize oneself with local laws and regulations regarding ammunition selection to ensure compliance and avoid potential legal issues.

Don't forget, choosing the proper self-defense ammunition is a decision that should not be taken lightly. It requires careful consideration of factors such as caliber, bullet type, weight, velocity, terminal performance, reliability, and legal considerations. By understanding the essence of each of these factors and how they contribute to overall effectiveness, individuals can make informed decisions that maximize their ability to defend themselves and others in life-threatening situations. Ultimately, the right choice of self-defense ammunition can provide peace of mind and confidence in one's ability to stay safe and secure in an unpredictable world.

Public Library

Private investigators rely on a wide range of resources to gather information, conduct research, and carry out their investigative duties effectively. While technological advancements have expanded access to digital databases and online resources, the importance of a private investigator having access to a public library cannot be overstated. Public libraries serve as invaluable repositories of knowledge, providing access to a diverse array of print and electronic resources, specialized databases, research materials, and expert assistance.

Understanding the significance of public library access for private investigators requires exploring the various ways in which these institutions support and enhance investigative efforts.

One of the primary benefits of public library access for private investigators is the wealth of information available within their collections. Public libraries house extensive collections of books, periodicals, newspapers, and other printed materials covering a wide range of subjects, including law, history, sociology, psychology, and forensics. These resources serve as valuable references for investigators seeking background information, context, or insights relevant to their cases. Whether researching legal precedents, exploring historical records, or studying behavioral patterns, public libraries offer a rich and diverse source of information to support investigative efforts.

Public libraries provide access to specialized databases and research tools that may not be readily available elsewhere. Many libraries subscribe to electronic databases, digital archives, and online research platforms that offer access to scholarly journals, academic publications, legal documents, and proprietary databases. These resources enable private investigators to conduct comprehensive research, access authoritative sources, and gather relevant information to support their investigative findings. Whether searching for court records, property deeds, business registrations, or academic studies, public library databases offer valuable insights and data for investigative purposes.

Additionally, public libraries serve as hubs of expertise and knowledge, offering access to professional librarians and subject matter experts who can provide guidance, assistance, and recommendations to private investigators. Librarians are skilled in information retrieval, research methodologies, and database searching techniques, making them valuable allies for investigators navigating complex or unfamiliar topics. Librarians can help identify relevant resources, formulate research strategies, and locate hard-to-find information, enhancing the efficiency and effectiveness of investigative efforts.

Public libraries offer a conducive environment for private investigators to conduct research, study, and work. Many libraries provide quiet study areas, computer workstations, and meeting rooms where investigators can focus, concentrate, and collaborate on their investigations. The tranquil atmosphere and supportive infrastructure of public libraries create an ideal setting for conducting research, analyzing evidence, and preparing reports, fostering productivity and concentration.

Public libraries play a vital role in promoting literacy, lifelong learning, and civic engagement within their communities. By providing free and open access to information, resources, and educational opportunities, public libraries empower individuals to pursue their intellectual curiosity, expand their knowledge, and develop critical thinking skills. For private investigators, access to public libraries not only facilitates their investigative work but also promotes professional development, continuous learning, and intellectual growth.

Ultimately, access to a public library is indispensable for private investigators, providing a wealth of resources, expertise, and support to enhance their investigative efforts. From extensive collections of print and electronic materials to specialized databases, research tools, and expert assistance, public libraries offer a rich and diverse array of resources to support investigative research, analysis, and decision-making. Public libraries serve as hubs of learning, collaboration, and community engagement, fostering a culture of inquiry, discovery, and lifelong learning. For private investigators committed to excellence, access to a public library is an essential asset that enhances their capabilities, expands their knowledge, and enriches their professional practice.

Court Records
Access to court records is essential for private investigators, providing valuable insights, evidence, and documentation crucial for conducting thorough and effective investigations. Court records contain a wealth of information related to legal proceedings, including civil and criminal cases, judgments, rulings, filings, and transcripts. Understanding the importance of access to court records for private investigators requires exploring the various ways in which these records support and enhance investigative efforts.

One of the primary benefits of access to court records for private investigators is the wealth of information contained within these documents. Court records provide detailed documentation of legal proceedings, including case histories, parties involved, allegations, evidence presented, and outcomes. This information serves as a valuable source of intelligence for investigators seeking to understand the background, context, and circumstances surrounding a particular case or individual. Whether researching prior legal issues, uncovering past misconduct, or identifying relevant parties, court records offer valuable insights to inform investigative strategies and decision-making.

Court records serve as a repository of evidence and documentation relevant to ongoing or potential investigations. These records may contain witness statements, affidavits, depositions, expert reports, and other materials that can corroborate findings, substantiate claims, or provide leads for further investigation. By accessing court records, private investigators can gather valuable evidence, documentations, and information to support their investigative findings and strengthen their cases.

Additionally, court records provide a valuable source of background information and context for individuals involved in legal proceedings. Private investigators often use court records to conduct background checks, verify identities, and assess the credibility and reputation of subjects under investigation. Whether researching criminal histories, civil litigation, bankruptcies, or restraining orders, court records offer valuable insights into a subject's past behavior, character, and associations, helping investigators assess risk and make informed decisions.

Court records serve as a tool for monitoring legal proceedings and tracking developments relevant to ongoing investigations. Private investigators can use court records to stay informed about new filings, hearings, rulings, and judgments related to their cases.

By monitoring court activity, investigators can anticipate potential challenges, identify emerging trends, and adjust their investigative strategies accordingly.

Thereto, court records provide private investigators with access to public information that may not be readily available through other channels. While certain aspects of court proceedings may be confidential or sealed, many court records are considered public records and are accessible to anyone upon request. This transparency ensures accountability, promotes transparency, and facilitates public oversight of the judicial system, empowering private investigators and other stakeholders to access information relevant to their interests and concerns.

In essence, access to court records is essential for private investigators, providing valuable insights, evidence, and documentation crucial for conducting thorough and effective investigations. Court records offer a wealth of information related to legal proceedings, including case histories, parties involved, evidence presented, and outcomes. By accessing court records, private investigators can gather valuable evidence, documentation, and information to support their investigative findings, strengthen their cases, and make informed decisions. Moreover, court records serve as a tool for monitoring legal proceedings, tracking developments, and staying informed about emerging trends and challenges relevant to ongoing investigations.

CHAPTER NINE
Office Setup

Setup: English *Origin 1890* - Set into place

In the realm of private investigation, professionalism, credibility, and trust are paramount. While some private investigators may operate as sole proprietors or independent contractors, there are compelling reasons why establishing and operating as a formal business entity can be advantageous. Let's delve into why a private investigator should consider operating as a business.

Operating as a business entity, such as a Limited Liability Company (LLC) or a corporation, provides crucial legal protection for private investigators. By separating personal assets from business liabilities, a formal business structure shields the individual investigator from personal liability in case of lawsuits or claims filed against the business. This protection is invaluable in a profession where legal risks and liabilities are inherent, offering peace of mind and financial security for the investigator.

Establishing a business entity lends credibility and professionalism to the private investigator's practice. Clients, attorneys, and other stakeholders often prefer to work with licensed businesses rather than individual freelancers or contractors. A formal business structure signals to potential clients that the investigator is committed to ethical standards, adheres to industry regulations, and operates with integrity and accountability. This enhanced credibility can be instrumental in attracting high-value clients, securing lucrative contracts, and building a reputable brand in the competitive field of private investigation.

Operating as a business entity allows private

investigators to create a distinct brand identity and implement targeted marketing strategies. A business name, logo, and website can establish a strong brand presence, differentiate the investigator from competitors, and attract potential clients. Additionally, business entities have more flexibility in marketing and advertising efforts, enabling them to reach their target audience through various channels such as social media, online directories, and industry associations. Effective branding and marketing initiatives can position the investigator as a trusted expert in their field and drive business growth and expansion.

Formal business structures facilitate operational efficiency and scalability for private investigators. By establishing clear roles, responsibilities, and workflows, a business entity can streamline administrative tasks, client communication, and case management processes. Furthermore, businesses have access to professional resources and support services, such as legal counsel, accounting, and technology solutions, to optimize their operations and maximize productivity. This operational efficiency allows investigators to focus on delivering high-quality investigative services, solving complex cases, and exceeding client expectations, ultimately driving profitability and success.

Operating as a business entity opens doors to a wealth of resources and opportunities for private investigators. Business associations, networking events, and industry conferences provide avenues for professional development, collaboration, and knowledge sharing. Additionally, business entities may qualify for government contracts, insurance coverage, and financing options that are not available to individual practitioners. By leveraging these resources and opportunities, private investigators can enhance their skills, expand their clientele, and position themselves for long-term success in the dynamic field of private investigation.

Establishing and operating as a business entity offers numerous advantages for private investigators seeking to thrive in their profession. From legal protection and credibility to branding and operational efficiency, the benefits of operating as a business are undeniable. By embracing a formal business structure, private investigators can safeguard their interests, elevate their reputation, and capitalize on opportunities for growth and advancement. In a competitive and demanding industry, operating as a business entity is not just a choice but a strategic imperative for success.

In the dynamic landscape of entrepreneurship, choosing the right business structure is paramount for success and sustainability. Among the myriad options available, Limited Liability Company (LLC) stands out as a popular choice, offering a multitude of benefits and strategic advantages. In this discourse, we delve into the importance and advantages of forming an LLC for businesses of all sizes and industries.

The modern business world demands agility, flexibility, and protection for its stakeholders. An LLC, with its blend of liability protection, tax advantages, and operational flexibility, emerges as an optimal solution. Let's explore why.

One of the primary reasons entrepreneurs opt for an LLC is the shield it provides against personal liability. Unlike sole proprietorships or general partnerships, where owners are personally liable for business debts and legal obligations, an LLC separates personal assets from business liabilities. This means that if the business faces lawsuits or debts, the personal assets of the LLC members (owners) are generally protected. Such protection fosters confidence among investors, encourages entrepreneurship, and mitigates the risk associated with venturing into new markets or industries.

LLCs offer unparalleled flexibility in taxation, allowing members to choose how they want their business to be taxed. By default, LLCs are pass-through entities, meaning profits and losses "pass through" the business to the owners' personal tax returns, avoiding double taxation. However, LLCs can elect to be taxed as corporations, providing options for optimizing tax efficiency based on the business's unique circumstances and goals. This flexibility empowers entrepreneurs to adapt to changing tax laws and maximize their bottom line.

Another significant advantage of forming an LLC is its operational flexibility. Unlike corporations, which have rigid structures and governance requirements, LLCs have fewer formalities and regulations. They offer greater flexibility in management, decision-making processes, and ownership structure. This versatility makes LLCs ideal for small businesses, startups, and family-owned enterprises, allowing them to focus on innovation and growth without being burdened by excessive administrative overhead.

Perception plays a crucial role in business success. Forming an LLC not only provides legal protection but also enhances the credibility and professionalism of a business. Having "LLC" in the company name signals to clients, customers, and partners that the business is legitimate, reputable, and committed to long-term success. This perception can be instrumental in attracting investors, securing partnerships, and fostering customer trust, ultimately contributing to the business's growth and sustainability.

Planning for the future is essential for any

business endeavor. LLCs offer greater flexibility in succession planning compared to other business structures. In the event of the death or departure of a member, LLC operating agreements can outline procedures for transferring ownership interests, ensuring continuity and stability for the business. This flexibility in ownership transition minimizes disruptions and safeguards the business's legacy for future generations.

Starting and maintaining an LLC is often more cost-effective than establishing a corporation. The registration fees and ongoing compliance requirements for LLCs are generally lower, making them accessible to entrepreneurs with limited resources. Additionally, LLCs can operate with fewer formalities and administrative burdens, reducing overhead costs and allowing businesses to allocate resources more efficiently. This cost-effectiveness makes LLCs an attractive option for startups, small businesses, and aspiring entrepreneurs looking to maximize their return on investment.

Access to capital is vital for business growth and expansion. Forming an LLC can enhance a business's ability to raise capital by offering various financing options. LLCs can issue membership interests to investors, raise funds through loans or lines of credit, or attract venture capital investment. Moreover, the limited liability protection offered by LLCs makes them more attractive to potential investors, as it mitigates their risk exposure. This increased access to capital empowers businesses to pursue opportunities for innovation, expansion, and market leadership.

Forming an LLC offers a myriad of benefits and strategic advantages for businesses seeking to thrive in today's competitive landscape. From liability protection and tax flexibility to operational freedom and credibility, the advantages of an LLC are evident across various dimensions. Whether you're a startup looking to establish a strong foundation or an established enterprise aiming for growth and scalability, choosing an LLC as your business structure can be a catalyst for success. By leveraging the benefits of an LLC, entrepreneurs can protect their assets, optimize their tax position, and position their businesses for long-term prosperity.

Filing with the state to form a business entity is a critical step in establishing a legal framework for your enterprise. Whether you're launching a small startup or expanding an existing venture, navigating the process of business formation with the state is essential for legitimacy, compliance, and protection. Here's a concise overview of the key aspects involved in filing with the state to form a business entity:

The first decision in filing with the state is selecting the most appropriate business structure for your needs. Common options include Limited Liability Company (LLC), Corporation (C-Corp or S-Corp), Partnership, and Sole Proprietorship. Each structure has unique characteristics regarding liability protection, taxation, management, and compliance requirements. Consider consulting with legal or financial professionals to determine the best fit for your business goals and circumstances.

Once you've chosen a business structure, you'll need to select a name for your entity and ensure its availability. Many states require businesses to reserve their chosen name before filing official paperwork. This process typically involves searching the state's business entity database to confirm name availability and submitting a name reservation application if necessary. Upon approval, you can proceed with registering your business name along with other required information.

After finalizing your business name and structure, you'll need to prepare and submit the required formation documents to the state. These documents often include Articles of Organization (for LLCs), Articles of Incorporation (for corporations), or Partnership Agreements (for partnerships). The content and format of these documents may vary depending on state laws and regulations. Ensure accuracy and completeness in preparing these documents to expedite the filing process and avoid potential delays or rejections.

Be aware of the filing fees associated with forming a business entity in your state, as these costs can vary widely depending on the entity type and jurisdiction. Additionally, familiarize yourself with the expected processing times for your filing. While some states offer expedited processing options for an additional fee, others may have longer turnaround times. Plan accordingly to ensure timely completion of the filing process and avoid unnecessary delays in launching your business.

Filing with the state to form a business entity is a foundational step in establishing your enterprise's legal framework and operational structure. By carefully navigating the process and adhering to state requirements, you can lay a solid foundation for your business's success while ensuring compliance with applicable laws and regulations.

Acquiring an insurance bond is a crucial requirement for many businesses operating in states across various industries. A surety bond serves as a form of protection for customers, clients, and the general public, ensuring financial compensation in case the bonded business fails to fulfill its obligations.

Here's a concise overview of the importance and process of acquiring an insurance bond to operate a business in the state:

Insurance bonds, also known as surety bonds, play a vital role in safeguarding consumers and stakeholders from potential financial losses due to non-performance or misconduct by a business. They provide assurance that the bonded business will fulfill its contractual obligations, adhere to industry regulations, and comply with applicable laws. By obtaining an insurance bond, businesses demonstrate their commitment to integrity, professionalism, and accountability, enhancing trust and confidence among customers, partners, and regulatory authorities.

There are various types of insurance bonds tailored to specific industries and purposes. Common examples include license and permit bonds, contractor bonds, fidelity bonds, performance bonds, and court bonds. The type of bond required depends on the nature of the business, its activities, and regulatory requirements set forth by the state or local authorities. It's essential for businesses to understand the specific bond requirements applicable to their operations and ensure compliance to avoid penalties or disruptions to their activities.

The process of obtaining an insurance bond typically involves several steps. First, businesses need to identify the type and amount of bond required for their operations. Next, they must select a reputable surety bond provider or insurance company authorized to issue bonds in the state. The bonding company will evaluate the business's financial stability, creditworthiness, and risk profile before issuing the bond. Once approved, the business will need to pay a premium, typically calculated as a percentage of the bond amount, to secure the bond coverage. Finally, the bond is filed with the appropriate state or local agency as proof of compliance with bonding requirements.

Acquiring an insurance bond is a fundamental aspect of operating a business in many states, serving as a protective measure for both businesses and consumers. By fulfilling bonding requirements and obtaining coverage from a reputable surety bond provider, businesses can demonstrate their commitment to ethical conduct, financial responsibility, and regulatory compliance, laying a solid foundation for long-term success and trust in the marketplace.

As businesses navigate the complexities of the modern marketplace, protecting against unforeseen risks and liabilities becomes paramount. Adequate insurance coverage serves as a crucial safeguard, providing financial security and peace of mind in the face of potential threats. In this comprehensive guide, we explore the various types of insurance coverage essential for businesses and considerations for determining the proper types and amounts of coverage.

Business insurance encompasses a wide range of policies designed to mitigate risks associated with operations, assets, liabilities, and personnel. From property and casualty insurance to liability and employee benefits coverage, businesses have diverse options to tailor their insurance portfolios to their specific needs and exposures. By understanding the various types of insurance coverage available, businesses can make informed decisions to protect their interests and assets comprehensively.

General liability insurance provides protection against third-party claims for bodily injury, property damage, and advertising injury. It covers legal expenses, settlements, and judgments arising from lawsuits alleging negligence, libel, slander, or copyright infringement. General liability insurance is essential for businesses of all sizes and industries, offering broad coverage against common risks encountered in daily operations.

Property insurance safeguards businesses against losses or damages to physical assets such as buildings, equipment, inventory, and furnishings. It covers perils including fire, theft, vandalism, and natural disasters, ensuring that businesses can recover and rebuild in the event of property damage or loss. Property insurance policies may also include business interruption coverage, reimbursing lost income and expenses during periods of suspended operations.

Also known as errors and omissions (E&O) insurance, professional liability insurance protects businesses and professionals against claims of negligence, errors, or omissions in the performance of professional services. It is particularly vital for consultants, contractors, healthcare providers, and other service-oriented businesses exposed to professional liability risks. Professional liability insurance covers legal defense costs and damages awarded in lawsuits alleging professional misconduct or inadequate performance.

Workers' compensation insurance provides coverage for medical expenses, lost wages, and disability benefits for employees injured or disabled on the job. It is a legal requirement in most states for businesses with employees, serving as a no-fault system to compensate workers for work-related injuries and illnesses. Workers' compensation insurance not only protects employees but also shields businesses from costly lawsuits related to workplace injuries.

In an increasingly digital world, cyber liability insurance is essential for businesses that collect, store, or transmit sensitive data. It provides coverage for expenses associated with data breaches, including notification costs, credit monitoring, forensic investigations, and legal fees. Cyber liability insurance also offers protection against liability claims arising from data breaches, such as lawsuits alleging negligence in safeguarding customer information.

Commercial auto insurance covers vehicles used for business purposes against accidents, collisions, and liability claims. It provides coverage for bodily injury and property damage liability, medical payments, and physical damage to owned, leased, or hired vehicles. Commercial auto insurance is essential for businesses with fleets, delivery vehicles, or employees who use their personal vehicles for work-related activities.

Directors and officers insurance protects corporate directors, officers, and executives from personal liability arising from decisions made in their professional capacities. It covers legal defense costs and damages resulting from lawsuits alleging mismanagement, breach of fiduciary duty, or other wrongful acts. D&O insurance is critical for attracting and retaining qualified directors and officers and shielding their personal assets from litigation risks.

Business interruption insurance, also known as business income insurance, provides coverage for lost income and operating expenses when a covered event disrupts normal business operations. It compensates businesses for lost revenue, payroll, rent, and other fixed expenses during periods of forced closure or temporary relocation. Business interruption insurance is particularly valuable for businesses vulnerable to natural disasters, such as hurricanes, floods, or earthquakes.

Determining Proper Types and Amounts of Coverage:

Conduct a comprehensive risk assessment to identify potential threats and vulnerabilities facing your business. Consider internal and external factors such as industry risks, geographical location, business size, operational activities, and regulatory requirements. Assess the likelihood and potential impact of various risks to prioritize insurance needs and allocate resources effectively.

Familiarize yourself with legal and regulatory requirements governing insurance coverage in your industry and jurisdiction. Some types of insurance, such as workers' compensation insurance or professional liability insurance, may be mandatory for businesses operating in certain states or industries. Ensure compliance with applicable laws and regulations to avoid penalties and legal liabilities.

Research industry best practices and standards for insurance coverage within your sector. Consult with industry associations, trade publications, and experienced professionals to understand common risks and recommended insurance solutions tailored to your industry. Benchmark against competitors and peers to ensure that your insurance coverage aligns with industry norms and standards.

Customize your insurance coverage to address the specific needs and exposures of your business. Work closely with insurance agents, brokers, or risk management consultants to design a comprehensive insurance portfolio that reflects your unique risk profile and risk tolerance. Consider factors such as business size, revenue, assets, liabilities, and growth projections when determining the appropriate types and amounts of coverage.

Evaluate coverage limits and deductibles carefully to strike the right balance between protection and affordability. Consider your business's financial resources, budget constraints, and potential loss scenarios when setting coverage limits and deductibles. Opt for adequate coverage limits to mitigate major risks and liabilities, while adjusting deductibles to manage premium costs and out-of-pocket expenses effectively.

Periodically review and reassess your insurance coverage to ensure that it remains aligned with your evolving business needs and objectives. Conduct regular risk assessments, evaluate changes in your business operations or external environment, and adjust your insurance portfolio accordingly. Stay informed about emerging risks, regulatory developments, and industry trends to proactively address potential gaps or deficiencies in your coverage.

Selecting the proper types and amounts of insurance coverage for business operations is a critical decision that requires careful consideration and strategic planning. By understanding the diverse types of insurance coverage available, conducting thorough risk assessments, and customizing insurance solutions to their specific needs, businesses can mitigate risks, protect their assets, and safeguard their long-term viability and success in today's dynamic business environment. Collaborate with experienced insurance professionals and industry experts to navigate the complexities of business insurance and build a robust risk management strategy that ensures resilience and continuity in the face of adversity.

Every office is different, setup accordingly. However, every office should have at minimum:

Fireproof filing cabinets play a crucial role in protecting vital documents, records, and valuables from the devastating effects of fires. In the event of a fire outbreak, these specialized cabinets offer a secure and reliable storage solution, ensuring that critical information remains intact and accessible. Here's why fireproof filing cabinets are essential for businesses:

Businesses rely on a wide range of documents and records for their day-to-day operations, including contracts, financial statements, personnel files, and legal documents. Losing these documents to fire can have catastrophic consequences, leading to disruptions, legal liabilities, and financial losses. Fireproof filing cabinets provide a secure repository for storing important documents, safeguarding them from fire damage and preserving their integrity and usability. By investing in fireproof storage solutions, businesses can mitigate the risk of data loss and ensure continuity in critical business processes.

Many industries and professions are subject to regulatory requirements governing the retention and protection of sensitive information. Failure to comply with these regulations can result in fines, penalties, and legal consequences. Fireproof filing cabinets help businesses meet regulatory compliance standards by providing a secure and tamper-resistant storage environment for confidential and sensitive documents. Whether it's healthcare records, financial data, or legal contracts, fireproof cabinets offer peace of mind that regulatory obligations are being met and data privacy is being upheld.

Beyond documents and records, businesses often store valuable assets and possessions that are susceptible to fire damage, such as cash, checks, jewelry, and electronic media. Fireproof filing cabinets offer a secure and fire-resistant solution for safeguarding these valuables, minimizing the risk of loss or destruction in the event of a fire. Whether it's protecting cash reserves in a retail store or securing backup drives in an office setting, fireproof cabinets provide an added layer of protection for critical assets and possessions.

Fire incidents can disrupt business operations and pose significant challenges to continuity and recovery efforts. By investing in fireproof filing cabinets, businesses enhance their disaster preparedness and resilience, ensuring that vital information and resources are protected during emergencies. With important documents and assets safely stored in fireproof cabinets, businesses can expedite recovery efforts, resume operations more quickly, and minimize downtime and productivity losses following a fire incident. Fireproof cabinets are an integral component of comprehensive disaster recovery plans, providing a reliable means of safeguarding critical assets and facilitating business continuity strategies.

Ultimately, fireproof filing cabinets offer businesses peace of mind and confidence in the security and integrity of their valuable assets and information. Knowing that important documents, records, and valuables are protected against fire damage provides reassurance to business owners, executives, employees, and stakeholders. This sense of security enables businesses to focus on their core activities, innovate, and grow without being unduly concerned about the potential impact of fire-related risks. Fireproof cabinets instill trust and reliability, reinforcing the commitment to safeguarding assets and ensuring the long-term success and sustainability of the business.

Fireproof filing cabinets are indispensable assets for businesses seeking to protect vital documents, records, and valuables from the destructive forces of fire. By providing a secure and fire-resistant storage solution, fireproof cabinets help preserve important information, comply with regulatory requirements, protect assets, and enhance disaster preparedness and recovery efforts. Investing in fireproof filing cabinets not only safeguards business continuity and resilience but also fosters peace of mind, confidence, and trust among stakeholders. As a critical component of comprehensive risk management and security strategies, fireproof cabinets are essential for businesses of all sizes and industries, ensuring that valuable assets and information remain protected and accessible in the face of fire-related risks.

Deploying a comprehensive security system, including video surveillance and alarm systems, is vital for safeguarding business offices against various threats and vulnerabilities. In today's dynamic business environment, where security risks are diverse and ever-evolving, businesses must prioritize the protection of their assets, employees, and operations. Here's why having a video surveillance system and alarm system is essential for business offices:

Video surveillance cameras act as a powerful deterrent against criminal activities such as theft, vandalism, and trespassing. The presence of visible cameras in and around the office premises sends a clear message to potential intruders that the area is under surveillance and that their actions are being monitored. This proactive approach to security helps deter opportunistic criminals and reduces the likelihood of unauthorized access or criminal incidents occurring on the premises.

Video surveillance systems enable real-time monitoring of the office environment, allowing security personnel or designated staff to observe activities and events as they unfold. In the event of suspicious behavior, unauthorized access, or security breaches, staff can promptly intervene or initiate appropriate response protocols to mitigate risks and prevent escalation. Additionally, modern video surveillance systems may feature advanced analytics and motion detection capabilities, alerting personnel to potential threats or anomalies automatically.

In the unfortunate event of security incidents or criminal activities occurring on the premises, video surveillance footage serves as valuable evidence for investigations, law enforcement inquiries, and insurance claims. High-definition cameras capture detailed images and footage of individuals, vehicles, and events, providing critical insights into the circumstances surrounding security breaches or incidents. This evidence can aid in identifying perpetrators, establishing timelines, and documenting the extent of damages or losses, facilitating swift and effective resolution of security-related matters.

Video surveillance systems enhance employee safety and accountability by promoting a secure and monitored work environment. Employees feel reassured knowing that their workplace is equipped with security measures that protect their well-being and assets. Moreover, video surveillance encourages adherence to company policies, procedures, and safety protocols, as employees are aware that their actions are being recorded and monitored. This fosters a culture of accountability, professionalism, and compliance within the organization, promoting a safer and more productive workplace environment.

Integrating video surveillance systems with

alarm systems enhances overall security effectiveness and responsiveness. Alarm systems provide an additional layer of protection by detecting unauthorized entry, perimeter breaches, or security breaches and triggering audible alarms or alerts. When integrated with video surveillance, alarm systems enable security personnel or designated staff to assess the situation visually, verify the nature of the alarm, and initiate appropriate response actions promptly. This seamless integration enhances situational awareness, reduces false alarms, and ensures a coordinated and effective security response.

For businesses operating in regulated industries or high-risk environments, implementing video surveillance and alarm systems may be necessary to comply with legal and regulatory requirements. These systems help businesses demonstrate due diligence in protecting their assets, employees, and customers, reducing the risk of liability claims and legal consequences resulting from security breaches or incidents. Additionally, having robust security measures in place can enhance the organization's reputation, credibility, and trustworthiness among stakeholders and the wider community.

Having a video surveillance system and alarm system is essential for business offices seeking to enhance security, deter criminal activities, and protect assets, employees, and operations. These integrated security solutions provide proactive monitoring, real-time incident response, evidence collection, and compliance assurance, safeguarding businesses against various security threats and vulnerabilities. By investing in robust security measures, businesses can create a safe, secure, and resilient environment conducive to productivity, innovation, and success.

High-security door locks are a fundamental

component of comprehensive physical security measures for businesses, providing a critical line of defense against unauthorized access, intrusions, and security breaches. Installing high-security locks on all exterior doors offers numerous benefits and reinforces the overall security posture of the premises. Here's why having high-security door locks on all exterior doors is essential for businesses:

High-security door locks are designed with advanced features and technologies to resist tampering, picking, drilling, and forced entry attempts. These locks utilize hardened materials, precision engineering, and complex keying mechanisms to withstand attacks and manipulation by unauthorized individuals. By deploying high-security locks on exterior doors, businesses significantly reduce the risk of break-ins, burglaries, and unauthorized access, deterring potential intruders and enhancing overall security effectiveness.

High-security door locks offer improved key control and access management capabilities, allowing businesses to implement restricted access policies and control who has keys to the premises. Key duplication is restricted to authorized personnel or certified locksmiths, minimizing the risk of unauthorized key copying and unauthorized access by former employees, contractors, or outsiders. By maintaining strict control over keys and access credentials, businesses can prevent unauthorized entry and maintain the integrity of their security protocols.

Many insurance providers require businesses to implement specific security measures, including high-security door locks, to qualify for coverage or obtain favorable insurance premiums. By installing high-security locks on all exterior doors, businesses demonstrate their commitment to risk mitigation and loss prevention, aligning with insurance industry standards and regulatory requirements. Compliance with insurance requirements not only protects businesses from financial losses resulting from security incidents but also ensures continuity of coverage and eligibility for potential claims reimbursement.

Ultimately, having high-security door locks on all exterior doors provides business owners, managers, and employees with peace of mind and confidence in the security and integrity of the premises. Knowing that exterior doors are equipped with robust locks that offer maximum protection against unauthorized access and intrusions instills a sense of security and trust in the workplace environment. This sense of security fosters a safe, productive, and conducive atmosphere for employees, customers, and stakeholders, contributing to overall satisfaction and well-being.

High-security door locks are indispensable assets for businesses seeking to enhance physical security, deter unauthorized access, and protect against security threats and vulnerabilities. By installing high-security locks on all exterior doors, businesses strengthen their defense mechanisms, control access to the premises, comply with insurance requirements, and foster a secure and confidence-inspiring environment for all stakeholders. Investing in high-quality, high-security door locks is a proactive and cost-effective measure that reinforces the overall security posture of the business and mitigates risks associated with unauthorized entry and intrusions.

In the modern workplace, the choice between wired and wireless connectivity for office computers is a crucial consideration. While Wi-Fi offers convenience and flexibility, wired connections provide reliability, security, and performance advantages that are indispensable for many business environments. In this comprehensive discussion, we explore the benefits and advantages of using wired office computers over Wi-Fi.

Wired connections offer unparalleled reliability and stability compared to Wi-Fi. Ethernet cables provide a direct and dedicated connection between computers and network devices, eliminating interference, signal degradation, and fluctuations in connection quality that are common with wireless networks. This stability ensures consistent network performance and minimizes the risk of downtime or disruptions in critical business operations, making wired connections ideal for environments where reliability is paramount.

Security is a top priority for businesses seeking to protect sensitive data, intellectual property, and proprietary information from unauthorized access and cyber threats. Wired connections offer enhanced security compared to Wi-Fi, as data transmitted over Ethernet cables is less susceptible to interception, eavesdropping, and hacking attempts. Unlike wireless signals that can be intercepted by nearby devices or compromised by malicious actors, wired connections provide a more secure communication channel, reducing the risk of data breaches and cyber attacks.

Wired connections deliver faster speeds and higher bandwidth capacity compared to Wi-Fi, making them ideal for bandwidth-intensive applications, large file transfers, and data-intensive tasks. Ethernet cables support Gigabit Ethernet and beyond, allowing for data transfer rates of up to 10 Gbps or more, depending on the network infrastructure. This high-speed connectivity enables employees to access and share resources, collaborate on projects, and interact with cloud-based applications without experiencing lag or latency issues commonly associated with wireless networks.

Latency, or the delay in data transmission between devices, can impact the responsiveness and performance of networked applications, especially in real-time communication and multimedia streaming scenarios. Wired connections minimize latency and lag by providing a direct and dedicated pathway for data transmission, eliminating the uncertainties and delays inherent in wireless communication. This low-latency connectivity is critical for demanding applications such as video conferencing, VoIP calls, online gaming, and virtual collaboration tools, where real-time interaction and responsiveness are essential.

Wired network infrastructure offers greater scalability and future-proofing capabilities compared to Wi-Fi, allowing businesses to accommodate growing bandwidth demands and evolving technology requirements. Ethernet-based networks can be easily expanded and upgraded by adding additional switches, routers, and cables to support increasing numbers of devices and users. Additionally, wired connections provide a more stable foundation for emerging technologies such as Internet of Things (IoT) devices, high-definition video streaming, and cloud computing, ensuring optimal performance and compatibility as businesses adopt new technologies and applications.

While the initial setup costs of wired network infrastructure may be higher than Wi-Fi, the long-term cost-effectiveness of wired connections often outweighs the upfront investment. Ethernet cables are relatively inexpensive and durable, requiring minimal maintenance and replacement compared to wireless access points and routers that may require periodic upgrades, troubleshooting, and security enhancements. Moreover, the reliability and performance advantages of wired connections can translate into productivity gains, reduced support overhead, and lower operational costs over time, making wired office computers a cost-effective and sustainable solution for businesses.

Lastly, using wired office computers over Wi-Fi offers numerous benefits and advantages that are essential for businesses seeking reliable, secure, and high-performance network connectivity. From enhanced reliability and security to faster speeds and reduced latency, wired connections provide a solid foundation for productivity, collaboration, and innovation in the modern workplace. By prioritizing wired network infrastructure, businesses can ensure seamless connectivity, protect sensitive data, and future-proof their technology investments, positioning themselves for success in today's digital economy. While Wi-Fi remains a convenient option for certain use cases, the reliability, security, and performance benefits of wired office computers make them the preferred choice for many businesses looking to optimize their network infrastructure and maximize operational efficiency.

Having an office printer scanner is indispensable for modern businesses seeking to streamline document management, improve productivity, and enhance workflow efficiency. Combining the functions of printing, scanning, copying, and sometimes faxing into a single device, office printer scanners offer numerous benefits and advantages that are essential for today's dynamic workplace. Here's why having an office printer scanner is beneficial:

Office printer scanners are versatile devices that serve multiple purposes, eliminating the need for separate equipment for printing, scanning, and copying tasks. With a single device, employees can print documents, digitize paper records, and create digital copies or backups effortlessly. This multi-functionality optimizes office space, reduces equipment clutter, and simplifies document management processes, enhancing overall efficiency and convenience in the workplace.

Investing in an office printer scanner can yield significant cost savings for businesses compared to purchasing individual devices for printing and scanning tasks. Consolidating multiple functions into a single device reduces upfront capital expenditure, maintenance costs, and consumables expenses associated with maintaining separate printers and scanners. Moreover, modern office printer scanners are designed for energy efficiency, reducing electricity consumption and operating costs over time, making them a cost-effective solution for businesses of all sizes.

Office printer scanners streamline document workflows and expedite task completion, resulting in improved productivity and efficiency for employees. With fast printing and scanning speeds, automatic document feeders, duplex printing/scanning capabilities, and intuitive user interfaces, these devices empower employees to accomplish tasks more quickly and effectively. Whether printing reports, scanning contracts, or copying presentations, office printer scanners enable seamless document handling and processing, minimizing downtime and maximizing productivity in the office.

Digital scanning capabilities provided by office printer scanners facilitate seamless collaboration and information sharing among team members. Scanned documents can be easily converted into digital formats such as PDFs or image files and shared via email, cloud storage, or network folders. This enables remote collaboration, document access from anywhere, and real-time collaboration on projects, regardless of physical location. By digitizing paper documents and fostering collaboration, office printer scanners promote efficiency, transparency, and teamwork within the organization.

In the end, having an office printer scanner is essential for businesses seeking to optimize document management, streamline workflows, and enhance productivity in the workplace. With their multi-functionality, cost-effectiveness, improved productivity, and enhanced collaboration capabilities, office printer scanners serve as indispensable tools for modern businesses of all sizes and industries. By investing in a high-quality office printer scanner and leveraging its features and capabilities, businesses can streamline operations, reduce costs, and stay competitive in today's fast-paced business environment.

Having a designated phone line for a private investigator's business office is essential for maintaining professionalism, managing communications effectively, and establishing credibility with clients. In a field where trust and confidentiality are paramount, a dedicated phone line serves as a direct point of contact for clients, facilitates efficient communication, and enhances the overall client experience. Here's why having a designated phone line is crucial for a private investigator's business office:

A dedicated phone line conveys a sense of professionalism and legitimacy, signaling to clients that the investigator operates a reputable and established business. It creates a distinct separation between personal and professional communications, reinforcing the credibility and professionalism of the business. By providing a professional point of contact, a designated phone line enhances the brand image and fosters trust and confidence among clients, contributing to long-term client relationships and business success.

Maintaining confidentiality and privacy is paramount in the private investigation industry, where sensitive information and sensitive matters are often discussed. A designated phone line ensures that client communications are handled securely and discreetly, minimizing the risk of unauthorized access or interception of sensitive information. By establishing clear protocols for handling client inquiries and consultations, a dedicated phone line helps safeguard client confidentiality and protect sensitive information from prying eyes or ears.

A designated phone line streamlines communication between the investigator and clients, enabling prompt response to inquiries, scheduling appointments, and addressing client concerns. With a dedicated phone line, clients can reach the investigator directly without having to navigate through receptionists or automated systems, fostering personalized and attentive client service. Additionally, a designated phone line allows the investigator to maintain better control over communication channels, ensuring that client inquiries are handled promptly and professionally, enhancing the overall client experience.

A dedicated phone line serves as a valuable marketing tool for promoting the investigator's business and enhancing brand recognition. Including the business phone number in marketing materials, advertisements, and online listings increases visibility and makes it easier for potential clients to contact the investigator. Consistent use of a designated phone line reinforces brand identity and makes the business more memorable to clients, leading to increased inquiries, referrals, and business opportunities.

To summarize, having a designated phone line for a private investigator's business office is essential for maintaining professionalism, managing communications effectively, and providing exceptional client service. By establishing a dedicated point of contact, the investigator can enhance brand image, safeguard client confidentiality, streamline communication, and promote business growth. Investing in a dedicated phone line demonstrates a commitment to professionalism, client satisfaction, and business success, making it a valuable asset for private investigators operating in today's competitive marketplace.

In the digital age, where online communication dominates, the traditional post office box (PO Box) remains a valuable asset for businesses of all sizes. Offering privacy, security, convenience, and flexibility, a PO Box serves as a reliable and versatile solution for managing mail and correspondence. In this comprehensive guide, we delve into the myriad benefits of using a PO Box for your business and explore how it can enhance efficiency, professionalism, and peace of mind.

One of the primary advantages of using a PO Box for business mail is enhanced privacy and security. Unlike a physical street address, which may expose your business location and personal details, a PO Box provides a discreet and anonymous mailing address. This helps protect your privacy, reduce the risk of identity theft, and prevent unwanted solicitations or inquiries. Additionally, PO Boxes are located within secure postal facilities, ensuring that your mail is safeguarded against theft, loss, or damage.

A PO Box lends an air of professionalism and credibility to your business, signaling to clients, partners, and stakeholders that you operate from a reputable and established address. Whether you're a small startup or a large corporation, having a dedicated PO Box enhances your brand image and instills confidence in your professionalism and reliability. It conveys a sense of permanence and stability, regardless of changes in physical location or office arrangements, enhancing your business's reputation and trustworthiness.

PO Boxes offer unparalleled flexibility and mobility, allowing businesses to receive mail and packages from anywhere, at any time. Whether you're relocating your office, traveling for business, or working remotely, your PO Box remains a constant and accessible point of contact for receiving mail. With convenient access hours and the option to forward mail to any location worldwide, PO Boxes accommodate the dynamic needs and lifestyles of modern businesses, ensuring uninterrupted mail delivery and communication.

Managing mail can be a time-consuming and challenging task for businesses, especially those receiving large volumes of correspondence. A PO Box simplifies mail management by providing a centralized location for receiving, sorting, and organizing mail. Instead of relying on multiple addresses or delivery points, businesses can consolidate their mail at a single PO Box address, streamlining mail handling processes and reducing the risk of mail loss or misplacement. This centralized approach enhances efficiency, productivity, and organization, enabling businesses to focus on core activities without being overwhelmed by mail-related tasks.

In addition to standard mail, PO Boxes offer secure package handling services, making them an ideal solution for businesses that receive shipments, parcels, or valuable items. Postal facilities equipped with PO Box services provide secure storage lockers or oversized mail compartments for receiving and retrieving packages safely. This eliminates the need for businesses to rely on doorstep delivery or unattended package drop-offs, reducing the risk of theft, damage, or missed deliveries. With secure package handling at a PO Box, businesses can receive shipments with confidence and peace of mind.

For many businesses, compliance with legal and regulatory requirements is a top priority. Using a PO Box for business mail can help meet these obligations by providing a reliable and verifiable mailing address for official correspondence, legal notices, and regulatory filings. PO Boxes offer a stable and standardized address format that meets postal standards and can be used for various business purposes, including licensing, permits, tax filings, and compliance documentation. By maintaining a PO Box, businesses ensure compliance with legal requirements while minimizing the risk of missed deadlines or communication errors.

Using a PO Box for business mail is a cost-effective solution compared to renting or leasing commercial office space solely for mail handling purposes. PO Box rental fees are typically affordable and transparent, with options available for businesses of all sizes and budgets. Additionally, the convenience and efficiency gained from using a PO Box can result in indirect cost savings by reducing administrative overhead, optimizing resource allocation, and improving operational efficiency. Overall, the cost-effectiveness of a PO Box makes it a practical and economical choice for businesses looking to manage mail effectively without breaking the bank.

It goes without saying, using a post office box (PO Box) for business mail offers a multitude of benefits that can enhance efficiency, professionalism, and peace of mind for businesses of all types and sizes. From privacy and security to professionalism and credibility, a PO Box provides a reliable and versatile solution for managing mail and correspondence. With flexibility, mobility, centralized mail management, secure package handling, legal compliance, and cost-effectiveness, a PO Box meets the diverse needs and priorities of modern businesses in today's dynamic marketplace. By leveraging the benefits of a PO Box, businesses can optimize their mail handling processes, strengthen their brand image, and focus on achieving their business goals with confidence and convenience.

CHAPTER TEN
<u>Other Gear</u>
(*Not Legal in all 50 States*)

Gear: Old Norse *Origin Gorvi* - Equipment

Audio Bug

Private investigators often employ various surveillance techniques to gather evidence, uncover information, and assist clients in legal matters. Among these techniques, the use of audio bugs, also known as covert listening devices or wiretaps, raises complex legal and ethical considerations. While audio surveillance can be a powerful tool in investigations, its legality is subject to stringent regulations and restrictions to protect individual privacy rights. In this comprehensive analysis, we delve into the legality of private investigators using audio bugs for surveillance, examining relevant laws, regulations, case precedents, and ethical guidelines.

Audio surveillance involves the use of listening devices to capture conversations, sounds, or other auditory information without the knowledge or consent of the parties being monitored. Private investigators may deploy audio bugs in various scenarios, including surveillance of suspected criminal activities, gathering evidence for civil litigation, monitoring employees or spouses for suspected misconduct, or conducting undercover operations for corporate clients.

The legality of private investigators using audio bugs for surveillance is governed by a complex framework of federal and state laws, as well as regulations issued by regulatory agencies and industry associations. Key legal considerations include:

1. **Federal Wiretap Act (Title III of the Omnibus Crime Control and Safe Streets Act of 1968)**: The

Wiretap Act regulates the interception of wire, oral, and electronic communications and establishes strict requirements for obtaining authorization to conduct audio surveillance. Under the Wiretap Act, private investigators must obtain a court order or warrant based on probable cause to intercept oral communications in most circumstances. Violations of the Wiretap Act can result in criminal penalties, civil liability, and suppression of illegally obtained evidence.

2. **State Wiretapping Laws**: In addition to federal law, each state has its own wiretapping statutes that govern the use of audio surveillance within its jurisdiction. State wiretapping laws may impose additional requirements, restrictions, or exceptions regarding the use of audio bugs by private investigators. It is essential for private investigators to familiarize themselves with the specific wiretapping laws and regulations applicable in the states where they operate to ensure compliance with legal requirements.

3. **One-Party Consent vs. Two-Party Consent States**: The United States follows a mixed approach to consent for audio surveillance, with some states requiring the consent of all parties to a conversation (two-party consent) and others only requiring the consent of one party (one-party consent). In one-party consent states, private investigators may legally record conversations in which they are participating without informing the other parties. However, in two-party consent states, all parties must consent to the recording for it to be lawful, unless exceptions apply.

4. **Exceptions and Exemptions**: The Wiretap Act and state wiretapping laws may include exceptions or exemptions for certain types of communications or individuals, such as law enforcement officers conducting authorized investigations, participants in

public meetings or gatherings, or individuals who have waived their privacy rights. Private investigators should carefully assess whether any exceptions or exemptions apply to their surveillance activities to ensure compliance with legal requirements.

Court decisions and legal interpretations play a significant role in shaping the legality of private investigators using audio bugs for surveillance. Landmark cases, appellate rulings, and judicial opinions have established important precedents and clarified legal standards regarding the use of audio surveillance techniques. These case precedents provide guidance on issues such as the interpretation of wiretapping laws, the admissibility of audio recordings as evidence in court proceedings, and the scope of privacy protections afforded to individuals.

In addition to legal requirements, private investigators must adhere to ethical principles and professional standards when using audio bugs for surveillance. Ethical considerations include:

Private investigators must respect the privacy rights of individuals and avoid unauthorized intrusions into their private affairs. This includes obtaining consent when required by law, minimizing the intrusion on privacy, and ensuring that surveillance activities are conducted in a manner that is proportionate to the investigative objectives.

Private investigators should be transparent about their surveillance activities and maintain accurate records documenting the use of audio bugs, including the dates, times, locations, and purposes of surveillance. Transparency and accountability foster trust and credibility with clients, regulatory authorities, and the public.

Private investigators must refrain from engaging in unlawful conduct or unethical practices when using audio bugs for surveillance. This includes avoiding unauthorized interceptions of communications, misrepresenting their identities or affiliations, and violating the rights of individuals under investigation.

Private investigators are bound by professional standards of conduct established by industry associations, regulatory bodies, and licensing boards. These standards may include guidelines for the lawful and ethical use of surveillance techniques, the protection of client confidentiality, and the maintenance of professional integrity.

The legality of private investigators using audio bugs for surveillance is subject to rigorous legal and ethical scrutiny, governed by a complex framework of laws, regulations, case precedents, and professional standards. While audio surveillance can be a valuable tool in investigations, private investigators must ensure strict compliance with applicable legal requirements, including obtaining consent when necessary, obtaining proper authorization, and adhering to privacy protections afforded by federal and state laws. By understanding the legal framework, exercising ethical judgment, and maintaining professionalism, private investigators can navigate the complexities of audio surveillance responsibly and effectively in pursuit of their investigative objectives.

Mini Camera Bug

Private investigators often rely on surveillance techniques to gather evidence, monitor activities, and assist clients in legal matters. Among these techniques, the use of mini spy cameras, also known as covert cameras or hidden cameras, can be a valuable tool for conducting discreet and effective investigations. However, the legality of using mini spy cameras in investigative activities is subject to various legal and ethical considerations. In this comprehensive analysis, we explore the legal framework governing the use of mini spy cameras by private investigators, examining relevant laws, regulations, case precedents, and ethical guidelines.

Mini spy cameras are small, discreet devices designed to capture audiovisual recordings covertly without the knowledge or consent of the subjects being monitored. These cameras come in various forms, including wearable devices, stationary objects, and concealed fixtures, allowing private investigators to discreetly observe and document activities in public or private settings. Mini spy cameras may be used in a wide range of investigative scenarios, including surveillance of suspected infidelity, workplace misconduct, insurance fraud, and criminal activities.

The legality of using mini spy cameras by private investigators is governed by a complex framework of federal and state laws, as well as regulations issued by regulatory agencies and industry associations. Key legal considerations include:

The use of mini spy cameras implicates privacy rights protected by the Fourth Amendment to the U.S. Constitution and state constitutions, as well as federal and state privacy statutes. Individuals generally have a reasonable expectation of privacy in areas where they have a heightened expectation of solitude or seclusion, such as their homes, hotel rooms, and private offices. Private investigators must ensure that their use of mini spy cameras complies with applicable privacy laws and respects the reasonable expectations of privacy of individuals under surveillance.

Mini spy cameras may also capture audio recordings in addition to video recordings, raising additional legal considerations related to wiretap laws and audio recording restrictions. Federal law and state wiretapping statutes regulate the interception of oral and electronic communications and impose strict requirements for obtaining consent to record conversations. Private investigators must be aware of the legal requirements for audio recordings in the jurisdictions where they operate and ensure compliance with applicable laws.

The United States follows a mixed approach to consent for audio recording, with some states requiring the consent of all parties to a conversation (two-party consent) and others only requiring the consent of one party (one-party consent). Private investigators must familiarize themselves with the consent requirements for audio recordings in the states where they conduct surveillance and ensure compliance with applicable laws.

The legality of using mini spy cameras may vary depending on whether surveillance occurs in public or private settings. In public settings where individuals have a diminished expectation of privacy, such as streets, parks, and shopping malls, the use of mini spy cameras may be less restricted. However, in private settings where individuals have a reasonable expectation of privacy, such as homes, hotel rooms, and private offices, the use of mini spy cameras may be subject to stricter legal limitations.

Court decisions and legal interpretations play a significant role in shaping the legality of using mini spy cameras by private investigators. Landmark cases, appellate rulings, and judicial opinions have established important precedents and clarified legal standards regarding the use of surveillance techniques. These case precedents provide guidance on issues such as the interpretation of privacy laws, the admissibility of video recordings as evidence in court proceedings, and the scope of privacy protections afforded to individuals.

In addition to legal requirements, private investigators must adhere to ethical principles and professional standards when using mini spy cameras in investigative activities. Ethical considerations include:

Private investigators must respect the privacy rights of individuals and avoid unwarranted intrusions into their private affairs. This includes minimizing the intrusion on privacy, avoiding surveillance in areas where individuals have a reasonable expectation of privacy, and ensuring that surveillance activities are conducted in a manner that is proportionate to the investigative objectives.

Private investigators should be transparent about their surveillance activities and maintain accurate records documenting the use of mini spy cameras, including the dates, times, locations, and purposes of surveillance. Transparency and accountability foster trust and credibility with clients, regulatory authorities, and the public.

Private investigators must refrain from engaging in unlawful conduct or unethical practices when using mini spy cameras in investigations. This includes obtaining proper authorization when required by law, respecting the rights of individuals under surveillance, and complying with legal and ethical standards governing the use of surveillance techniques.

Private investigators should consider the potential harms and consequences of using mini spy cameras, including the impact on individual privacy, reputation, and well-being. Surveillance activities should be conducted with sensitivity and discretion, taking into account the potential for unintended consequences or collateral damage to innocent parties.

As a final point, the legal use of mini spy cameras by private investigators is subject to stringent legal and ethical considerations, governed by a complex framework of laws, regulations, case precedents, and professional standards. While mini spy cameras can be a valuable tool for conducting discreet and effective investigations, private investigators must ensure strict compliance with applicable privacy laws, consent requirements, and ethical principles. By understanding the legal framework, exercising ethical judgment, and maintaining professionalism, private investigators can use mini spy cameras responsibly and effectively in pursuit of their investigative objectives, while respecting the rights and privacy of individuals under surveillance.

Parabolic Microphone
Private investigators often employ various surveillance techniques to gather evidence, monitor activities, and assist clients in legal matters. Among these techniques, the use of parabolic microphones, also known as shotgun microphones or directional microphones, can be a powerful tool for capturing audio from a distance. However, the legality of using parabolic microphones in investigative activities is subject to stringent legal and ethical considerations. In this comprehensive analysis, we explore the legal framework governing the use of parabolic microphones by private investigators, examine relevant laws, regulations, case precedents, and ethical guidelines, and discuss the challenges and limitations associated with their use.

Parabolic microphones are specialized audio recording devices designed to capture sound from a distance by focusing and amplifying sound waves using a parabolic dish. These devices are equipped with highly sensitive microphones and directional capabilities, allowing private investigators to capture clear audio recordings of conversations, ambient noise, or other auditory information from a distance. Parabolic microphones are commonly used in surveillance operations, stakeouts, and undercover investigations to gather evidence, monitor activities, and gather intelligence.

The legality and ethical of using parabolic microphones by private investigators is governed by a complex framework similar to that of audio bugs and spy cameras in which they are regulated by federal and state laws, as well as regulations issued by regulatory agencies and industry associations.

Despite their effectiveness, the use of parabolic microphones in private investigations poses several challenges and limitations:

1. **Range and Sensitivity**: Parabolic microphones have limited range and sensitivity, making them less effective in noisy environments or at long distances. Environmental factors such as wind, background noise, and interference can affect the quality of audio recordings captured by parabolic microphones, limiting their utility in certain surveillance scenarios.

2. **Line of Sight Requirements**: Parabolic microphones rely on line-of-sight communication to capture audio from a distance, requiring an unobstructed view of the target area. Physical barriers such as walls, foliage, or obstacles can obstruct the path of sound waves and diminish the effectiveness of

parabolic microphones, necessitating careful positioning and placement to optimize performance.

3. **Legal and Ethical Concerns**: The use of parabolic microphones raises legal and ethical concerns regarding privacy rights, consent requirements, and compliance with wiretapping laws. Private investigators must navigate these complexities carefully and ensure strict adherence to legal and ethical standards to avoid potential legal liability, suppression of evidence, or damage to professional reputation.

4. **Technical Expertise and Training**: Effective use of parabolic microphones requires technical expertise and specialized training to operate the equipment properly, analyze audio recordings, and interpret the results accurately. Private investigators must invest time and resources in acquiring the necessary skills and knowledge to maximize the effectiveness of parabolic microphones in investigative activities.

The legal use of parabolic microphones by private investigators is subject to stringent legal and ethical considerations, governed by a complex framework of laws, regulations, case precedents, and professional standards. While parabolic microphones can be a valuable tool for capturing audio from a distance in investigative activities, private investigators must ensure strict compliance with applicable privacy laws, consent requirements, and ethical principles. By understanding the legal framework, exercising ethical judgment, and addressing the challenges and limitations associated with their use, private investigators can leverage parabolic microphones effectively and responsibly in pursuit of their investigative objectives, while respecting the rights and privacy of individuals under surveillance.

Drone w/ camera

As mentioned in Chapter Eight, use drones with extreme caution. The legal considerations surrounding the use of drones in surveillance are multifaceted. Regulations govern airspace usage, privacy rights, and data collection. Drone operators must adhere to Federal Aviation Administration (FAA) guidelines, obtain proper licensing, and comply with local laws regarding drone operation. Additionally, surveillance conducted with drones must respect individuals' privacy rights, ensuring that data collection remains within legal boundaries. Understanding and adhering to these regulations is crucial to avoid legal repercussions and protect the rights of both the drone operator and those being surveilled.

R/C Vehicle w/ camera

Drones and remote-controlled vehicles (RCVs) share several legal considerations when used for surveillance operations, as both technologies involve capturing images or recordings of individuals or property. While drones are unmanned aerial vehicles capable of autonomous flight, RCVs are ground-based vehicles controlled remotely by an operator. Despite their differences in operation and capabilities, both drones and RCVs are subject to similar legal frameworks and regulations governing their use in surveillance activities. In this discussion, we explore the legal commonalities between drones and RCVs in the context of surveillance operations.

One of the primary legal considerations for both drones and RCVs is privacy law, particularly concerning individuals' reasonable expectation of privacy. Surveillance conducted using drones or RCVs must adhere to privacy laws that protect individuals from unwarranted intrusions into their private affairs. Whether capturing images or recordings from the air or ground, operators of drones and RCVs must respect individuals' privacy rights and avoid conducting surveillance in areas where individuals have a reasonable expectation of privacy, such as their homes, yards, or other private spaces.

In some jurisdictions, the use of surveillance devices, including drones and RCVs, may require the consent of the individuals being surveilled. This is particularly relevant when capturing audio recordings or conducting surveillance in areas where individuals have a reasonable expectation of privacy. Operators of drones and RCVs must ensure compliance with consent requirements to avoid legal challenges or allegations of privacy violations. Obtaining explicit consent from individuals before conducting surveillance with drones or RCVs can help mitigate legal risks and ensure compliance with applicable laws.

Both drones and RCVs may be equipped with audio recording capabilities, raising legal considerations related to wiretapping laws and audio recording restrictions. Federal and state wiretapping statutes regulate the interception of oral communications and impose strict requirements for obtaining consent to record conversations. Operators of drones and RCVs must be aware of the legal requirements for audio recordings in the jurisdictions where they operate and ensure compliance with applicable laws. Unauthorized interception of oral communications using drones or RCVs can result in legal liability and suppression of illegally obtained evidence.

Drones, being aerial vehicles, are subject to Federal Aviation Administration (FAA) regulations governing their operation in the National Airspace System (NAS). These regulations include requirements for drone registration, pilot certification, airspace restrictions, and operational limitations. While RCVs do not operate in airspace regulated by the FAA, they may still be subject to local ordinances or regulations governing their use in public spaces. Operators of both drones and RCVs must adhere to applicable regulations to ensure safe and lawful operation and avoid legal penalties or enforcement actions.

Both drones and RCVs may be subject to public nuisance and trespass laws when operated inappropriately or intrusively. Surveillance conducted using drones or RCVs must respect property rights and avoid interfering with individuals' use and enjoyment of their property. Operators of drones and RCVs must refrain from flying or driving over private property without permission and should exercise caution to avoid causing disturbances or disruptions to others. Violations of public nuisance or trespass laws can result in legal liabilities and civil lawsuits against operators.

In conclusion, drones and remote-controlled vehicles (RCVs) share several legal considerations when used for surveillance operations, including privacy laws, consent requirements, wiretapping laws, FAA regulations, and public nuisance and trespass laws. Operators of drones and RCVs must navigate these legal complexities carefully to ensure compliance with applicable laws and regulations and avoid legal liabilities or enforcement actions. By understanding and adhering to legal requirements, operators can conduct surveillance operations responsibly and lawfully, respecting individuals' privacy rights and protecting themselves from legal risks and challenges.

GPS Tracker (real time)

Private investigators often rely on GPS trackers as a valuable tool for conducting surveillance, monitoring activities, and gathering evidence in legal matters. However, the use of GPS trackers raises complex legal and ethical considerations, as it involves tracking individuals' movements and collecting location data. In this comprehensive analysis, we explore the legal framework governing the use of GPS trackers by private investigators, examine relevant laws, regulations, case precedents, and ethical guidelines, and discuss the challenges and limitations associated with their use.

GPS trackers, or Global Positioning System trackers, are electronic devices that use satellite signals to determine and record the precise location of a target vehicle or asset. These devices are typically small, discreet, and easily concealable, allowing private investigators to monitor the movements of vehicles, individuals, or objects covertly. GPS trackers can provide real-time tracking data, historical location records, speed information, and other relevant metrics, enabling private investigators to gather valuable evidence and intelligence for their investigations.

The legality of using GPS trackers by private investigators is governed by a complex framework of federal and state laws, as well as regulations issued by regulatory agencies and industry associations. Key legal considerations include:

The use of GPS trackers implicates privacy rights protected by federal and state wiretapping statutes, which regulate the interception of wire, oral, and electronic communications. The U.S. Supreme Court's decision in United States v. Jones (2012) established that attaching a GPS tracker to a vehicle constitutes a search under the Fourth Amendment to the U.S. Constitution and may require a warrant based on probable cause. State wiretapping laws may impose additional requirements or restrictions on the use of GPS trackers, depending on the jurisdiction.

In light of the Jones decision, private investigators should be aware that attaching a GPS tracker to a vehicle without the owner's consent or a valid warrant may constitute an unlawful search under the Fourth Amendment. While the exact legal requirements for obtaining a warrant may vary depending on the circumstances and jurisdiction, private investigators should err on the side of caution and obtain proper authorization whenever possible to avoid potential legal challenges or suppression of evidence.

In some jurisdictions, obtaining the consent of the vehicle owner or authorized user may serve as a legal basis for using a GPS tracker. However, consent must be freely given, voluntary, and informed to be valid under the law. Private investigators should obtain written consent from the vehicle owner or authorized user before deploying a GPS tracker to ensure compliance with legal requirements and minimize the risk of legal liability.

Certain exceptions or exemptions may apply to the use of GPS trackers in specific circumstances, such as law enforcement investigations, emergency situations, or consent-based tracking. Private investigators should familiarize themselves with applicable legal exceptions and exemptions in their jurisdiction to determine the legality of using GPS trackers in their investigations.

Court decisions and legal interpretations play a significant role in shaping the legality of using GPS trackers by private investigators. Landmark cases, appellate rulings, and judicial opinions have established important precedents and clarified legal standards regarding the use of surveillance techniques. These case precedents provide guidance on issues such as the interpretation of Fourth Amendment protections, the admissibility of GPS tracking data as evidence in court proceedings, and the scope of privacy rights afforded to individuals.

In addition to legal requirements, private investigators must adhere to ethical principles and professional standards when using GPS trackers in investigative activities. Ethical considerations include:

Private investigators must respect the privacy rights of individuals and avoid unwarranted intrusions into their private affairs. This includes minimizing the intrusion on privacy, obtaining proper authorization when required by law, and ensuring that GPS tracking activities are conducted in a manner that is proportionate to the investigative objectives.

Private investigators should be transparent about their use of GPS trackers and maintain accurate records documenting the deployment, operation, and retrieval of tracking devices. Transparency and accountability foster trust and credibility with clients, regulatory authorities, and the public.

Private investigators must refrain from engaging in unlawful conduct or unethical practices when using GPS trackers in investigations. This includes obtaining proper authorization, respecting individuals' privacy rights, and complying with legal and ethical standards governing the use of surveillance techniques.

Despite their effectiveness, the use of GPS trackers in private investigations poses several challenges and limitations:

GPS trackers require power to operate, and battery life can vary depending on the device's size, design, and features. Private investigators must ensure that tracking devices are adequately powered and maintained to prevent disruptions or failures in tracking operations.

GPS trackers may experience signal interference or accuracy issues in certain environments, such as urban areas with tall buildings or remote locations with limited satellite coverage. Private investigators should consider potential signal disruptions and inaccuracies when deploying GPS trackers and verify the reliability of tracking data.

GPS tracking data may contain sensitive information about individuals' movements and activities, raising concerns about data security and privacy. Private investigators must take appropriate measures to safeguard tracking data, protect it from unauthorized access or disclosure, and comply with applicable data protection laws and regulations.

The use of GPS trackers in private investigations carries legal risks, including potential liability for privacy violations, trespassing, or unauthorized surveillance. Private investigators should seek legal advice, obtain proper authorization, and adhere to legal and ethical standards to mitigate legal liability and litigation risks associated with GPS tracking activities.

Lastly, the legal considerations for private investigators using GPS trackers are complex and multifaceted, governed by a combination of federal and state laws, regulations, case precedents, and ethical guidelines. While GPS trackers can be a valuable tool for gathering evidence and conducting surveillance in investigations, private investigators must navigate legal requirements, obtain proper authorization, and adhere to ethical standards to ensure compliance with the law and protect individuals' rights. By understanding the legal framework, addressing ethical considerations, and mitigating challenges and limitations associated with GPS tracking, private investigators can leverage this technology effectively and responsibly in pursuit of their investigative objectives.

CHAPTER ELEVEN
Sock Puppet

Puppet: *Latin Origin pupa* - an inanimate figure controlled by a master

Establish an individuals network of proven associates and where they hangout.

The tools described herein can be dangerous when used for nefarious purposes. It is you the readers responsibility to take care to ensure that while using these tools and other tools like these that you are diligent in compliance with the laws for your ares.

In the realm of cybersecurity, a "sock puppet" refers to a covert online identity created and controlled by a malicious actor for deceptive or manipulative purposes. Essentially, it's a fake persona used to interact with others online while hiding the true identity of the individual or group behind it. The term "sock puppet" originates from the idea of using a puppet to disguise the hand controlling it.

Characteristics of Sock Puppets:

1. **Fictitious Identity**: A sock puppet typically has a fabricated persona with a fake name, profile picture, background, and personal details. These details are carefully crafted to appear genuine and credible to unsuspecting individuals.

2. **Deceptive Intent**: The primary purpose of a sock puppet is to deceive others into believing that the persona is a real person with legitimate interests, opinions, or affiliations. This deception may involve engaging in conversations, participating in online communities, or sharing content to manipulate perceptions or influence behavior.

3. **Anonymity and Secrecy**: Sock puppets are

often created and operated anonymously to conceal the true identity of the individual or group behind them. This anonymity allows malicious actors to avoid detection, attribution, or accountability for their actions.

4. **Automation and Coordination**: In some cases, sock puppets may be automated using bots or scripts to perform repetitive tasks or interact with multiple users simultaneously. Additionally, multiple sock puppets may be coordinated by a single operator or group to amplify messages, spread disinformation, or harass targeted individuals.

Uses of Sock Puppets in Cybersecurity:

1. **Social Engineering**: Sock puppets are frequently used in social engineering attacks to manipulate users into disclosing sensitive information, clicking on malicious links, or installing malware. By posing as a trusted individual or authority figure, a sock puppet can exploit human psychology and trust to deceive unsuspecting victims.

2. **Disinformation Campaigns**: Sock puppets are deployed in disinformation campaigns to spread false or misleading information, manipulate public opinion, or sow discord and division within online communities. These campaigns may target political, social, or cultural issues to advance a particular agenda or undermine trust in institutions.

3. **Cyber Espionage**: In espionage operations, sock puppets may be used to infiltrate target networks, gather intelligence, or conduct reconnaissance on potential targets. By posing as employees, contractors, or business partners, sock puppets can gain access to sensitive information or exploit vulnerabilities in cybersecurity defenses.

4. **Online Harassment and Trolling**: Sock puppets are employed in online harassment and trolling campaigns to intimidate, harass, or bully individuals or groups. These campaigns may involve coordinated attacks, threats, or abusive behavior intended to silence dissenting voices or suppress free expression.

5. **Credential Theft and Account Takeover**: Sock puppets may be used to trick users into revealing their login credentials or personal information through phishing scams or other deceptive tactics. Once obtained, these credentials can be used to compromise accounts, steal sensitive data, or conduct further cyber attacks.

Countermeasures and Mitigation Strategies:

1. **User Education and Awareness**: Educating users about the risks of interacting with unknown or suspicious individuals online can help prevent them from falling victim to sock puppet attacks. Teaching users to recognize common tactics used by sock puppets, such as unsolicited friend requests, suspicious links, or requests for personal information, can empower them to stay vigilant and avoid potential threats.

2. **Technical Controls and Monitoring**: Implementing technical controls, such as spam filters, content moderation tools, and intrusion detection systems, can help detect and block sock puppet activity. Monitoring online communities, social media platforms, and communication channels for suspicious behavior or anomalous patterns can enable early detection and response to potential threats.

3. **Authentication and Verification**: Requiring users to verify their identities through multi-factor

authentication, CAPTCHA challenges, or identity verification processes can help mitigate the risk of sock puppet attacks. Authenticating users' identities and ensuring that they are who they claim to be can enhance trust and credibility in online interactions.

4. **Reporting and Response Mechanisms**: Establishing reporting mechanisms and response procedures for users to report suspicious activity or abusive behavior can facilitate timely intervention and mitigation of sock puppet attacks. Providing users with channels to report incidents, flag suspicious accounts, or seek assistance from moderators or administrators can help address threats effectively.

5. **Collaboration and Information Sharing**: Collaboration among cybersecurity professionals, law enforcement agencies, and online platforms is essential for combating sock puppet activity effectively. Sharing threat intelligence, best practices, and mitigation strategies can enhance collective efforts to identify and disrupt sock puppet operations, protect users, and safeguard online communities from harm.

It should be noted that sock puppets when used for bad purposes, represent a significant threat to cybersecurity, privacy, and online safety, posing risks to individuals, organizations, and society as a whole. Understanding the characteristics, uses, and countermeasures associated with sock puppets is essential for mitigating the risks they pose and protecting against their malicious activities. By raising awareness, implementing preventive measures, and fostering collaboration among stakeholders, we can work together to detect, deter, and defend against sock puppet attacks and uphold the integrity and security of online environments.

To generate a Sock Puppet with good intentions,

as a private investigator; create a name, obtain a phone number an identity (date of birth, etc), an email account and social media accounts.

Over a period of time you will need to craft the 'puppet' and bring it to life by putting content online via social media accounts. At the very least the following accounts should be activated: Facebook, Instagram, KIK, Pinterest, Reddit, SnapChat, CashApp, LinkedIn

Lastly, you should be creating multiple puppets, each puppet with their own unique identity and social media accounts. The purpose of this for the investigator is that the socket puppet with an identity of a C-level executive would not seem like the perfect candidate to use when you are attempting to knowledge about a typical blue collar worker that takes his kids to public park on the weekend and drives a used Corolla.

CHAPTER TWELVE
Moonlighting / Side Work

Work: Middle English *Origin Weorc* - To fulfill duties

Process serving

Becoming a legal process server is a career path that requires dedication, attention to detail, and a thorough understanding of the legal system. In this comprehensive guide, we'll explore the role of a legal process server, the steps to becoming one, the responsibilities involved, and the challenges and rewards of the profession.

A legal process server is an individual tasked with delivering legal documents to parties involved in court proceedings. These documents may include subpoenas, summons, complaints, writs, and other legal notices. The role of a process server is critical to the legal system, as it ensures that all parties are properly notified of their rights and responsibilities under the law.

Steps to Becoming a Legal Process Server

1. Understand the Requirements:

Before pursuing a career as a process server, it's essential to understand the legal requirements in your jurisdiction. Some states may have specific licensing or certification requirements, while others may have no formal regulations.

2. Obtain Necessary Training:

While formal training may not be required in all jurisdictions, it can be beneficial to complete a process server training program or course. These programs typically cover topics such as legal procedures, ethics, safety protocols, and practical skills for serving documents effectively.

3. Research Legal Process Serving Laws:

Familiarize yourself with the laws and regulations governing legal process serving in your area. This includes understanding the rules for proper service of process, timelines for delivery, and any restrictions or limitations that may apply.

4. Obtain Required Licenses or Certifications:

If your jurisdiction requires process servers to be licensed or certified, you'll need to complete the necessary application process and meet any eligibility requirements. This may include passing a background check, submitting fingerprints, or providing proof of training.

5. Develop Necessary Skills:

To be successful as a process server, you'll need strong communication, organization, and problem-solving skills. You should also be detail-oriented, able to work independently, and comfortable navigating various types of situations and environments.

6. Invest in Equipment:

As a process server, you'll need certain tools and equipment to perform your job effectively. This may include a reliable vehicle for travel, a smartphone or GPS device for navigation, and basic office supplies such as envelopes, stamps, and legal forms.

7. Build a Professional Network:

Networking is crucial in the legal process serving industry. Establish relationships with attorneys, law firms, court personnel, and other professionals who may require your services. Networking can help you secure clients, expand your business, and stay informed about industry trends and opportunities.

8. Start Your Business:

If you choose to work independently as a process server, you'll need to set up your own business entity, such as a sole proprietorship or LLC. This involves registering your business with the appropriate authorities, obtaining any necessary permits or licenses, and establishing a system for managing finances and taxes.

Responsibilities of a Legal Process Server

1. Serving Legal Documents:

The primary responsibility of a process server is to deliver legal documents to the individuals or entities named in the documents. This may involve locating the recipient, confirming their identity, and physically handing them the documents in accordance with legal requirements.

2. Documenting Service:

After serving documents, process servers must complete an affidavit or proof of service form documenting the details of the service. This includes information such as the date, time, location, and method of service, as well as any relevant observations or interactions with the recipient.

3. Following Legal Procedures:

Process servers must adhere to strict legal procedures when serving documents to ensure that service is valid and legally binding. This may include serving documents within specified timeframes, using approved methods of service, and following any special instructions or requirements outlined in the documents.

4. Maintaining Confidentiality:

Process servers often handle sensitive legal documents and personal information, so it's essential to maintain confidentiality and privacy at all times. This includes safeguarding documents from unauthorized access and ensuring that sensitive information is not disclosed to third parties.

5. Providing Court Testimony:

In some cases, process servers may be required to testify in court regarding the service of process. This may involve providing testimony about the details of the service, confirming the authenticity of documents, and answering questions from attorneys or judges.

Challenges and Rewards of Being a Legal Process Server

Challenges:

Serving legal documents can sometimes be risky, especially if the recipient is hostile or confrontational. Process servers must be prepared to handle difficult situations and prioritize their safety at all times.

Process servers must ensure that service is

performed in strict compliance with legal requirements to avoid challenges to the validity of service or legal repercussions.

Workload can be unpredictable in the legal process serving industry, with busy periods followed by lulls in activity. Process servers must be flexible and able to adapt to changing demands.

Serving legal documents often involves delivering unwelcome news or initiating legal proceedings that may be emotionally challenging for the recipients. Process servers must approach their work with empathy and professionalism.

Rewards:

Process servers play a crucial role in ensuring that the legal system operates effectively by ensuring that all parties are properly notified of their rights and responsibilities.

Process serving offers flexibility in terms of schedule and workload, allowing individuals to work independently and manage their own businesses.

Every day as a process server brings new challenges and opportunities to interact with a diverse range of people and situations.

Process serving provides opportunities for professional growth and development, allowing individuals to build valuable skills and experience in the legal field.

Becoming a legal process server is a rewarding career path that offers opportunities for individuals with a strong work ethic, attention to detail, and dedication to upholding the principles of the legal system. By following the steps outlined in this guide, aspiring process servers can embark on a fulfilling journey in the legal profession, serving as vital conduits of justice and ensuring that due process is upheld for all.

Bounty hunter

Bail enforcement agents, also known as bounty hunters, play a crucial role in the criminal justice system by tracking down and apprehending individuals who have failed to appear in court after posting bail. In this comprehensive guide, we'll explore the responsibilities, requirements, challenges, and rewards of being a bail enforcement agent.

Bail enforcement agents are hired by bail bondsmen to locate and apprehend fugitives who have skipped bail. When individuals are released from custody on bail, they are required to appear in court for their scheduled hearings. If they fail to appear, the court may issue a warrant for their arrest, and the bail bond company becomes responsible for locating and returning the fugitive to custody.

The primary responsibility of a bail enforcement agent is to locate fugitives who have skipped bail. This may involve conducting surveillance, interviewing witnesses, and using investigative techniques to track down the whereabouts of the fugitive.

Once a fugitive has been located, the bail enforcement agent is responsible for apprehending them and returning them to custody. This may involve making a physical arrest or coordinating with law enforcement agencies to facilitate the surrender of the fugitive.

Bail enforcement agents must exercise caution and professionalism at all times when apprehending fugitives. They must ensure that their actions are legal and compliant with applicable laws and regulations, and they must prioritize the safety of themselves and others involved in the apprehension.

Bail enforcement agents are required to maintain accurate records of their activities, including details of their investigations, communications with law enforcement agencies, and any arrests or apprehensions made. This documentation may be used as evidence in court proceedings or to support claims for compensation from bail bond companies.

Bail enforcement agents may be required to testify in court regarding their actions and the circumstances surrounding the apprehension of fugitives. This may involve providing testimony about their investigative methods, the events leading up to the apprehension, and any relevant details about the fugitive's case.

In many states, bail enforcement agents are required to be licensed and undergo specialized training before they can legally work in the field. This training may cover topics such as state laws and regulations, investigative techniques, self-defense, and firearms safety. In Texas, the current requirement to become a bounty hunter is simply become a licensed private investigator.

Bail enforcement agents must pass a background check to ensure that they have no criminal record or history of unethical behavior that would disqualify them from working in the field.

Bail enforcement agents must be physically fit and able to perform the duties of the job, which may include conducting surveillance, apprehending fugitives, and engaging in physical confrontations if necessary.

Bail enforcement agents must have a thorough understanding of the legal system, including laws related to bail, fugitive recovery, and the use of force. They must also be familiar with the rights of individuals accused of crimes and the procedures for apprehending fugitives in compliance with the law.

Challenges:

Safety Risks:** Bail enforcement agents often work in high-risk environments and may encounter dangerous individuals or situations while apprehending fugitives.

Legal and Ethical Considerations:** Bail enforcement agents must navigate complex legal and ethical issues when apprehending fugitives, including ensuring that their actions are legal and compliant with applicable laws and regulations.

Emotional Toll:** Apprehending fugitives can be emotionally taxing, especially when dealing with individuals who may be desperate or hostile.

Uncertainty of Work:** The workload of a bail enforcement agent can be unpredictable, with periods of intense activity followed by periods of relative calm.

Rewards:

Sense of Accomplishment:** Successfully apprehending fugitives and returning them to custody can provide a sense of accomplishment and fulfillment for bail enforcement agents.

Financial Rewards:** Bail enforcement agents are typically compensated for their services, either through a fee structure or a percentage of the bail bond amount.

Variety of Work:** Every day as a bail enforcement agent brings new challenges and opportunities to apply skills and expertise in tracking down fugitives and apprehending them.

Contribution to Justice:** Bail enforcement agents play a vital role in ensuring that individuals accused of crimes are held accountable for their actions and appear in court as required by law.

Becoming a bail enforcement agent is a challenging and rewarding career path that requires dedication, skill, and a commitment to upholding the principles of the criminal justice system. By meeting the requirements outlined in this guide and navigating the challenges of the profession with professionalism and integrity, bail enforcement agents can make a meaningful contribution to the legal system and help ensure that justice is served.

Notary public
Becoming a notary public is an esteemed profession that carries significant responsibilities and opportunities for service within the legal and business communities. In this comprehensive guide, we'll explore the role of a notary public, the steps to becoming one, the duties and responsibilities involved, as well as the challenges and rewards of the profession.

A notary public is an official appointed by the state government to serve as an impartial witness to the signing of legal documents. The primary function of a notary public is to verify the identity of signers, ensure the willingness of parties to sign documents, and administer oaths or affirmations when required.

Before pursuing a career as a notary public, it's essential to understand the requirements in your state. Each state has its own eligibility criteria, application process, and regulations governing notary publics.

In general, to become a notary public, you must meet certain eligibility requirements, such as being at least 18 years old, being a legal resident of the state, and not having a felony conviction on your record.

Some states require individuals to complete a notary education course or training program before applying for a notary commission. These courses cover topics such as notary laws and regulations, best practices for notarizing documents, and ethical considerations.

To become a notary public, you must submit an application to the appropriate state agency, along with the required fee. The application typically requires information about your personal background, education, and any previous notary commissions.

In some states, applicants may be required to pass a notary examination to demonstrate their knowledge of notary laws and procedures. The examination may be administered online or in-person and may cover topics such as legal terminology, document preparation, and identification verification.

After receiving approval for your notary commission, you'll need to obtain a notary bond and supplies, such as a notary seal, journal, and official notary stamp. These items are essential for performing notarial acts and maintaining accurate records of your notary transactions.

Before performing notarial acts, you must take an oath of office in the presence of a qualified official, such as a judge or clerk of court. The oath typically involves swearing or affirming to uphold the duties and responsibilities of a notary public in accordance with state laws.

One of the primary responsibilities of a notary public is to verify the identity of signers before notarizing documents. This may involve examining government-issued identification, such as a driver's license or passport, to confirm the signer's identity and ensure they are of legal age to sign.

Notary publics serve as impartial witnesses to the signing of legal documents. They must observe the signing process to ensure that all parties are willingly and knowingly executing the document in accordance with legal requirements.

In some cases, notary publics are required to administer oaths or affirmations to individuals swearing to the truthfulness of statements made in a document. This may involve asking the individual to swear or affirm that the information provided is accurate and truthful.

Notary publics are required to maintain accurate records of their notarial acts, including details such as the date, time, location, and type of document notarized, as well as the identity of the signers. These records serve as a permanent record of the notarial transaction and may be used as evidence in legal proceedings.

Notary publics play a crucial role in preventing fraud by ensuring the integrity and authenticity of legal documents. They must exercise diligence and attention to detail when performing notarial acts to guard against fraudulent activity.

Challenges:

Notary publics may be held legally liable for errors or omissions in their notarial acts, so it's essential to exercise caution and follow proper procedures at all times.

Notary laws and regulations vary from state to state and may change over time, requiring notary publics to stay informed and up-to-date on the latest legal requirements.

Becoming a notary public requires an investment of time and money for education, training, and supplies, as well as ongoing expenses for maintaining your commission.

Rewards:

Being a notary public is a prestigious designation that demonstrates professionalism, integrity, and trustworthiness within the legal and business communities.

Notary publics enjoy flexibility in their work schedules and locations, as they can perform notarial acts at various times and locations to accommodate the needs of clients.

Notary publics provide a valuable service to their communities by facilitating the execution of legal documents and ensuring the integrity of important transactions.

Notary publics can generate additional income by charging fees for their notarial services, which can be a lucrative source of revenue, especially for those who work independently.

Becoming a notary public is a rewarding career path that offers opportunities for service, professional growth, and financial success. By following the steps outlined in this guide and embracing the responsibilities and challenges of the profession, aspiring notary publics can embark on a fulfilling journey in the legal and business communities, serving as trusted witnesses to the execution of important legal documents and upholding the integrity of the notarial process.

Finger printing
Becoming a professional fingerprint technician involves mastering the art and science of collecting, analyzing, and interpreting fingerprints for various purposes, including criminal investigations, background checks, and identification verification. In this comprehensive guide, we'll explore the role of a fingerprint technician, the skills and training required, the responsibilities involved, and the challenges and rewards of the profession.

A professional fingerprint technician, also known as a fingerprint examiner or forensic identification specialist, plays a critical role in law enforcement, forensic science, and other fields that rely on fingerprint analysis. The primary responsibility of a fingerprint technician is to collect, process, and analyze fingerprint evidence to aid in criminal investigations and other legal proceedings.

Fingerprint analysis requires a keen eye for detail and the ability to identify unique ridge patterns, minutiae points, and other characteristics that distinguish one fingerprint from another.

Fingerprint technicians must be proficient in using specialized equipment and software for fingerprint collection, processing, and analysis. This may include fingerprint brushes, powders, chemicals, cameras, scanners, and computer databases.

A solid understanding of human anatomy and physiology is essential for interpreting fingerprint patterns and understanding how they are formed on the skin's surface.

Fingerprint technicians must possess strong analytical skills to interpret complex fingerprint patterns, compare prints for identification purposes, and draw conclusions based on the evidence.

Effective communication skills are crucial for collaborating with law enforcement agencies, presenting findings in court, and providing expert testimony as needed.

Fingerprint technicians must adhere to strict ethical standards and guidelines to ensure the integrity and accuracy of their work. This includes maintaining confidentiality, avoiding conflicts of interest, and following established protocols and procedures.

Fingerprint technicians are responsible for collecting fingerprints from crime scenes, evidence items, and individuals for identification purposes. This may involve using various techniques, such as dusting, lifting, or photographing prints, depending on the nature of the evidence and the surface texture.

Once collected, fingerprints must be processed to enhance their clarity and detail for analysis. This may involve applying powders, chemicals, or other substances to reveal latent prints and using specialized equipment to capture high-resolution images.

Fingerprint technicians analyze collected prints to identify unique ridge patterns, minutiae points, and other features that can be used for comparison and identification. This may involve manually examining prints under a microscope or using automated software for computerized analysis.

Fingerprint technicians compare collected prints to known prints from databases or reference sources to determine if there is a match. This process requires meticulous attention to detail and may involve side-by-side comparisons, overlaying prints, and using specialized software for pattern recognition.

Fingerprint technicians document their findings in detailed reports, including descriptions of collected prints, analysis results, and conclusions drawn from the evidence. These reports may be used as evidence in criminal investigations, court proceedings, and other legal matters.

Fingerprint technicians may be called upon to testify in court as expert witnesses to provide opinions and interpretations of fingerprint evidence. This requires clear and concise communication skills, as well as the ability to explain complex technical concepts to judges and jurors.

Fingerprint analysis can be highly complex and time-consuming, requiring meticulous attention to detail and extensive training and experience.

Fingerprint technicians must adhere to strict legal and ethical standards when handling evidence, maintaining chain of custody, and presenting findings in court.

Keeping up with advances in fingerprint technology and forensic science requires ongoing training and professional development.

Working with fingerprint evidence from crime scenes can be emotionally challenging, especially when dealing with cases involving violence or tragedy.

Fingerprint technicians play a vital role in criminal investigations and legal proceedings, helping to identify suspects, exonerate the innocent, and ensure that justice is served.

Fingerprint analysis offers intellectual stimulation and the opportunity to apply scientific principles and analytical skills to real-world problems.

Fingerprint technicians have opportunities for professional growth and advancement through training, certification, and specialization in areas such as latent print examination, crime scene analysis, or digital forensics.

Fingerprint technicians have the satisfaction of knowing that their work has a direct impact on public safety, law enforcement efforts, and the administration of justice.

CHAPTER THIRTEEN
<u>Resources</u>

Resource: *Latin Origin resurere* - Rise again

WEBSITES

This list is by no means considered comprehensive, this is only a small segment.

TLO
TransUnion's TLOxp database represents a paradigm shift in the realm of investigative and risk management tools. TLOxp stands for "TransUnion Location-based Online investigative Experience," reflecting its focus on providing comprehensive and actionable intelligence for businesses, law enforcement agencies, and government entities.

This database harnesses the power of big data analytics and cutting-edge technology to aggregate vast amounts of information from public records, proprietary sources, and online sources. From criminal records and property ownership to social media activity and financial history, TLOxp offers a wealth of data to inform decision-making and mitigate risk.

One of the key strengths of TLOxp is its advanced search capabilities, allowing users to quickly and efficiently uncover connections and patterns that might otherwise remain hidden. Its intuitive interface and customizable search parameters empower users to tailor their inquiries to specific needs, whether it's locating individuals, verifying identities, or conducting due diligence on businesses.

Moreover, TLOxp prioritizes data security and compliance with stringent privacy regulations, ensuring that sensitive information is handled responsibly and ethically. Through ongoing innovation and investment in technology, TransUnion continues to enhance the capabilities of TLOxp, staying ahead of emerging threats and evolving needs in an increasingly complex landscape.

In essence, TransUnion's TLOxp database represents a powerful tool for navigating the modern data landscape, offering actionable insights and unparalleled access to information to support informed decision-making and mitigate risk effectively.

IRB

IRBsearch.com is a versatile and comprehensive online platform designed to provide access to a vast array of public records and investigative tools. Catering to professionals in various fields such as law enforcement, private investigation, legal services, and risk management, IRBsearch.com offers a wealth of information to support due diligence, background checks, and investigative work.

The platform boasts an extensive database that aggregates data from numerous sources, including court records, property records, criminal databases, and more. Users can quickly and efficiently search for individuals, businesses, and assets, with options to narrow down results based on specific criteria.

One of IRBsearch.com's standout features is its user-friendly interface, which allows for intuitive navigation and streamlined search processes. Whether conducting a basic background check or delving into more complex investigative work, users can easily access the information they need, saving time and effort in the process.

IRBsearch.com prioritizes data security and compliance, ensuring that sensitive information is handled with the utmost care and in accordance with relevant regulations. This commitment to privacy and security instills confidence in users, knowing that their searches are conducted responsibly and ethically.

Overall, IRBsearch.com stands as a valuable resource for professionals across various industries, providing access to comprehensive public records and investigative tools to support informed decision-making and mitigate risks effectively.

U.S. Sanctions list
The website sanctionssearch.ofac.treas.gov, maintained by the Office of Foreign Assets Control (OFAC) under the U.S. Department of the Treasury, serves as a critical tool for private investigators in conducting thorough and compliant investigations. OFAC administers and enforces economic and trade sanctions based on U.S. foreign policy and national security goals. Here's how private investigators can leverage this resource:

1. **Screening for Sanctioned Individuals and Entities**: Private investigators can use the OFAC search tool to screen individuals and entities against the OFAC Specially Designated Nationals (SDN) List. This list includes individuals, groups, and entities subject to various sanctions programs, including those related to terrorism, narcotics trafficking, and proliferation of weapons of mass destruction. By cross-referencing subjects against this list, investigators can identify potential risks or connections to sanctioned parties.

2. **Identifying Red Flags in Financial Transactions**: Private investigators often analyze financial records and transactions as part of their investigations. By using OFAC's search tool, investigators can identify any matches to sanctioned

individuals or entities involved in financial transactions. This can uncover illicit activities such as money laundering or terrorist financing, providing valuable insights into the subjects under investigation.

3. **Verifying Identities and Affiliations**: OFAC's search tool can help private investigators verify the identities and affiliations of individuals and entities. By confirming whether a subject appears on the SDN List or other OFAC sanctions lists, investigators can assess the subject's potential involvement in prohibited activities or associations with sanctioned parties.

4. **Ensuring Compliance with Regulations**: Private investigators must adhere to legal and regulatory requirements when conducting investigations. By using OFAC's search tool, investigators can ensure compliance with sanctions regulations and avoid inadvertently engaging with sanctioned individuals or entities. This helps mitigate legal risks and ensures that investigations are conducted ethically and responsibly.

All in all, sanctionssearch.ofac.treas.gov is a valuable resource for private investigators, offering a means to screen individuals and entities, identify red flags in financial transactions, verify identities and affiliations, and ensure compliance with sanctions regulations. By leveraging this tool effectively, investigators can enhance the efficiency and accuracy of their investigations while mitigating legal and regulatory risks.

PimEyes
Pimeyes.com is a powerful online tool that utilizes facial recognition technology to conduct reverse image searches, enabling users to locate and identify individuals across the internet. This platform offers a range of features that can be particularly

valuable for private investigators:

1. **Identifying Persons of Interest**: Private investigators can upload images of individuals they are investigating to Pimeyes.com to conduct reverse image searches. This can help identify social media profiles, websites, or other online sources where the person's image appears, providing valuable leads for further investigation.

2. **Tracking Online Presence**: Pimeyes.com allows investigators to track the online presence of individuals by identifying where their images have been posted. This can help uncover connections, associations, or activities that may be relevant to the investigation.

3. **Verifying Identities**: By comparing images obtained during investigations with those found on Pimeyes.com, investigators can verify the identities of individuals and confirm whether they are using aliases or false identities.

4. **Gathering Evidence**: Pimeyes.com can be a valuable tool for gathering evidence, such as identifying individuals involved in fraudulent activities, online harassment, or other illicit behavior.

As a whole, Pimeyes.com offers private investigators a valuable resource for conducting online investigations, tracking individuals' online presence, verifying identities, and gathering evidence to support their investigations. By leveraging facial recognition technology and reverse image searches, investigators can enhance the efficiency and effectiveness of their investigative efforts.

OpenGovUS
Private investigators often rely on open

government data to access valuable information for their investigations, and opengovus.com serves as a centralized platform to streamline this process. With its user-friendly interface and comprehensive database, opengovus.com offers several benefits to private investigators:

1. **Access to Public Records**: Opengovus.com provides access to a wide range of public records, including property records, business filings, court documents, and more. Private investigators can leverage this information to gather key insights into individuals, businesses, or properties involved in their investigations.

2. **Background Checks**: Private investigators frequently conduct background checks as part of their investigations, and opengovus.com offers a wealth of information to support this process. Investigators can access criminal records, bankruptcy filings, professional licenses, and other pertinent data to assess the background and credibility of individuals under investigation.

3. **Due Diligence**: Opengovus.com enables private investigators to perform due diligence on businesses, individuals, or properties involved in various transactions or legal matters. By accessing relevant government records and filings, investigators can identify potential risks, conflicts of interest, or regulatory compliance issues.

4. **Tracking Legal Proceedings**: Private investigators may use opengovus.com to track legal proceedings, including civil lawsuits, criminal cases, and administrative actions. This can provide valuable insights into the legal history and activities of individuals or businesses under investigation.

By and large, opengovus.com serves as a valuable resource for private investigators, offering access to public records, facilitating background checks and due diligence, and providing insights into legal proceedings. By leveraging the information available on this platform, investigators can enhance the efficiency and effectiveness of their investigations.

OpenCorporates

Private investigators frequently rely on opencorporates.com as a vital resource in their investigations, particularly when conducting corporate research and due diligence. Opencorporates.com offers access to a vast database of corporate information from jurisdictions around the world, making it an invaluable tool for uncovering connections, identifying beneficial owners, and assessing the legitimacy of businesses.

One of the primary uses of opencorporates.com for private investigators is conducting background checks on companies and their principals. By searching the database, investigators can access details such as company registration information, corporate structure, directors, shareholders, and financial data. This enables them to verify the authenticity of businesses and assess any potential risks or red flags.

Opencorporates.com allows investigators to track corporate relationships and affiliations, helping to uncover hidden connections or conflicts of interest. This can be particularly useful in cases involving fraud, money laundering, or other illicit activities where individuals may attempt to conceal their involvement through complex corporate structures.

Opencorporates.com provides private investigators with a powerful tool for conducting corporate research and due diligence, enabling them to gather critical information to support their investigations effectively. By leveraging the wealth of data available on this platform, investigators can uncover valuable insights and make informed decisions in their pursuit of truth and justice.

Google Earth
Private investigators can utilize Google Earth as a versatile and powerful tool to support various aspects of their investigations. Here's how:

1. **Surveillance Planning**: Google Earth allows investigators to virtually scout locations from the comfort of their office. They can use satellite imagery and street view to assess the layout of an area, identify entry and exit points, and plan surveillance operations effectively. By familiarizing themselves with the surroundings beforehand, investigators can minimize risks and maximize the chances of success during fieldwork.

2. **Locating Addresses and Properties**: Google Earth enables investigators to locate addresses and properties with precision using its search feature. By entering an address or landmark, investigators can view the property from different angles, assess its surroundings, and gather valuable contextual information. This can be especially useful when conducting skip tracing or asset searches.

3. **Gathering Intelligence**: Investigators can use Google Earth to gather intelligence on specific locations relevant to their investigations. This includes identifying nearby businesses, landmarks, transportation hubs, and other points of interest that may be relevant to the case. By understanding the geographical context, investigators can uncover potential leads or connections that may have otherwise

gone unnoticed.

4. **Mapping Connections**: Google Earth's ability to overlay multiple layers of data allows investigators to map out connections and relationships visually. They can mark locations associated with key individuals, events, or activities, and visualize how they relate to each other spatially. This can help investigators identify patterns, trends, or areas of interest that merit further investigation.

5. **Documenting Evidence**: Google Earth allows investigators to capture and document visual evidence directly from the platform. They can take screenshots of satellite imagery, street view images, or custom maps to preserve relevant information for their case files. This documentation can serve as valuable corroborating evidence or aid in presenting findings to clients or in court.

Google Earth is a valuable resource for private investigators, offering a range of features to support surveillance planning, location identification, intelligence gathering, mapping connections, and documenting evidence. By leveraging the platform's capabilities, investigators can enhance the efficiency and effectiveness of their investigations across various domains.

Google Maps
Google Maps is an invaluable tool for private investigators, offering a wealth of features to support various aspects of their investigations:

1. **Address and Location Verification**: Private investigators often need to verify addresses or locations associated with their cases. Google Maps allows them to enter an address and obtain precise location information, including satellite imagery, street

view, and real-time traffic updates. This helps investigators confirm the accuracy of information provided by clients or witnesses and plan their investigative activities effectively.

2. **Surveillance Planning**: Google Maps enables investigators to plan surveillance operations by familiarizing themselves with the layout of an area. They can use satellite imagery to assess the terrain, identify potential vantage points, and plan entry and exit routes. Street view provides additional insights into the surroundings, allowing investigators to scout locations without physically being there.

3. **Route Planning and Navigation**: When conducting fieldwork, private investigators rely on efficient route planning and navigation to save time and resources. Google Maps offers reliable turn-by-turn directions, real-time traffic updates, and alternative route suggestions to help investigators navigate unfamiliar areas efficiently. This ensures they reach their destinations promptly and minimize the risk of detection during surveillance operations.

4. **Location Intelligence**: Google Maps provides valuable location intelligence that can aid in investigations. Investigators can use features like "Nearby Places" to identify businesses, landmarks, or points of interest near a specific location. This helps them gather additional context and identify potential leads or connections relevant to their cases.

5. **Geospatial Analysis**: Google Maps offers advanced geospatial analysis capabilities that allow investigators to visualize data spatially. They can overlay multiple layers of information, such as addresses, demographics, crime statistics, and historical data, to identify patterns, trends, or correlations. This helps investigators uncover insights

that may not be apparent through traditional methods of analysis.

Largely, Google Maps is an indispensable tool for private investigators, offering features for address verification, surveillance planning, route navigation, location intelligence, and geospatial analysis. By leveraging the platform's capabilities, investigators can enhance the efficiency and effectiveness of their investigations across various domains.

Vehicle History VIN Check

Private investigators can leverage vehiclehistory.com as a valuable resource to obtain critical information about vehicles, aiding them in various aspects of their investigations:

1. **Vehicle Identification**: Private investigators often need to identify vehicles associated with their cases. Vehiclehistory.com allows them to search for vehicles using their VIN (Vehicle Identification Number) or license plate number. This enables investigators to obtain detailed information about the vehicle's make, model, year, specifications, and history.

2. **Ownership History**: Vehiclehistory.com provides access to the ownership history of vehicles, allowing investigators to track ownership transfers and identify previous owners. This information can be valuable in cases involving asset searches, fraud investigations, or disputes over vehicle ownership.

3. **Title and Lien Records**: Private investigators can access title and lien records for vehicles through vehiclehistory.com. This helps them verify the legal status of a vehicle's title and identify any existing liens or encumbrances. Investigators can use this information to assess the financial history of the vehicle and uncover potential red flags, such as

unpaid loans or salvage titles.

4. **Accident and Damage History**: Vehiclehistory.com offers access to accident and damage history reports for vehicles, providing insights into their past incidents and repairs. Investigators can use this information to assess the vehicle's condition, evaluate its value, and determine if it has been involved in any suspicious or criminal activities.

5. **Recall Information**: Private investigators can access recall information for vehicles through vehiclehistory.com. This helps them identify any safety recalls issued by manufacturers and determine if a vehicle is subject to any outstanding recalls. Investigators can use this information to assess the safety and reliability of the vehicle and investigate potential liability issues.

Finally, vehiclehistory.com is a valuable tool for private investigators, offering access to a wealth of information about vehicles, including identification, ownership history, title and lien records, accident and damage history, and recall information. By leveraging this platform, investigators can enhance their investigations and make informed decisions in cases involving vehicles.

National Insurance VIN Check
The National Insurance Crime Bureau (NICB) provides a valuable tool for private investigators through its VINCheck service, allowing them to access critical information about vehicles to support their investigations.

1. **Vehicle Identification**: Private investigators often need to identify vehicles involved in their cases. VINCheck allows investigators to enter a vehicle's VIN (Vehicle Identification Number) and obtain detailed

information about the vehicle, including its make, model, year, and specifications. This enables investigators to accurately identify vehicles associated with their investigations.

2. **Theft and Salvage History**: VINCheck provides access to theft and salvage history records for vehicles. Investigators can determine if a vehicle has been reported stolen or salvaged, providing insights into its legal status and potential risks. This information is crucial for cases involving stolen property, insurance fraud, or disputes over vehicle ownership.

3. **Insurance Claims**: Private investigators can access insurance claims history for vehicles through VINCheck. This allows investigators to identify any previous insurance claims filed for the vehicle, including information about accidents, repairs, and damage. By reviewing insurance claims history, investigators can assess the vehicle's condition and determine if it has been involved in any suspicious or fraudulent activities.

4. **Title and Lien Records**: VINCheck provides access to title and lien records for vehicles, allowing investigators to verify the vehicle's legal status and ownership history. Investigators can determine if there are any existing liens or encumbrances on the vehicle's title, providing insights into its financial history and potential liabilities.

5. **Recall Information**: VINCheck allows investigators to access recall information for vehicles, including safety recalls issued by manufacturers. Investigators can determine if a vehicle is subject to any outstanding recalls, helping them assess the vehicle's safety and reliability. This information is crucial for cases involving defective vehicles or liability

issues.

To point, VINCheck is a valuable tool for private investigators, offering access to critical information about vehicles, including identification, theft and salvage history, insurance claims, title and lien records, and recall information. By leveraging this service, investigators can enhance their investigations and make informed decisions in cases involving vehicles.

Federal Bureau of Prisons Inmate Locator
      The Federal Bureau of Prisons (BOP) Inmate Locator tool is a valuable resource for private investigators conducting various types of investigations. By accessing this online database, investigators can obtain crucial information about individuals who are currently incarcerated in federal prisons across the United States.

      This tool allows investigators to search for inmates by their name or BOP register number, providing details such as their current location, custody status, offense history, and projected release date. This information can be invaluable for investigations involving criminal cases, background checks, and asset searches.

      For example, private investigators may use the BOP Inmate Locator to verify the incarceration status of individuals involved in legal disputes, gather information about their criminal history, or track down witnesses or suspects in ongoing investigations.

      Additionally, the tool can aid in due diligence processes by helping investigators assess the credibility and reliability of individuals involved in business transactions or personal matters. Overall, the BOP Inmate Locator serves as a valuable tool for private investigators, providing access to critical information that can support their investigations and help them achieve their investigative objectives.

BRB Public Records Search

Private investigators often rely on a wide array of resources to gather information crucial to their investigations. One such resource is public record websites, which provide access to a wealth of information that can be invaluable in uncovering leads, verifying identities, and building cases. BRB Publications is a prominent provider of resources for accessing public records, offering a variety of free resources and tools for private investigators and other professionals. In this comprehensive guide, we'll explore how private investigators can use BRB Publications' public record sites to enhance their investigative efforts.

Understanding Public Records

Public records are documents and information maintained by government agencies and other organizations that are accessible to the public. These records cover a wide range of topics, including criminal records, court documents, property records, business filings, and more. Public record websites aggregate and organize this information, making it easier for individuals, businesses, and professionals like private investigators to access and utilize in their work.

BRB Publications' Free Resources

BRB Publications offers a variety of free resources and tools designed to help individuals and professionals access public records more easily and effectively. These resources include:

State Public Record Websites:

BRB Publications provides links to state-specific public record websites, allowing users to access public records from various government agencies and organizations within each state. These websites typically offer access to a wide range of records, including criminal records, court records, property records, and more.

Federal Public Record Websites:

In addition to state-specific resources, BRB Publications provides links to federal public record websites, where users can access records maintained by federal agencies and organizations. These websites offer access to federal court records, bankruptcy filings, property records, and other federal-level information.

International Public Record Websites:

For investigators working on cases with an international component, BRB Publications also provides links to international public record websites. These websites offer access to public records from countries around the world, allowing investigators to gather information relevant to their cases across borders.

Industry-Specific Resources:

BRB Publications offers industry-specific resources for accessing public records, tailored to the needs of professionals in various fields. These resources include links to public record websites focused on specific industries, such as real estate, finance, insurance, and more.

Educational Materials:

In addition to providing links to public record websites, BRB Publications offers educational materials and guides to help users navigate the complexities of accessing public records. These materials cover topics such as understanding different types of public records, conducting effective searches, and interpreting the information obtained.

How Private Investigators Use BRB Publications' Public Record Sites

1. Background Checks:

Private investigators often conduct background checks as part of their investigations, and public record websites can be valuable tools for gathering information about individuals' criminal history, court records, property ownership, and more. By using BRB Publications' public record sites, investigators can access comprehensive databases of public records to verify identities, uncover past behaviors, and assess potential risks.

2. Asset Searches:

In cases involving financial investigations or litigation, private investigators may need to conduct asset searches to identify and locate assets owned by individuals or businesses. Public record websites can provide access to property records, business filings, liens, and other financial information that may be relevant to asset searches. BRB Publications' resources can help investigators navigate the complexities of accessing these records and gather the information needed to trace assets effectively.

3. Skip Tracing:

Skip tracing is the process of locating individuals who have gone missing or are attempting to avoid detection, often for legal or financial reasons. Public record websites can be valuable tools for skip tracing, providing access to a variety of records that may contain information about individuals' current or previous addresses, employment history, and more. By using BRB Publications' public record sites, investigators can access databases of public records from multiple sources to track down individuals and locate potential leads.

4. Due Diligence:

In cases involving business transactions, mergers, acquisitions, or partnerships, private investigators may need to conduct due diligence to assess the background and credibility of individuals or companies involved. Public record websites can provide access to a wealth of information about businesses, including corporate filings, business licenses, litigation history, and more. By using BRB Publications' resources, investigators can gather the information needed to conduct thorough due diligence and mitigate risks for their clients.

5. Legal Support:

Public record websites can be valuable tools for gathering evidence and supporting legal proceedings. Whether it's obtaining court records, verifying property ownership, or accessing other relevant information, public record sites can provide the documentation needed to build a strong case or support legal arguments. BRB Publications' resources can help investigators access the records and information necessary to support their clients' legal objectives effectively.

Challenges and Considerations

While public record websites offer valuable resources for private investigators, there are also challenges and considerations to keep in mind:

1. Data Accuracy:

Not all public records may be accurate or up to date, and information obtained from public record websites should be verified whenever possible. Private investigators must exercise caution and diligence when using public record sites to ensure the accuracy and reliability of the information obtained.

2. Privacy Concerns:

Public record websites may contain sensitive personal information about individuals, and investigators must be mindful of privacy laws and regulations when accessing and using this information. It's essential to follow ethical guidelines and legal requirements to protect individuals' privacy rights and avoid unauthorized use or disclosure of personal data.

3. Legal Compliance:

Private investigators must ensure that their use of public record websites is legal and compliant with applicable laws and regulations. This may include adhering to restrictions on accessing certain types of records, obtaining consent when required, and using information obtained from public record sites appropriately in their investigations.

4. Technical Skills:

Navigating public record websites and

conducting effective searches may require technical skills and familiarity with online databases and search tools. Private investigators should invest time in learning how to use these resources effectively to maximize their utility in their investigations.

Conclusion: BRB Publications' public record sites offer valuable resources for private investigators, providing access to a wealth of information that can be crucial to their investigations. By leveraging these resources effectively, investigators can gather the information needed to verify identities, conduct background checks, trace assets, locate individuals, and support legal proceedings. However, it's essential for investigators to exercise caution, diligence, and legal compliance when using public record websites to ensure the accuracy, reliability, and ethical use of the information obtained. With the right skills, knowledge, and resources, private investigators can harness the power of public record sites to enhance their investigative efforts and achieve successful outcomes for their clients.

SSN Validator

SSNValidator.com is a valuable tool for investigators, providing access to a variety of tools and resources for verifying Social Security Numbers (SSNs) and conducting background checks. In this guide, we'll explore how investigators can use SSNValidator.com to enhance their investigative efforts and gather critical information for their cases.

SSNValidator.com is an online platform that offers a range of tools and services for verifying SSNs and conducting background checks. The platform provides access to a database of SSN records, allowing users to verify the validity of SSNs, confirm individuals' identities, and gather information about their background, employment history, and more.

One of the primary uses of SSNValidator.com for investigators is SSN verification. Investigators can use the platform to validate SSNs and confirm whether they are valid and associated with the correct individual. This can be valuable for verifying identities, conducting background checks, and ensuring the accuracy of information obtained during investigations.

SSNValidator.com offers background check services that allow investigators to gather information about individuals' criminal history, employment history, financial records, and more. By using the platform's background check tools, investigators can access comprehensive reports containing information from various sources, helping them uncover relevant details for their cases.

Investigators can use SSNValidator.com to verify individuals' identities and ensure that the information provided is accurate and up to date. This can be particularly useful in cases involving fraud, identity theft, or other situations where individuals may attempt to conceal their true identities or misrepresent themselves.

SSNValidator.com provides access to individuals' address history, allowing investigators to track their movements and identify potential leads or connections relevant to their investigations. By accessing address history records, investigators can uncover patterns, trends, or associations that may be significant to their cases.

Investigators can use SSNValidator.com to gather information about individuals' employment history, including past employers, job titles, and dates of employment. This can be valuable for conducting background checks, verifying resumes, or investigating individuals' financial status and credibility.

SSNValidator.com offers access to individuals' financial records, including credit reports, bankruptcy filings, and other financial information. Investigators can use this information to assess individuals' financial status, identify potential liabilities or risks, and uncover evidence of financial misconduct or fraud.

SSNValidator.com provides access to individuals' legal records, including court filings, civil judgments, and other legal documents. Investigators can use this information to gather evidence, track legal proceedings, and uncover relevant details about individuals' legal history and activities.

While SSNValidator.com offers valuable tools and resources for investigators, there are also considerations and limitations to keep in mind:

As with any database or online platform, the accuracy of the information provided by SSNValidator.com may vary. Investigators should verify information obtained from the platform through additional sources whenever possible to ensure its accuracy and reliability.

Investigators must ensure that their use of SSNValidator.com is legal and compliant with applicable laws and regulations. This may include adhering to privacy laws, obtaining consent when required, and using information obtained from the platform appropriately in their investigations.

Investigators should always prioritize ethical considerations when using SSNValidator.com and other investigative tools. This includes respecting individuals' privacy rights, avoiding unauthorized access to sensitive information, and using information obtained from the platform responsibly and ethically.

SSNValidator.com offers valuable tools and resources for investigators, providing access to SSN verification services, background checks, address history records, employment history, financial records, legal records, and more. By leveraging the platform's capabilities, investigators can enhance their investigative efforts, verify individuals' identities, conduct comprehensive background checks, and gather critical information for their cases. However, it's essential for investigators to exercise caution, diligence, and legal compliance when using SSNValidator.com and other investigative tools to ensure the accuracy, reliability, and ethical use of the information obtained. With the right skills, knowledge, and resources, investigators can harness the power of SSNValidator.com to achieve successful outcomes for their clients and contribute to the pursuit of truth and justice.

PACER U.S. Court Records
PACER (Public Access to Court Electronic Records) is a valuable tool for investigators, providing access to a vast repository of federal court documents and case information. In this guide, we'll explore how investigators can utilize PACER to enhance their investigative efforts and gather critical information for their cases.

PACER is an online platform that allows users to access electronic court records from the federal courts, including district, bankruptcy, and appellate courts. The platform provides access to a wide range of documents and information, including case dockets, pleadings, motions, judgments, and opinions. PACER is widely used by attorneys, researchers, journalists, and investigators to access court records and track legal proceedings.

PACER allows investigators to conduct comprehensive research on federal court cases, including civil and criminal proceedings. Investigators can search for cases by party name, case number, or other criteria and access detailed case dockets containing information about the parties involved, case filings, court orders, and more. This information can be invaluable for gathering background information, identifying key players, and understanding the context of a case.

Investigators can use PACER to monitor ongoing litigation and track the progress of court cases in real-time. By setting up alerts and notifications for specific cases or parties, investigators can stay informed about new filings, court hearings, and other developments as they occur. This allows investigators to proactively monitor cases relevant to their investigations and respond quickly to new developments.

PACER provides access to a wide range of court documents and filings, including pleadings, motions, briefs, opinions, and orders. Investigators can use the platform to retrieve and download these documents directly from the court's electronic filing system. This allows investigators to obtain copies of court filings, review legal arguments, and analyze case strategies as part of their investigative research.

PACER can be a valuable tool for conducting background checks on individuals and businesses involved in federal court cases. Investigators can search for cases involving specific parties or entities and review case dockets to gather information about their legal history, litigation activity, and involvement in federal court proceedings. This information can be useful for assessing individuals' credibility, identifying potential risks, and uncovering relevant details for investigative purposes.

PACER allows investigators to conduct due diligence on parties involved in legal transactions, business deals, or other activities with potential legal implications. By searching for cases involving specific parties or entities, investigators can assess their litigation history, legal disputes, and other relevant factors that may impact the transaction or deal. This information can help investigators identify potential risks, evaluate the credibility of parties, and make informed decisions about their involvement in the matter.

While PACER offers valuable resources for investigators, there are also considerations and limitations to keep in mind:

PACER charges users a fee for accessing court documents and case information, typically on a per-page basis. Investigators should budget for these costs and consider the financial implications of accessing large volumes of documents or conducting extensive research on the platform.

PACER only provides access to federal court records and does not include information from state or local courts. Investigators may need to use other resources or databases to access court records from state or local jurisdictions as needed for their investigations.

Investigators must ensure that their use of PACER is legal and compliant with applicable laws and regulations. This includes adhering to PACER's terms of use, respecting individuals' privacy rights, and using information obtained from the platform responsibly and ethically.

Navigating PACER and conducting effective searches may require technical skills and familiarity with online databases and search tools. Investigators should invest time in learning how to use the platform effectively to maximize its utility in their investigations.

PACER is a valuable tool for investigators, providing access to a vast repository of federal court documents and case information. By leveraging PACER's capabilities, investigators can conduct comprehensive research, monitor ongoing litigation, retrieve court documents, conduct background checks, and perform due diligence on parties involved in legal transactions. However, it's essential for investigators to be mindful of the costs, data availability, legal compliance, and technical considerations associated with using PACER to ensure the accuracy, reliability, and ethical use of the information obtained. With the right skills, knowledge, and resources, investigators can harness the power of PACER to enhance their investigative efforts and achieve successful outcomes for their clients.

Sex Offender Registry
The National Sex Offender Public Website (NSOPW) is a powerful tool for private investigators, providing access to a comprehensive database of sex offender registry information from across the United States. In this guide, we'll explore how private investigators can utilize NSOPW to enhance their investigative efforts and gather critical information for their cases.

NSOPW is a free online resource that allows users to search for sex offenders by name, location, or other criteria. The website aggregates sex offender registry information from all 50 states, the District of Columbia, Puerto Rico, Guam, and various tribal jurisdictions, providing a centralized database of sex offender records accessible to the public.

NSOPW allows private investigators to conduct comprehensive background checks on individuals by searching for sex offender registry information. Investigators can search for sex offenders by name, address, or other identifying information to determine if individuals have a history of sexual offenses and are listed on the registry. This information can be invaluable for assessing individuals' credibility, identifying potential risks, and uncovering relevant details for investigative purposes.

In cases involving personal or professional relationships, business transactions, or other activities with potential legal implications, private investigators can use NSOPW to conduct due diligence on parties involved. By searching for sex offenders associated with specific individuals or entities, investigators can assess their background, evaluate potential risks, and make informed decisions about their involvement in the matter.

NSOPW allows users to search for sex offenders by location, including specific addresses, neighborhoods, or geographic areas. Private investigators can use this feature to assess the prevalence of sex offenders in a particular area, identify potential risks for clients or businesses operating in the area, and gather information about sex offender residency restrictions or other relevant factors.

In cases involving victims of sexual offenses, private investigators can use NSOPW to provide support and advocacy for victims and their families. By accessing sex offender registry information, investigators can assist victims in identifying perpetrators, tracking their movements, and taking steps to ensure their safety and well-being. This can include coordinating with law enforcement agencies, providing resources and referrals, and helping victims navigate the legal process.

NSOPW can be a valuable tool for assessing potential risks and vulnerabilities in various contexts, including residential communities, schools, workplaces, and other settings. Private investigators can use sex offender registry information to identify individuals who may pose a risk to others in these environments and take appropriate precautions to mitigate potential dangers. This can include implementing safety measures, conducting security assessments, and providing recommendations for risk management.

NSOPW can provide valuable support for legal proceedings, including criminal investigations, civil litigation, and other legal matters involving sexual offenses. Private investigators can use sex offender registry information to gather evidence, establish patterns of behavior, and support legal arguments in court. This can help strengthen cases, corroborate witness testimony, and achieve successful outcomes for clients seeking justice or compensation.

While NSOPW offers valuable resources for private investigators, there are also considerations and limitations to keep in mind:

The accuracy of sex offender registry information can vary, and investigators should verify information obtained from NSOPW through additional sources whenever possible. This may include contacting law enforcement agencies, reviewing court records, or conducting interviews with relevant parties to confirm details and corroborate evidence.

NSOPW contains sensitive information about individuals who have been convicted of sexual offenses, and investigators must handle this information with care and respect for individuals' privacy rights. It's essential to use sex offender registry information responsibly and ethically, following legal and ethical guidelines to protect individuals' privacy and avoid unauthorized use or disclosure of personal data

Investigators must ensure that their use of NSOPW is legal and compliant with applicable laws and regulations. This may include adhering to privacy laws, obtaining consent when required, and using information obtained from NSOPW appropriately in their investigations. It's essential to understand the legal requirements and restrictions associated with accessing and using sex offender registry information to avoid potential legal issues or liabilities.

When using NSOPW in cases involving victims of sexual offenses, investigators must approach the matter with sensitivity and compassion for the individuals involved. It's essential to prioritize the well-being and dignity of victims and their families, providing support and advocacy in a respectful and empathetic manner.

NSOPW is a valuable tool for private investigators, providing access to a comprehensive database of sex offender registry information from across the United States. By leveraging NSOPW's capabilities, investigators can conduct background checks, due diligence, location-based searches, victim advocacy, risk assessment, and legal support in cases involving sexual offenses. However, it's essential for investigators to be mindful of considerations and limitations associated with using NSOPW, including data accuracy, privacy concerns, legal compliance, and victim sensitivity. With the right approach, private investigators can utilize NSOPW to enhance their investigative efforts and achieve successful outcomes for their clients while upholding the principles of justice and integrity.

Intelligence X

IntelX.io is a powerful tool that private investigators can leverage to gather valuable intelligence and conduct thorough investigations. In this comprehensive guide, we'll explore how private investigators can utilize IntelX.io to enhance their investigative efforts, gather critical information, and achieve successful outcomes for their cases.

IntelX.io is an online platform that provides access to a vast repository of data from a variety of sources, including the web, databases, and other digital sources. The platform offers powerful search capabilities, allowing users to conduct comprehensive searches for information related to individuals, organizations, events, and more. IntelX.io aggregates data from a wide range of sources, including websites, social media platforms, public records, and dark web forums, providing users with access to valuable intelligence that may not be available through traditional sources.

IntelX.io is a valuable tool for gathering open-source intelligence (OSINT) on individuals, organizations, events, and more. Private investigators can use the platform to conduct comprehensive searches for information related to their investigations, including social media profiles, online mentions, news articles, blog posts, and other publicly available data. By aggregating data from a variety of sources, IntelX.io provides investigators with a comprehensive view of their subjects, helping them uncover relevant details and identify potential leads for their cases.

IntelX.io can be used to conduct thorough background checks on individuals and organizations involved in investigations. Private investigators can search for information related to a subject's personal and professional history, including employment records, education history, criminal records, financial records, and more. By gathering comprehensive background information, investigators can assess the credibility and reliability of individuals, identify potential risks, and uncover relevant details for their cases.

IntelX.io is a valuable tool for conducting due diligence on individuals and organizations involved in business transactions, partnerships, or other activities with potential legal or financial implications. Private investigators can search for information related to a subject's business history, corporate affiliations, regulatory filings, litigation history, and more. By conducting thorough due diligence, investigators can assess the integrity and reliability of parties involved in transactions, identify potential risks, and make informed decisions about their involvement in the matter.

IntelX.io provides access to data from a variety of digital sources, including websites, social media platforms, and dark web forums. Private investigators can use the platform to conduct cyber investigations, gathering information related to cyber threats, data breaches, online fraud, and other cybercrimes. By monitoring online activity and gathering intelligence from digital sources, investigators can identify potential threats, track cybercriminals, and gather evidence to support legal proceedings.

IntelX.io can be used to gather competitive intelligence on businesses, industries, and markets. Private investigators can search for information related to competitors, market trends, industry developments, and more. By analyzing data from a variety of sources, investigators can identify market opportunities, assess competitors' strategies, and gather insights to inform business decisions.

IntelX.io can be a valuable tool for supporting legal proceedings and litigation. Private investigators can use the platform to gather evidence, conduct research, and gather intelligence relevant to legal cases. By accessing data from a variety of sources, investigators can uncover relevant information, track legal developments, and gather evidence to support legal arguments.

While IntelX.io offers valuable resources for private investigators, there are also considerations and limitations to keep in mind:

As with any online platform, the accuracy of the information provided by IntelX.io may vary. Investigators should verify information obtained from the platform through additional sources whenever possible to ensure its accuracy and reliability.

Investigators must ensure that their use of IntelX.io is legal and compliant with applicable laws and regulations. This includes adhering to privacy laws, obtaining consent when required, and using information obtained from the platform responsibly and ethically.

Navigating IntelX.io and conducting effective searches may require technical skills and familiarity with online databases and search tools. Investigators should invest time in learning how to use the platform effectively to maximize its utility in their investigations.

IntelX.io is a valuable tool for private investigators, providing access to a vast repository of data from a variety of sources. By leveraging IntelX.io's capabilities, investigators can gather valuable intelligence, conduct thorough investigations, and achieve successful outcomes for their cases. However, it's essential for investigators to be mindful of the considerations and limitations associated with using IntelX.io and to ensure that their use of the platform is legal, ethical, and compliant with applicable laws and regulations. With the right skills, knowledge, and resources, investigators can harness the power of IntelX.io to enhance their investigative efforts and achieve successful outcomes for their clients.

Who Is

Who.is is a versatile tool utilized by a wide range of users, including private investigators, to gather valuable information about domain names, websites, and their associated entities. This platform provides a comprehensive suite of services that empower investigators to conduct domain name searches, uncover ownership details, assess website history, and perform various other investigative tasks. In this guide, we will delve into how private investigators can effectively leverage Who.is to enhance their investigative efforts, gather critical intelligence, and achieve successful outcomes for their cases.

Who.is is a web-based platform designed to provide insights into domain names and websites. It offers a variety of tools and services tailored to meet the needs of users seeking information about the ownership, history, and status of domain names. By aggregating data from various sources, Who.is offers a comprehensive database of domain name records, allowing users to perform domain searches, access ownership information, and explore related details.

Private investigators can utilize Who.is to perform domain name searches, enabling them to gather information about specific domain names and their associated entities. By entering a domain name into the search bar, investigators can retrieve valuable details such as domain ownership, registration status, creation date, expiration date, and more. This information can provide insights into the identity of website owners, their location, and their contact information, helping investigators to identify potential leads and gather intelligence for their cases.

Who.is allows investigators to access ownership details for domain names, providing information about the individuals or organizations behind specific websites. Investigators can obtain details such as the name of the domain owner, their email address, postal address, phone number, and administrative contact information. This information can be instrumental in identifying and locating individuals associated with suspicious or fraudulent websites, enabling investigators to pursue further inquiries and take appropriate action as needed.

Who.is offers access to historical data for domain names, allowing investigators to track changes and modifications over time. By reviewing historical records, investigators can gain insights into the evolution of a website, including changes in ownership, registration details, hosting providers, and other relevant information. This historical perspective can be valuable for assessing the credibility and reliability of websites, identifying patterns of behavior, and uncovering potential red flags or inconsistencies.

Who.is enables investigators to conduct in-depth analysis of websites, including assessing their reputation, trustworthiness, and legitimacy. By analyzing domain name records, registration details, and other relevant information, investigators can evaluate the authenticity of websites and identify potential risks or threats. This analysis can help investigators to assess the credibility of online sources, identify fraudulent websites, and mitigate risks for their clients.

Who.is serves as a valuable research tool for private investigators, providing access to a wealth of information about domain names and websites. Investigators can use the platform to gather intelligence, verify identities, uncover connections, and perform various other investigative tasks. Whether conducting due diligence, background checks, or fraud investigations, Who.is offers a comprehensive suite of services to support investigators in their efforts to gather critical intelligence and achieve successful outcomes for their cases.

While Who.is offers valuable resources for private investigators, there are also considerations and limitations to keep in mind:

As with any online platform, the accuracy of the information provided by Who.is may vary. Investigators should verify information obtained from the platform through additional sources whenever possible to ensure its accuracy and reliability.

Investigators must ensure that their use of Who.is is legal and compliant with applicable laws and regulations. This includes adhering to privacy laws, obtaining consent when required, and using information obtained from the platform responsibly and ethically.

Navigating Who.is and interpreting domain name

records may require technical skills and familiarity with internet protocols and domain registration processes. Investigators should invest time in learning how to use the platform effectively to maximize its utility in their investigations.

Who.is is a valuable tool for private investigators, providing access to a wealth of information about domain names and websites. By leveraging Who.is's capabilities, investigators can gather valuable intelligence, perform domain name searches, access ownership details, analyze website history, and conduct various other investigative tasks. However, it's essential for investigators to be mindful of the considerations and limitations associated with using Who.is and to ensure that their use of the platform is legal, ethical, and compliant with applicable laws and regulations. With the right skills, knowledge, and resources, investigators can harness the power of Who.is to enhance their investigative efforts and achieve successful outcomes for their cases.

Social Mention
        Social Mention (https://mention.com) is a powerful tool that offers real-time social media search and analysis, enabling private investigators to monitor online conversations, track brand mentions, and gather valuable intelligence from various social media platforms. In this comprehensive guide, we'll explore how private investigators can effectively leverage Social Mention to enhance their investigative efforts, gather critical information, and achieve successful outcomes for their cases.

        Social Mention is a free web-based platform that provides real-time search and analysis of social media content. It offers a comprehensive search engine that aggregates user-generated content from various social media platforms, including Twitter, Facebook,

YouTube, Instagram, and more. Social Mention allows users to search for keywords, hashtags, and phrases to monitor online conversations, track brand mentions, and analyze sentiment across social media channels.

Social Mention enables private investigators to monitor social media conversations in real-time, providing insights into trending topics, emerging issues, and public sentiment. Investigators can use the platform to track keywords, hashtags, and phrases relevant to their investigations, allowing them to stay informed about online discussions, news events, and developments related to their cases.

Private investigators can leverage Social Mention to monitor brand mentions and track online reputation for individuals, businesses, or organizations. By monitoring mentions of specific brands, products, or services, investigators can assess public perception, identify potential risks, and detect instances of brand misuse, infringement, or defamation.

Social Mention offers valuable insights into competitors' activities, allowing private investigators to gather competitive intelligence and analyze market trends. Investigators can track mentions of competitors' brands, products, or services to identify strengths, weaknesses, opportunities, and threats in the marketplace. This information can help investigators to develop effective strategies, benchmark performance, and gain a competitive edge in their investigations.

Social Mention provides valuable data on social media influencers, enabling private investigators to identify individuals or accounts with significant influence and reach. Investigators can analyze mentions, engagement, and sentiment surrounding influencers to assess their impact, credibility, and relevance to their investigations. This information can help investigators to identify potential sources of information, collaborators, or influencers who may be relevant to their cases.

Social Mention offers sentiment analysis tools that allow investigators to analyze the tone and sentiment of online conversations. Investigators can assess public sentiment towards specific topics, brands, or individuals, helping them to gauge public perception, identify potential risks, and detect emerging issues or trends. Sentiment analysis can provide valuable insights into public opinion, sentiment trends, and sentiment shifts, helping investigators to make informed decisions and take proactive measures in their investigations.

Social Mention enables private investigators to monitor online conversations during crisis situations, enabling them to track emerging issues, assess public sentiment, and identify potential risks or threats. Investigators can monitor keywords, hashtags, or phrases related to crisis events, allowing them to stay informed about developments, disseminate information, and manage reputational risks effectively.

While Social Mention offers valuable resources for private investigators, there are also considerations and limitations to keep in mind:

Social Mention may not provide comprehensive coverage of all social media platforms or sources. Investigators should be aware of potential gaps in data coverage and consider using additional tools or sources to supplement their social media monitoring efforts.

As with any social media monitoring tool, the accuracy of the information provided by Social Mention may vary. Investigators should verify information obtained from the platform through additional sources whenever possible to ensure its accuracy and reliability.

Investigators must ensure that their use of Social Mention is legal and compliant with applicable privacy laws and regulations. This includes obtaining consent when required, respecting individuals' privacy rights, and using information obtained from the platform responsibly and ethically.

Social Mention is a valuable tool for private investigators, providing real-time social media search and analysis capabilities to monitor online conversations, track brand mentions, and gather valuable intelligence from various social media platforms. By leveraging Social Mention's capabilities, investigators can stay informed about online discussions, track brand mentions, analyze sentiment, and gather competitive intelligence to enhance their investigative efforts and achieve successful outcomes for their cases. However, it's essential for investigators to be mindful of the considerations and limitations associated with using Social Mention and to ensure that their use of the platform is legal, ethical, and compliant with applicable laws and regulations. With the right skills, knowledge, and resources, investigators can harness the power of Social Mention to enhance their investigative efforts and achieve successful outcomes for their cases.

Who Posted What
WhoPostedWhat.com is a valuable tool for private investigators, offering insights into social media activity, monitoring online conversations, and gathering intelligence from various social media platforms. In this guide, we'll explore how private investigators can effectively leverage WhoPostedWhat.com to enhance

their investigative efforts, gather critical information, and achieve successful outcomes for their cases.

WhoPostedWhat.com is a web-based platform that provides social media monitoring and analytics services. It offers real-time search and analysis capabilities, allowing users to monitor social media activity, track mentions of specific keywords or hashtags, and analyze trends across various social media platforms. WhoPostedWhat.com aggregates data from sources such as Twitter, Facebook, Instagram, YouTube, and more, providing users with valuable insights into online conversations, public sentiment, and emerging issues.

WhoPostedWhat.com enables private investigators to monitor social media activity in real-time, providing insights into trending topics, emerging issues, and public sentiment. Investigators can track mentions of specific keywords, hashtags, or phrases relevant to their investigations, allowing them to stay informed about online discussions, news events, and developments related to their cases.

Private investigators can leverage WhoPostedWhat.com to track mentions of specific keywords or phrases across social media platforms. By monitoring keywords relevant to their investigations, investigators can identify relevant conversations, track online activity, and gather intelligence from various sources. This information can help investigators to identify potential leads, uncover relevant details, and track the progress of their investigations.

WhoPostedWhat.com offers hashtag analysis tools that allow investigators to analyze trends and activity surrounding specific hashtags. Investigators can track the usage of hashtags relevant to their investigations, identify influential users, and monitor discussions related to specific topics or events. This hashtag analysis can provide valuable insights into public sentiment, emerging issues, and trends on social media platforms.

WhoPostedWhat.com enables investigators to monitor social media users and track their online activity across multiple platforms. Investigators can track the activity of specific users, including their posts, comments, likes, and interactions. This user monitoring can help investigators to identify individuals of interest, track their online behavior, and gather intelligence relevant to their investigations.

WhoPostedWhat.com offers sentiment analysis tools that allow investigators to analyze the tone and sentiment of online conversations. Investigators can assess public sentiment towards specific topics, brands, or individuals, helping them to gauge public perception, identify potential risks, and detect emerging issues or trends. Sentiment analysis can provide valuable insights into public opinion, sentiment trends, and sentiment shifts, helping investigators to make informed decisions and take proactive measures in their investigations.

WhoPostedWhat.com enables investigators to analyze trends and patterns across social media platforms. Investigators can track changes in online activity, identify emerging trends, and analyze the impact of specific events or topics on social media platforms. Trend analysis can help investigators to anticipate developments, identify opportunities, and adapt their investigative strategies accordingly.

While WhoPostedWhat.com offers valuable resources for private investigators, there are also considerations and limitations to keep in mind:

WhoPostedWhat.com may not provide comprehensive coverage of all social media platforms or sources. Investigators should be aware of potential gaps in data coverage and consider using additional tools or sources to supplement their social media monitoring efforts.

As with any social media monitoring tool, the accuracy of the information provided by WhoPostedWhat.com may vary. Investigators should verify information obtained from the platform through additional sources whenever possible to ensure its accuracy and reliability.

Investigators must ensure that their use of WhoPostedWhat.com is legal and compliant with applicable privacy laws and regulations. This includes obtaining consent when required, respecting individuals' privacy rights, and using information obtained from the platform responsibly and ethically.

WhoPostedWhat.com is a valuable tool for private investigators, providing social media monitoring and analytics capabilities to track online conversations, monitor brand mentions, and gather intelligence from various social media platforms. By leveraging WhoPostedWhat.com's capabilities, investigators can stay informed about online discussions, track mentions of specific keywords or hashtags, analyze trends, and gather valuable intelligence to enhance their investigative efforts. However, it's essential for investigators to be mindful of the considerations and limitations associated with using WhoPostedWhat.com and to ensure that their use of the platform is legal, ethical, and compliant with applicable laws and regulations. With the right skills, knowledge, and resources, investigators can harness the power of WhoPostedWhat.com to enhance their investigative efforts and achieve successful outcomes for their cases.

Board Reader

Boardreader is a powerful tool for private investigators, offering access to a vast repository of online discussions, forums, and message boards. In this guide, we'll explore how private investigators can effectively utilize Boardreader to gather valuable intelligence, monitor online conversations, and uncover critical information for their investigations.

Boardreader is an online search engine that specializes in indexing and searching online forums and message boards. It aggregates content from a wide range of discussion platforms, including forums, bulletin boards, and community websites, allowing users to search for topics, keywords, or phrases across multiple sources. Boardreader offers advanced search capabilities, enabling users to filter results by date, forum, language, and other criteria to find relevant discussions quickly and efficiently.

Boardreader is a valuable tool for conducting online investigations, allowing private investigators to monitor discussions, track trends, and gather intelligence from various online forums and communities. Investigators can search for keywords, topics, or individuals relevant to their investigations, enabling them to identify potential leads, gather evidence, and uncover critical information from online discussions.

Boardreader can be used to monitor discussions and conversations across social media platforms, providing insights into public sentiment, opinions, and trends. Investigators can search for hashtags, mentions, or topics related to their investigations, allowing them to track online conversations, identify influencers, and gauge public sentiment towards specific individuals, brands, or events.

Boardreader offers valuable insights into competitors' activities, allowing investigators to gather competitive intelligence and analyze market trends. Investigators can search for discussions related to competitors' products, services, or brands, enabling them to identify strengths, weaknesses, opportunities, and threats in the marketplace. This information can help investigators to develop effective strategies, benchmark performance, and gain a competitive edge in their investigations.

Boardreader enables private investigators to monitor brand mentions and track online reputation for individuals, businesses, or organizations. Investigators can search for discussions related to specific brands, products, or services, allowing them to assess public perception, identify potential risks, and detect instances of brand misuse, infringement, or defamation.

Boardreader can be a valuable tool for monitoring online conversations during crisis situations, enabling investigators to track emerging issues, assess public sentiment, and identify potential risks or threats. Investigators can search for keywords, hashtags, or phrases related to crisis events, allowing them to stay informed about developments, disseminate information, and manage reputational risks effectively.

While Boardreader offers valuable resources for private investigators, there are also considerations and limitations to keep in mind:

Boardreader may not provide comprehensive coverage of all online forums and message boards. Investigators should be aware of potential gaps in data coverage and consider using additional tools or sources to supplement their online monitoring efforts.

As with any online search engine, the accuracy of the information provided by Boardreader may vary. Investigators should verify information obtained from the platform through additional sources whenever possible to ensure its accuracy and reliability.

Investigators must ensure that their use of Boardreader is legal and compliant with applicable laws and regulations. This includes adhering to privacy laws, obtaining consent when required, and using information obtained from the platform responsibly and ethically.

Boardreader is a valuable tool for private investigators, providing access to a wealth of online discussions, forums, and message boards. By leveraging Boardreader's capabilities, investigators can gather valuable intelligence, monitor online conversations, and uncover critical information for their investigations. However, it's essential for investigators to be mindful of the considerations and limitations associated with using Boardreader and to ensure that their use of the platform is legal, ethical, and compliant with applicable laws and regulations. With the right skills, knowledge, and resources, investigators can harness the power of Boardreader to enhance their investigative efforts and achieve successful outcomes for their cases.

CarNet AI
Carnet.ai is a sophisticated online platform that serves as a valuable resource for private investigators, offering advanced capabilities in data analysis, risk assessment, and investigative research. This comprehensive guide will explore how private investigators can effectively utilize Carnet.ai to

enhance their investigative efforts, gather critical information, and achieve successful outcomes for their cases.

Carnet.ai is an AI-powered platform designed to assist investigators in analyzing and interpreting vast amounts of data from diverse sources. It employs cutting-edge machine learning algorithms and natural language processing techniques to extract actionable insights, identify patterns, and uncover hidden connections within complex datasets. Carnet.ai offers a range of features and tools tailored to meet the needs of investigative professionals, including data enrichment, risk scoring, entity resolution, and relationship mapping.

Carnet.ai enables private investigators to enrich their datasets with additional context and relevant information, enhancing the depth and accuracy of their analyses. Investigators can upload datasets containing structured or unstructured data, such as names, addresses, phone numbers, or textual documents, and Carnet.ai will automatically enrich the data with additional attributes, such as social media profiles, business affiliations, criminal records, or financial information. This enriched data can provide valuable insights and facilitate more comprehensive investigations.

Carnet.ai offers risk scoring capabilities that allow investigators to assess the risk associated with individuals, organizations, or transactions. Investigators can input relevant data into the platform, and Carnet.ai will analyze the data using advanced algorithms to assign a risk score based on various factors, such as reputation, credibility, compliance, or financial stability. This risk scoring process can help investigators prioritize their investigative efforts, identify high-risk entities, and focus resources on areas of greatest concern.

Carnet.ai facilitates entity resolution by identifying and linking related entities within complex datasets. Investigators often encounter challenges when dealing with data containing multiple references to the same individual, organization, or entity. Carnet.ai employs sophisticated entity resolution algorithms to identify duplicate records, reconcile inconsistencies, and link related entities together. This process helps investigators build more accurate profiles, identify connections, and uncover relationships that may be crucial to their investigations.

Carnet.ai enables private investigators to visualize and explore relationships between entities using interactive relationship mapping tools. Investigators can input data into the platform, and Carnet.ai will analyze the data to identify connections, associations, and interactions between individuals, organizations, or entities. Investigators can then visualize these relationships using intuitive graphical representations, such as network graphs or link charts, allowing them to identify patterns, detect anomalies, and uncover hidden connections that may be relevant to their investigations.

Carnet.ai leverages predictive analytics to forecast future events, trends, or behaviors based on historical data and patterns. Investigators can input historical data into the platform, and Carnet.ai will analyze the data using machine learning algorithms to identify patterns, trends, or anomalies. By extrapolating from this analysis, Carnet.ai can generate predictive models that anticipate future outcomes, identify potential risks, or highlight emerging trends. This predictive capability can help investigators anticipate developments, mitigate risks, and proactively address issues before they escalate.

While Carnet.ai offers valuable resources for private investigators, there are also considerations and limitations to keep in mind:

Investigators must ensure that their use of Carnet.ai complies with applicable data privacy laws and regulations. This includes obtaining consent when required, protecting sensitive information, and using data obtained from the platform responsibly and ethically.

As with any data analysis platform, the accuracy of the information provided by Carnet.ai may vary. Investigators should verify information obtained from the platform through additional sources whenever possible to ensure its accuracy and reliability.

Navigating Carnet.ai and interpreting data analysis results may require technical skills and familiarity with data analysis tools and techniques. Investigators should invest time in learning how to use the platform effectively to maximize its utility in their investigations.

Carnet.ai is a powerful platform that offers advanced capabilities in data analysis, risk assessment, and investigative research for private investigators. By leveraging Carnet.ai's AI-powered features and tools, investigators can enrich their datasets, assess risk, resolve entities, map relationships, and generate predictive insights to enhance their investigative efforts and achieve successful outcomes for their cases. However, it's essential for investigators to be mindful of the considerations and limitations associated with using Carnet.ai and to ensure that their use of the platform is legal, ethical, and compliant with applicable laws and regulations. With the right skills, knowledge, and resources, investigators can harness the power of Carnet.ai to augment their investigative capabilities and achieve successful outcomes for their clients.

Associations

Texas Association of Licensed Investigators
In the vast expanse of the Lone Star State, where tales of intrigue and suspense echo through the canyons and across the plains, there exists a bastion of professionalism and expertise - the Texas Association of Licensed Investigators (TALI). Established as a beacon of excellence in the field of private investigation, TALI stands as a testament to the unwavering commitment of its members to uphold the highest standards of integrity, ethics, and proficiency in their craft.

Founded on the principles of camaraderie and collaboration, TALI serves as a unifying force for licensed investigators across the state of Texas. Its origins can be traced back to a time when the need for a unified voice within the profession became increasingly apparent, giving rise to an organization dedicated to fostering fellowship, promoting education, and advancing the interests of its members.

At the heart of TALI lies a deep-seated commitment to professionalism and continuing education. Through a comprehensive array of training programs, seminars, and conferences, the association equips its members with the knowledge, skills, and resources necessary to excel in their field. From the latest investigative techniques to emerging legal trends, TALI ensures that its members remain at the forefront of their profession, adeptly navigating the ever-changing landscape of private investigation with confidence and competence.

What truly sets TALI apart is its unwavering dedication to ethical conduct and adherence to the highest standards of integrity. As licensed investigators, members of the association are bound by a strict code of ethics, ensuring that each inquiry is conducted with honesty, impartiality, and respect for the rights of all parties involved. By upholding these principles, TALI not only safeguards the reputation of the profession but also earns the trust and confidence of clients and stakeholders alike.

In addition to its role as a provider of education and training, TALI also serves as a powerful advocate for the rights and interests of licensed investigators across Texas. Through legislative initiatives, lobbying efforts, and grassroots activism, the association works tirelessly to promote the recognition and professionalization of the private investigation industry. By championing policies that enhance licensure standards, protect consumer rights, and combat illegal practices, TALI ensures that the voice of its members is heard loud and clear in the corridors of power.

One of the hallmarks of TALI is its unwavering commitment to community engagement and public service. Recognizing the importance of giving back to the communities they serve, members of the association actively participate in a wide range of philanthropic endeavors, from volunteering at local charities to organizing fundraisers for worthy causes. Whether it's providing pro bono services to victims of crime or supporting initiatives to combat human trafficking, TALI members embody the spirit of compassion and altruism, proving that the true measure of success lies not in the cases they solve, but in the lives they touch along the way.

In an age where technology reigns supreme, TALI remains steadfast in its dedication to traditional investigative methods. While the digital revolution has undoubtedly transformed the landscape of private investigation, the association firmly believes in the importance of combining cutting-edge technology with time-tested investigative techniques. From surveillance operations to witness interviews, TALI members leverage a diverse array of tools and tactics to uncover the truth, unraveling the mysteries that lie hidden beneath the surface with skill and precision.

As the sun sets over the rugged terrain of Texas, casting long shadows across the sprawling landscape, the members of TALI continue their vigil, ever watchful, ever vigilant. For in a state where secrets abound and mysteries linger just beyond the horizon, it is their unwavering commitment to excellence and integrity that sets them apart. In the hallowed halls of the Texas Association of Licensed Investigators, the pursuit of truth knows no bounds, and the quest for justice knows no rest.

Associated Security Services & Investigators of Texas
In the vast expanse of the Lone Star State, where the winds whisper tales of resilience and determination, there exists a bastion of security and integrity - the Associated Security Services & Investigators of Texas (ASSI-TX). Rooted in a rich history of service and commitment, ASSI-TX stands as a formidable guardian of safety and professionalism, uniting security professionals and investigators in a common pursuit of excellence.

Established as a beacon of reliability and trust, ASSI-TX traces its origins to a time when the need for a unified platform for security services and investigative expertise became increasingly evident. Founded on principles of collaboration, education, and advocacy, the association serves as a cornerstone of the security industry in Texas, providing its members with the tools, resources, and support they need to thrive in a challenging and dynamic environment.

At the heart of ASSI-TX lies a steadfast commitment to professionalism and ethical conduct. Members of the association, comprising security professionals, private investigators, and allied experts, adhere to a strict code of ethics, ensuring that each undertaking is conducted with integrity, transparency, and respect for the rights of all parties involved. By upholding these principles, ASSI-TX not only safeguards the reputation of the security industry but also fosters trust and confidence among clients, stakeholders, and the public at large.

Central to the mission of ASSI-TX is its dedication to continuous learning and professional development. Through a comprehensive range of training programs, seminars, and workshops, the association equips its members with the knowledge, skills, and expertise needed to excel in their respective fields. From security risk assessments to surveillance techniques, ASSI-TX ensures that its members remain at the forefront of industry best practices, adeptly navigating the evolving landscape of security and investigation with confidence and competence.

What sets ASSI-TX apart is its unwavering commitment to collaboration and mutual support. As a diverse community of security professionals and investigators, members of the association have access to a wealth of knowledge and expertise, enabling them to leverage collective insights and experiences to overcome challenges and seize opportunities. Through networking events, forums, and online communities, ASSI-TX fosters a culture of camaraderie and cooperation, empowering its members to achieve their goals and advance their careers.

In addition to its role as a hub for professional development, ASSI-TX also serves as a powerful advocate for the interests of its members and the broader security industry. Through legislative advocacy, public outreach, and community engagement, the association works tirelessly to promote policies and initiatives that enhance the effectiveness, professionalism, and accountability of security services and investigations in Texas. By advocating for licensure standards, regulatory reforms, and industry best practices, ASSI-TX ensures that the voice of its members is heard and respected in the halls of government and beyond.

Integral to the ethos of ASSI-TX is its unwavering commitment to community service and public safety. Recognizing the importance of giving back to the communities they serve, members of the association actively participate in a wide range of philanthropic endeavors, from volunteering at local events to providing security services for charitable organizations. Whether it's supporting disaster relief efforts or helping to ensure the safety of public gatherings, ASSI-TX members embody the spirit of service and citizenship, demonstrating that the true measure of success lies not in individual achievements, but in the positive impact they have on the lives of others.

As the sun sets over the vast plains of Texas, casting long shadows across the rugged landscape, the members of ASSI-TX continue their vigil, ever watchful, ever vigilant. For in a state where challenges abound and threats lurk just beyond the horizon, it is their unwavering commitment to integrity and professionalism that sets them apart. In the hallowed halls of the Associated Security Services & Investigators of Texas, the pursuit of safety knows no bounds, and the quest for excellence knows no rest.

National Council of Investigation & Security Services

In the intricate web of security and investigation across the United States, one organization stands as a beacon of professionalism and excellence: the National Council of Investigation & Security Services (NCISS). Founded on principles of integrity, collaboration, and advocacy, NCISS serves as a unifying force for security and investigative professionals, fostering a community dedicated to upholding the highest standards of competence and ethics in the industry.

Established in recognition of the need for a cohesive voice to represent the interests of security and investigation practitioners nationwide, NCISS has a rich history dating back to its inception. As a leading trade association, it has played a pivotal role in shaping the landscape of the security and investigation profession, advocating for legislative reforms, promoting industry best practices, and providing a platform for education and networking.

At its core, NCISS is committed to promoting professionalism and ethical conduct among its members. Through a comprehensive code of ethics and standards of practice, the association ensures that its members adhere to principles of honesty, integrity, and respect for individual rights in their professional endeavors. By upholding these principles, NCISS not only safeguards the reputation of the industry but also fosters trust and confidence among clients, stakeholders, and the public at large.

Central to the mission of NCISS is its dedication to education and professional development. Through a diverse array of training programs, seminars, and conferences, the association equips its members with the knowledge, skills, and resources needed to excel in their respective fields. From advanced investigative techniques to cutting-edge security strategies, NCISS ensures that its members remain at the forefront of industry trends, enabling them to adapt to evolving challenges and opportunities with confidence and competence.

What sets NCISS apart is its commitment to collaboration and mutual support. As a national organization representing a diverse range of security and investigation professionals, NCISS provides its members with access to a vast network of colleagues, mentors, and industry experts. Through online forums, regional meetings, and national conferences, members have the opportunity to exchange insights, share best practices, and collaborate on complex cases, fostering a culture of camaraderie and cooperation that transcends geographic boundaries.

In addition to its role as a provider of education and networking opportunities, NCISS serves as a powerful advocate for the interests of its members and the broader security and investigation industry. Through legislative advocacy, public outreach, and coalition building, the association works tirelessly to promote policies and initiatives that enhance the effectiveness, professionalism, and accountability of security and investigation services nationwide. By engaging with policymakers, law enforcement agencies, and regulatory bodies, NCISS ensures that the voice of its members is heard and respected in matters affecting the industry.

Integral to the ethos of NCISS is its commitment to community service and public safety. Recognizing the importance of giving back to the communities they serve, members of the association actively participate in a wide range of philanthropic endeavors, from volunteering at local events to providing security services for charitable organizations. Whether it's supporting disaster relief efforts or assisting law enforcement agencies with missing persons cases, NCISS members embody the spirit of service and citizenship, demonstrating that the true measure of success lies not in individual achievements, but in the positive impact they have on the lives of others.

As the sun sets over the diverse landscape of the United States, casting long shadows across bustling cities and tranquil countryside alike, the members of NCISS continue their vigil, ever watchful, ever vigilant. For in a country where security threats are ever-present and the pursuit of justice knows no bounds, it is their unwavering commitment to integrity and expertise that sets them apart. In the hallowed halls of the National Council of Investigation & Security Services, the quest for excellence knows no rest, and the defense of truth and justice knows no compromise.

Council of International Investigators
In the intricate tapestry of global security and investigation, one organization stands as a beacon of excellence and collaboration: the Council of International Investigators (CII). With its roots tracing back to a shared vision of fostering international cooperation and promoting professional standards, CII serves as a unifying force for private investigators and security professionals across the globe, dedicated to upholding the highest ethical and operational standards in the field.

Established in recognition of the increasingly interconnected nature of crime and security threats, CII has emerged as a leading authority in the realm of international investigation. Through its diverse membership base, spanning continents and cultures, the association fosters a dynamic community of professionals united by a common commitment to excellence, integrity, and mutual support.

At its core, CII is guided by a steadfast commitment to professionalism and ethical conduct. Members of the association, hailing from diverse backgrounds and disciplines, adhere to a strict code of ethics that upholds principles of honesty, integrity, and respect for individual rights in their professional endeavors. By promoting these values, CII not only safeguards the reputation of the investigative profession but also fosters trust and confidence among clients, stakeholders, and the public at large.

Central to the mission of CII is its dedication to education and knowledge sharing. Through a robust program of training seminars, conferences, and workshops, the association provides its members with access to the latest tools, techniques, and insights in the field of investigation. From advanced surveillance tactics to cross-border legal considerations, CII ensures that its members remain at the forefront of industry best practices, enabling them to navigate the complex landscape of international investigation with confidence and competence.

What sets CII apart is its commitment to fostering collaboration and cooperation among its members. As an international organization, CII provides its members with a unique opportunity to connect with colleagues from around the world, exchange ideas, and collaborate on complex cases that transcend national borders. Through regional meetings, online forums, and international conferences, members have the opportunity to build lasting relationships and leverage collective expertise to tackle the most challenging investigative assignments.

In addition to its role as a provider of education and networking opportunities, CII serves as a powerful advocate for the interests of its members and the broader investigative community. Through its engagement with policymakers, law enforcement agencies, and regulatory bodies, the association works tirelessly to promote policies and initiatives that enhance the effectiveness, professionalism, and accountability of investigative services worldwide. By advocating for regulatory reforms, promoting industry standards, and combating illegal practices, CII ensures that the voice of its members is heard and respected on the global stage.

Integral to the ethos of CII is its commitment to community service and social responsibility. Recognizing the importance of giving back to the communities they serve, members of the association actively participate in a wide range of philanthropic endeavors, from volunteering at local charities to providing pro bono investigative services for humanitarian causes. Whether it's supporting efforts to combat human trafficking or assisting with disaster relief efforts, CII members embody the spirit of service and compassion, demonstrating that the true measure of success lies not in individual achievements, but in the positive impact they have on the lives of others.

As the sun sets on cities and villages around the world, casting long shadows across bustling metropolises and remote landscapes alike, the members of CII continue their vigil, ever watchful, ever vigilant. For in a world where crime knows no borders and security threats transcend national boundaries, it is their unwavering commitment to integrity and expertise that sets them apart. In the hallowed halls of the Council of International Investigators, the pursuit of truth knows no bounds, and the defense of justice knows no compromise.

International Private Investigators Union

In the labyrinth of global mysteries and clandestine operations, one organization stands as a bastion of professionalism and collaboration: the International Private Investigators Union (IPIU). Rooted in a shared commitment to excellence and integrity, the IPIU serves as a unifying force for private investigators around the world, fostering a community dedicated to upholding the highest standards of ethics and proficiency in the field.

Established in recognition of the increasingly interconnected nature of crime and security challenges, the IPIU has emerged as a leading advocate for the investigative profession on the international stage. With its diverse membership spanning continents and cultures, the union provides a platform for private investigators to exchange ideas, share best practices, and collaborate on cases that transcend national borders.

At its core, the IPIU is guided by a steadfast commitment to professionalism and ethical conduct. Members of the union, representing a wide range of investigative specialties and backgrounds, adhere to a strict code of ethics that emphasizes principles of honesty, integrity, and respect for individual rights in their professional endeavors. By upholding these values, the IPIU not only safeguards the reputation of the investigative profession but also fosters trust and confidence among clients, stakeholders, and the public at large.

Central to the mission of the IPIU is its dedication to education and professional development. Through a comprehensive program of training seminars, workshops, and conferences, the union equips its members with the knowledge, skills, and resources needed to excel in their respective fields.

From advanced investigative techniques to emerging trends in digital forensics, the IPIU ensures that its members remain at the forefront of industry best practices, enabling them to navigate the complex landscape of international investigation with confidence and competence.

What sets the IPIU apart is its commitment to fostering collaboration and cooperation among its members. As an international organization, the union provides a unique opportunity for private investigators to connect with colleagues from around the world, exchange insights, and collaborate on cases that require a global perspective. Through online forums, regional meetings, and international conferences, members have the opportunity to build lasting relationships and leverage collective expertise to tackle the most challenging investigative assignments.

In addition to its role as a provider of education and networking opportunities, the IPIU serves as a powerful advocate for the interests of its members and the broader investigative community. Through its engagement with policymakers, law enforcement agencies, and regulatory bodies, the union works tirelessly to promote policies and initiatives that enhance the effectiveness, professionalism, and accountability of investigative services worldwide. By advocating for regulatory reforms, promoting industry standards, and combating illegal practices, the IPIU ensures that the voice of its members is heard and respected on the global stage.

Integral to the ethos of the IPIU is its commitment to community service and social responsibility. Recognizing the importance of giving back to the communities they serve, members of the union actively participate in a wide range of philanthropic endeavors, from volunteering at local charities to providing pro bono investigative services for humanitarian causes. Whether it's supporting efforts to combat human trafficking or assisting with disaster relief efforts, the IPIU members embody the spirit of service and compassion, demonstrating that the true measure of success lies not in individual achievements, but in the positive impact they have on the lives of others.

As the sun sets on cities and landscapes around the world, casting long shadows across bustling metropolises and remote villages alike, the members of the International Private Investigators Union continue their vigil, ever watchful, ever vigilant. For in a world where crime knows no borders and security threats transcend national boundaries, it is their unwavering commitment to integrity and expertise that sets them apart. In the hallowed halls of the IPIU, the pursuit of truth knows no bounds, and the defense of justice knows no compromise.

Magazines

This list is by no means considered comprehensive, this is only a small segment.

Professional Investigator Magazine
In the dynamic world of private investigation, staying informed and connected is paramount to success. Among the plethora of resources available to professionals in the field, PIMagazine.com stands out as a trusted source of news, insights, and resources tailored specifically to the needs of private investigators.

PIMagazine.com serves as the online counterpart to the renowned Private Investigator Magazine, a publication dedicated to providing industry professionals with the latest trends, techniques, and best practices in the field of private investigation. With its online platform, PIMagazine.com offers an array of features designed to inform, educate, and empower private investigators in their pursuit of excellence.

Upon landing on PIMagazine.com, visitors are greeted with a clean and intuitive interface designed for ease of navigation. The homepage typically features a selection of featured articles, news updates, and upcoming events relevant to the private investigation community. A user-friendly menu allows visitors to explore different sections of the website, including articles, resources, forums, and subscription options.

At the heart of PIMagazine.com lies its rich and diverse content offerings. From in-depth articles and case studies to expert interviews and industry analysis, the website covers a wide range of topics relevant to private investigators of all levels of experience. Whether it's exploring the latest investigative techniques, discussing legal and ethical considerations, or sharing success stories from the field, PIMagazine.com provides a wealth of valuable insights to its readers.

One of the highlights of PIMagazine.com is its extensive collection of articles and features written by industry experts and seasoned professionals. These articles cover a broad spectrum of subjects, including surveillance, digital forensics, skip tracing, background checks, and more. Whether readers are looking to enhance their investigative skills, stay informed about emerging trends, or gain practical advice for running a successful investigative business, they can find valuable information within the pages of PIMagazine.com.

In addition to articles and features, PIMagazine.com offers a variety of resources and tools designed to support private investigators in their daily operations. These may include downloadable templates for reports and documentation, links to relevant legal statutes and regulations, directories of investigative agencies and suppliers, and access to training and certification programs. By providing access to these resources, PIMagazine.com empowers investigators to streamline their workflow, improve efficiency, and deliver superior results to their clients.

Beyond its role as a repository of information, PIMagazine.com fosters a sense of community among private investigators through its online forums and discussion boards. These forums provide a platform for professionals to connect with peers, share experiences, ask questions, and seek advice on a wide range of topics related to the investigative profession. By facilitating dialogue and collaboration, PIMagazine.com helps to create a supportive and collaborative environment where investigators can learn from one another and grow together.

For those looking to dive deeper into the world of private investigation, PIMagazine.com offers various subscription options that provide access to premium content, exclusive features, and additional resources. Subscribers may receive access to digital editions of Private Investigator Magazine, discounts on training and events, invitations to networking opportunities, and other benefits designed to enhance their professional development and success.

All things considered, PIMagazine.com serves as an invaluable resource for private investigators seeking to stay informed, connected, and empowered in their profession. With its diverse range of content offerings, user-friendly interface, and commitment to community engagement, the website remains a trusted source of information and inspiration for investigative professionals around the world. Whether you're a seasoned investigator looking to stay ahead of the curve or a newcomer seeking guidance and support, PIMagazine.com has something to offer to help you succeed in your investigative endeavors.

Working P.I. Magazine
In the dynamic world of private investigation, access to resources, job opportunities, and networking platforms is essential for professionals to thrive. Among the plethora of websites catering to the needs of private investigators, WorkingPIMag.com emerges as a promising platform dedicated to connecting investigators with job opportunities, industry insights, and professional development resources. In this comprehensive guide, we delve into the features, offerings, and benefits of WorkingPIMag.com, exploring how it serves as a valuable tool for private investigators worldwide.

WorkingPIMag.com is an online platform specifically designed to cater to the needs of private investigators seeking job opportunities, career advancement resources, and industry insights. Serving as a hub for professionals in the field, the website aims to bridge the gap between employers and job seekers while providing a range of resources to support the professional development and success of investigators.

Upon visiting WorkingPIMag.com, users are greeted with a user-friendly interface designed for easy navigation and accessibility. The homepage typically features a range of features, including job listings, industry news, professional development resources, and networking opportunities. A clear and intuitive menu allows users to explore different sections of the website, including job listings, training programs, forums, and subscription options.

WorkingPIMag.com offers a variety of features and offerings tailored to the needs of private investigators:

One of the primary features of WorkingPIMag.com is its extensive database of job listings for private investigators. Employers from various sectors, including corporate, legal, and government, post job opportunities for investigators with different skill sets and experience levels. Job seekers can browse through listings, filter based on criteria such as location and specialization, and apply directly through the platform.

In addition to job listings, WorkingPIMag.com provides valuable insights into industry trends, best practices, and regulatory updates. Articles, blog posts, and case studies authored by industry experts offer readers valuable perspectives on topics such as surveillance techniques, digital forensics, legal considerations, and business management strategies.

WorkingPIMag.com offers a range of resources to support the professional development of private investigators. This may include access to training programs, certification courses, webinars, and workshops designed to enhance investigative skills, expand knowledge, and stay abreast of industry advancements. Additionally, the platform may provide downloadable templates, guides, and tools to streamline investigative processes and improve efficiency.

Networking is crucial for professional growth and career advancement, and WorkingPIMag.com facilitates connections among investigators through online forums, discussion boards, and networking events. These platforms allow users to engage with peers, share experiences, seek advice, and build relationships within the investigative community.

WorkingPIMag.com may offer subscription options that provide access to premium features, exclusive content, and additional benefits. Subscribers may receive priority access to job listings, discounts on training programs, invitations to networking events, and personalized support from the platform's team.

WorkingPIMag.com fosters a sense of community among private investigators by providing opportunities for engagement, collaboration, and support. Through its online forums, discussion boards, and networking events, users can connect with peers, share insights, and seek advice on a wide range of topics related to the investigative profession. Additionally, the platform may offer support services, such as career counseling, mentorship programs, and job placement assistance, to help investigators navigate their career paths effectively.

WorkingPIMag.com serves as a valuable resource for private investigators seeking job opportunities, industry insights, and professional development resources. With its user-friendly interface, comprehensive features, and commitment to community engagement, the platform empowers investigators to advance their careers, expand their knowledge, and connect with peers in the field. Whether you're a seasoned investigator looking for your next career opportunity or a newcomer seeking guidance and support, WorkingPIMag.com offers a range of tools and resources to help you succeed in your investigative endeavors.

Pursuit Magazine

PursuitMag.com is a leading online publication dedicated to the field of private investigation and related professions. With its extensive array of articles, resources, and insights, PursuitMag.com serves as a central hub for professionals seeking to stay informed, connected, and inspired in their work. In this comprehensive guide, we'll delve into the various aspects of PursuitMag.com, exploring its content offerings, community engagement, and impact on the investigative industry.

PursuitMag.com is the digital arm of Pursuit Magazine, a respected publication that has been serving the investigative community for years. Founded by professionals with deep roots in the industry, PursuitMag.com has established itself as a trusted source of information and inspiration for private investigators, law enforcement professionals, legal professionals, and others engaged in the pursuit of truth and justice.

Upon visiting PursuitMag.com, visitors are greeted with a clean, user-friendly interface designed to facilitate easy navigation and exploration. The homepage typically features a selection of featured articles, news updates, and highlights from the world of investigation. A streamlined menu allows visitors to access different sections of the website, including articles, resources, podcasts, and more.

At the heart of PursuitMag.com lies its rich and diverse content offerings. From in-depth articles and case studies to expert interviews and industry analysis, the website covers a wide range of topics relevant to professionals in the investigative field. Whether readers are interested in surveillance techniques, digital forensics, skip tracing, or legal considerations, they can find valuable insights and information within the pages of PursuitMag.com.

PursuitMag.com boasts an extensive collection of articles and features written by industry experts, seasoned professionals, and thought leaders. These articles cover a broad spectrum of subjects, including investigative techniques, industry trends, legal developments, and more. Whether readers are looking to enhance their skills, stay informed about emerging issues, or gain practical advice for their work, they can find valuable content tailored to their needs on PursuitMag.com.

In addition to articles and features, PursuitMag.com offers a variety of resources and tools designed to support professionals in their investigative work. These resources may include downloadable templates for reports and documentation, links to relevant laws and regulations, directories of investigative agencies and suppliers, and access to training and certification programs. By providing access to these resources, PursuitMag.com empowers professionals to improve their efficiency, effectiveness, and success in their work.

PursuitMag.com also features podcasts and multimedia content that provide additional insights and perspectives on the world of investigation. These podcasts may feature interviews with industry experts, discussions on current events and issues, and explorations of cutting-edge techniques and technologies. By offering a variety of formats and voices, PursuitMag.com ensures that its audience can engage with content in ways that suit their preferences and interests.

Beyond its role as a source of information, PursuitMag.com fosters a sense of community among professionals in the investigative field. Through its online forums, social media channels, and networking events, the website provides opportunities for professionals to connect, collaborate, and share experiences. By facilitating dialogue and interaction, PursuitMag.com helps to build a supportive and inclusive community where professionals can learn from one another, exchange ideas, and support one another in their work.

For those looking to dive deeper into the world of investigation, PursuitMag.com offers various subscription options that provide access to premium content, exclusive features, and additional resources. Subscribers may receive access to digital editions of Pursuit Magazine, discounts on training and events, invitations to networking opportunities, and other benefits designed to enhance their professional development and success.

Finally, PursuitMag.com is a valuable resource for professionals in the investigative field, providing a wealth of information, insights, and resources to support their work. With its diverse content offerings, engaging community, and commitment to excellence, PursuitMag.com continues to serve as a trusted source of inspiration and guidance for professionals seeking to excel in their careers. Whether you're a seasoned investigator or a newcomer to the field, PursuitMag.com has something to offer to help you succeed in your investigative endeavors.

Security Magazine

SecurityMagazine.com stands as a digital fortress in the ever-evolving landscape of security, offering a wealth of resources, insights, and news to professionals and enthusiasts alike. As a leading online platform dedicated to security topics, the website serves as a hub for information, analysis, and community engagement in the field of security.

SecurityMagazine.com is a comprehensive online resource catering to a diverse audience interested in security-related topics. Whether you're a security professional, a business owner, a government official, or a concerned citizen, the website provides valuable content and resources to help you stay informed and prepared in an increasingly complex security landscape.

Upon visiting SecurityMagazine.com, visitors are greeted with a user-friendly interface designed for easy navigation and accessibility. The homepage typically features a curated selection of articles, news updates, and multimedia content covering a wide range of security-related topics. A menu bar and search function allow users to explore different sections of the website, including articles, news, features, and resources.

SecurityMagazine.com boasts a diverse array of content offerings, catering to the diverse interests and needs of its audience. From in-depth articles and analysis to breaking news updates and expert interviews, the website covers a broad spectrum of security-related topics, including cybersecurity, physical security, risk management, emergency preparedness, and more. Whether you're looking for insights into emerging threats, best practices for security implementation, or thought leadership on industry trends, SecurityMagazine.com delivers timely and relevant content to its readers.

One of the primary attractions of SecurityMagazine.com is its extensive collection of articles and features written by industry experts, thought leaders, and seasoned professionals. These articles delve into a wide range of security-related subjects, providing valuable insights, analysis, and practical advice to readers. Whether you're seeking guidance on securing your organization's network infrastructure, mitigating physical security risks, or navigating regulatory compliance requirements, you can find authoritative information within the pages of SecurityMagazine.com.

In addition to feature articles and analysis, SecurityMagazine.com delivers timely news updates and alerts on the latest developments in the security industry. From data breaches and cyberattacks to geopolitical events and regulatory changes, the website keeps readers informed about breaking news and emerging trends that may impact their security strategies and operations. By providing up-to-date information and analysis, SecurityMagazine.com helps its audience stay ahead of the curve in an ever-changing security landscape.

SecurityMagazine.com offers a variety of resources and tools to help security professionals enhance their knowledge, skills, and capabilities. These resources may include whitepapers, case studies, webinars, podcasts, and downloadable templates for security assessments and planning. By providing access to these resources, SecurityMagazine.com empowers security professionals to deepen their understanding of key concepts, explore new technologies and methodologies, and implement effective security strategies within their organizations.

Beyond its role as a repository of information, SecurityMagazine.com fosters a sense of community among security professionals through its interactive features and engagement opportunities. The website may host forums, discussion boards, and social media channels where readers can connect with peers, share insights, and exchange ideas on a wide range of security-related topics. By facilitating dialogue and collaboration, SecurityMagazine.com helps to create a supportive and knowledge-sharing environment where security professionals can learn from one another and collectively address the challenges facing the industry.

To conclude, SecurityMagazine.com stands as an indispensable resource for security professionals and enthusiasts seeking to stay informed, connected, and empowered in the field of security. With its diverse content offerings, user-friendly interface, and commitment to community engagement, the website remains a trusted source of information and inspiration for security professionals around the world. Whether you're looking to stay abreast of the latest industry trends, deepen your knowledge of security best practices, or connect with like-minded professionals, SecurityMagazine.com has something to offer to help you succeed in your security endeavors.

Sample Case File

In the realm of investigations, whether in law enforcement, private investigation, or corporate security, the creation of a detailed case file serves as the cornerstone of success. A meticulously crafted case file not only organizes evidence and information but also provides a roadmap for investigators to follow, guiding them through the complexities of their inquiry. In this article, we delve into the critical components and best practices for creating a comprehensive case file that lays the groundwork for a successful investigation.

1. Understanding the Purpose of a Case File**

Before delving into the intricacies of creating a

case file, it's essential to understand its purpose. A case file serves as a centralized repository of all relevant information pertaining to an investigation. It documents every aspect of the inquiry, from initial leads and evidence collection to witness statements and analysis. By consolidating information in a single location, a case file ensures that investigators have quick and easy access to the data they need to make informed decisions and progress the investigation effectively.

2. Gathering and Organizing Information**

The first step in creating a detailed case file is to gather all pertinent information related to the investigation. This includes any reports, documents, photographs, videos, or other evidence collected during the course of the inquiry. It's crucial to organize this information in a logical and systematic manner, using file folders, digital folders, or database software, depending on the nature of the investigation.

3. Establishing Case File Sections**

To maintain clarity and organization, a case file should be divided into distinct sections, each addressing a specific aspect of the investigation. Common sections may include:

- Case Overview: A brief summary of the investigation, including the nature of the case, key objectives, and relevant dates.
- Incident Reports: Detailed accounts of any incidents or events related to the investigation, including dates, times, locations, and involved parties.
- Evidence: A comprehensive inventory of all evidence collected during the investigation, including descriptions, chain of custody documentation, and analysis reports.

- Witnesses: Contact information, statements, and interviews with witnesses or persons of interest.
- Interviews: Transcripts or summaries of interviews conducted with individuals relevant to the investigation, including suspects, victims, and witnesses.
- Analysis and Findings: An analysis of the evidence collected and findings of the investigation, including any conclusions or recommendations.
- Legal and Regulatory: Any legal documents, court orders, or regulatory requirements relevant to the investigation.

4. Documenting Details and Observations**

A detailed case file should include thorough documentation of all details and observations relevant to the investigation. This may include descriptions of physical evidence, timelines of events, observations made during surveillance, or notes from interviews. It's essential to record information accurately and objectively, using clear and concise language that can be easily understood by others.

5. Maintaining Chain of Custody**

Chain of custody refers to the chronological documentation of the handling, custody, and control of evidence throughout the investigation process. Maintaining a clear and unbroken chain of custody is critical to ensuring the admissibility and reliability of evidence in legal proceedings. As such, a detailed case file should include documentation of the chain of custody for each piece of evidence collected, including who collected it, where and when it was collected, and any transfers or changes in custody that occurred.

6. Updating and Reviewing the Case File**

A case file is a living document that should be

continuously updated and reviewed throughout the course of the investigation. Investigators should regularly add new information, update existing records, and review the file for accuracy and completeness. Additionally, periodic reviews of the case file can help identify any gaps or inconsistencies in the investigation and guide further inquiry or analysis.

In conclusion, creating a detailed case file is essential for the success of any investigation. By gathering and organizing information, establishing clear sections, documenting details and observations, maintaining chain of custody, and regularly updating and reviewing the file, investigators can create a comprehensive record of their inquiry that serves as a roadmap for progress and decision-making. A well-crafted case file not only enhances the efficiency and effectiveness of an investigation but also ensures its integrity and reliability, laying the groundwork for a successful resolution.

Case File Templet

Import data to include: Client name, client contact information, retainer fee, reimbursements, mileage, cost per day, minimum days guaranteed, service type, release agreement, GPS authorization, legal, arbitration, police reports, doctor reports, background reports, social media info., etc

Contract Tips:
Algodocs.com
Algodocs.com offers a comprehensive suite of document automation tools that streamline the process of creating, editing, and managing documents. With its user-friendly interface and robust features, Algodocs.com empowers users to create professional-looking documents quickly and efficiently.

One of the key features of Algodocs.com is its intuitive document editor, which allows users to create and customize documents with ease. The editor offers a wide range of formatting options, templates, and design elements, enabling users to tailor their documents to their specific needs. Whether creating a business proposal, legal contract, or marketing brochure, users can leverage Algodocs.com to produce high-quality documents that make a lasting impression.

In addition to its document editing capabilities, Algodocs.com also offers powerful collaboration tools that facilitate teamwork and communication. Users can easily share documents with colleagues, clients, or collaborators and collaborate in real-time on document edits and revisions. The platform also offers version control features, allowing users to track changes, revert to previous versions, and maintain a clear audit trail of document revisions.

Algodocs.com also offers advanced document automation features that help users streamline repetitive tasks and increase productivity. Users can create custom document templates, automate document generation based on predefined variables, and integrate with other software systems to automate workflows. By automating document creation and management processes, Algodocs.com helps users save time, reduce errors, and improve efficiency.

Another standout feature of Algodocs.com is its robust security measures that ensure the confidentiality and integrity of user data. The platform employs state-of-the-art encryption techniques to protect sensitive information and offers granular access controls that enable users to restrict access to documents based on user roles and permissions. With

Algodocs.com, users can trust that their documents are safe and secure at all times.

Overall, Algodocs.com is a versatile document automation platform that offers a wide range of features to help users create, edit, and manage documents more effectively. With its intuitive interface, powerful collaboration tools, advanced automation capabilities, and robust security measures, Algodocs.com is the ideal solution for individuals and businesses looking to streamline their document workflows and boost productivity.

Docusign.com

Docusign.com revolutionizes the way businesses handle document transactions by offering a comprehensive electronic signature solution. As a pioneer in the field of e-signatures, DocuSign has transformed traditional paper-based workflows into streamlined digital processes, empowering organizations to accelerate transactions, reduce costs, and enhance customer experiences.

At the core of DocuSign's offerings is its intuitive electronic signature platform, which enables users to sign, send, and manage documents securely and efficiently. With DocuSign, users can electronically sign documents from any device, anywhere, at any time, eliminating the need for printing, scanning, and mailing paper documents. This flexibility not only saves time but also reduces the environmental impact associated with paper-based processes.

One of the key advantages of DocuSign is its ease of use. The platform offers a simple and intuitive interface that guides users through the signing process step by step. Whether signing a contract, approving a purchase order, or authorizing a transaction, users can sign documents with just a few clicks, using their finger, mouse, or stylus. DocuSign also supports multiple authentication options, including SMS verification and biometric authentication, to ensure the security and integrity of electronic signatures.

In addition to electronic signatures, DocuSign offers a suite of powerful features designed to streamline document workflows and improve efficiency. Users can create custom templates, automate document routing and approval processes, and integrate with other business applications to seamlessly transfer data and documents between systems. DocuSign's advanced analytics and reporting tools provide insights into document status, completion rates, and signer behavior, enabling organizations to optimize their processes and drive better business outcomes.

DocuSign also prioritizes security and compliance, offering industry-leading encryption, authentication, and data protection measures to safeguard sensitive information. The platform complies with global regulations and standards, including GDPR, HIPAA, and SOC 2 Type II, giving users peace of mind knowing that their documents are secure and compliant.

Furthermore, DocuSign offers a range of integrations with popular business applications, including Salesforce, Microsoft Office 365, and Google Workspace, allowing users to seamlessly incorporate electronic signatures into their existing workflows. This interoperability enables organizations to maximize the value of their investments in technology and leverage DocuSign's capabilities across their entire business ecosystem.

Overall, DocuSign.com is a game-changer for

organizations looking to digitize their document processes and streamline their operations. With its user-friendly interface, powerful features, robust security, and seamless integrations, DocuSign empowers businesses to accelerate transactions, reduce costs, and deliver superior customer experiences in today's digital world.

Okta.com

Okta.com stands as a leading identity platform, empowering organizations to securely connect the right people to the right technologies. With its suite of innovative identity management solutions, Okta.com enables businesses to streamline access management, enhance security, and improve user experiences across their entire digital ecosystem.

At the heart of Okta.com's offerings is its Identity Cloud platform, which provides a centralized hub for managing user identities, access policies, and authentication methods. Through Okta's platform, organizations can seamlessly integrate with a wide range of applications, directories, and systems, allowing users to access the tools and resources they need with ease and efficiency.

One of the key features of Okta.com is its Single Sign-On (SSO) functionality, which enables users to access multiple applications with a single set of credentials. With SSO, users can log in once and gain access to all their authorized applications, eliminating the need to remember multiple passwords and reducing the risk of password-related security incidents. This not only enhances user productivity but also strengthens security by reducing the likelihood of password reuse and credential theft.

In addition to SSO, Okta.com offers a range of advanced authentication methods to ensure secure access to sensitive resources. These include multi-factor authentication (MFA), adaptive authentication, and biometric authentication, which provide additional layers of security beyond traditional password-based authentication. By implementing these advanced authentication methods, organizations can protect against unauthorized access and mitigate the risk of data breaches.

Okta.com also provides comprehensive access management capabilities, allowing organizations to define and enforce granular access policies based on user roles, permissions, and contextual factors. Administrators can easily configure access controls, manage user lifecycles, and revoke access privileges in real-time, ensuring that only authorized users have access to sensitive data and resources.

Also, Okta.com prioritizes security and compliance, offering industry-leading encryption, data protection, and compliance controls to safeguard sensitive information. The platform complies with global regulations and standards, including GDPR, HIPAA, and SOC 2 Type II, giving organizations peace of mind knowing that their identity management solution is secure and compliant.

Simultaneously, Okta.com offers seamless integrations with a wide range of business applications, directories, and systems, including cloud-based applications, on-premises systems, and legacy platforms. This interoperability enables organizations to leverage Okta's identity management capabilities across their entire technology stack, driving efficiency, and consistency in their identity management practices.

So, Okta.com is a powerful identity platform that enables organizations to securely connect users to technologies, streamline access management, and enhance security across their digital ecosystem. With its comprehensive features, robust security, and seamless integrations, Okta.com empowers businesses to achieve their identity management goals and drive success in today's digital world.

Entrust.com

Entrust.com stands at the forefront of digital security solutions, providing organizations worldwide with cutting-edge technologies to safeguard their digital identities, data, and transactions. With a focus on trust, innovation, and reliability, Entrust.com offers a comprehensive suite of identity and access management, encryption, and authentication solutions designed to protect against evolving cyber threats and ensure secure digital experiences.

Central to Entrust.com's offerings is its Identity as a Service (IDaaS) platform, which provides organizations with a centralized and scalable solution for managing digital identities across their entire ecosystem. Through the IDaaS platform, organizations can streamline identity lifecycle management, enforce access controls, and mitigate the risk of unauthorized access to critical systems and data.

One of the key features of Entrust.com's IDaaS platform is its robust authentication capabilities, which enable organizations to implement multi-factor authentication (MFA) and adaptive authentication methods to verify the identities of users accessing their systems and applications. By combining factors such as passwords, biometrics, and device identifiers, Entrust.com helps organizations strengthen security while maintaining a seamless user experience.

In addition to authentication, Entrust.com offers a range of encryption solutions to protect sensitive data at rest, in transit, and in use. From data encryption and tokenization to secure communication protocols and cryptographic key management, Entrust.com provides organizations with the tools they need to safeguard their data against unauthorized access and data breaches.

Entrust.com prioritizes compliance and regulatory requirements, offering solutions that help organizations achieve and maintain compliance with industry standards and regulations such as GDPR, HIPAA, and PCI DSS. Through comprehensive auditing and reporting capabilities, Entrust.com enables organizations to demonstrate compliance with confidence and ease.

Moreover, Entrust.com offers seamless integrations with a wide range of business applications, systems, and devices, enabling organizations to leverage its security solutions across their entire technology stack. Whether deploying on-premises, in the cloud, or in hybrid environments, Entrust.com provides organizations with the flexibility and scalability they need to adapt to evolving business requirements and technology landscapes.

Entrust.com is a trusted partner for organizations seeking to enhance their digital security posture and protect against cyber threats. With its comprehensive suite of identity and access management, encryption, and authentication solutions, Entrust.com empowers organizations to safeguard their digital identities, data, and transactions while maintaining compliance with regulatory requirements and delivering secure digital experiences to their users.

Important details to remember to ask and include in

your client interview:

Who
        Who else
        Who else
What
        They did they do or are doing
        What do they drive
        What routes do they take
Where
        Did it or will it happen
        Where do they work
When
        Did it or will it happen
        Do they travel
Why
        Are they doing it
How
        Are they doing it

NETWORKING

Lawyers
     Accident
     Criminal
     Family

District Attorney

Business Network Groups
     Chamber of Commerce
     BNI
     Rotary
     Lions
     Kiwanis

City Police

County Sheriff Department

State Police

Reporters

Coroner

Skip Tracers

Used Car Dealers

Insurance Agents

Private Investigators

BIOGRAPHY

In the shadowy realm of clandestine inquiries and concealed truths, there exists two figures whose expertise has illuminated the darkest corners of human behavior. With over four decades of experience in investigation between them, David Arndt and Bruce Nowlin stand as a paragon of diligence, perseverance, and astute observation. Through their unwavering commitment to uncovering the truth, they have navigated a labyrinth of mysteries, shedding light on the enigmatic and the obscure. David and Bruce hopes every reader takes this captivating journey through the maze, on their way to become a fellow master of the clandestine arts.

David Arndt and Bruce Nowlin were both born with an innate curiosity and a keen eye for detail, traits that would later define their illustrious career. Bruce born and raised in Texas and David in Oregon, both of their childhoods followed similar paths. They were marked with an insatiable thirst for knowledge and an unwavering determination to decipher the world's mysteries. It was during their formative years that they developed a fascination with human behavior and the intricate web of motivations that drive it.

Fueled by a passion for unraveling enigma's of the universe, Bruce Nowlin pursued a degree in organizational psychology and David Arndt pursued criminal justice, schooling laid the groundwork for their future endeavors. Their academic pursuits complemented their early careers prior to private investigation, Bruce in construction safety and David in law enforcement. Their formative careers helped fortified their investigative and surveillance techniques, forensic analysis, and interrogation tactics.

Armed with knowledge and determination, David Arndt and Bruce Nowlin embarked on their maiden voyage into the realm of private investigation. Private Investigation cases can range from matrimonial disputes to corporate espionage, each presenting its own set of complexities and intrigues. Through dogged determination and meticulous attention to detail, they have earned a reputation for their ability to unearth the truth, no matter how well-concealed.

Over the years, David and Bruce have encountered a myriad of challenges, from elusive suspects to labyrinthine legal proceedings. Yet, with each obstacle, they have emerged stronger and more resilient, resolved and unshaken by the adversities each faced. Along the way, Bruce and David have achieved several milestones, including the resolution of hundreds of cases and the development of innovative investigative techniques. Their unwavering commitment to their craft have earned them the respect of their peers and the admiration of their clients.

As David Arndt and Bruce Nowlin reflect on their illustrious careers, they can take pride in the legacy they have built and the impact they have made on the lives of those whom they have served. Through their unwavering pursuit of truth and justice, they have brought closure to countless individuals and businesses, restoring faith in the power of perseverance and integrity. Their journey serves as an inspiration to aspiring investigators and a testament to the enduring importance of diligence and determination in the face of adversity.

In the annals of private investigation, David Arndt and Bruce Nowlin will stand as a beacon of excellence, their name synonymous with integrity, perseverance, and unwavering dedication to the pursuit of truth. Through four decades of relentless pursuit, they have unravelled the mysteries of the human psyche and illuminated the darkest corners of human behavior. As they continue their journey, they vow to remain committed to upholding the principles that have guided them thus far, knowing that the pursuit of truth is a lifelong endeavor, and one that takes unwavering resolve.